Property Rights, Planning and Markets

To Belinda, Maggie, Frances, Sophia, Chloe and Samuel

Property Rights, Planning and Markets

Managing Spontaneous Cities

Chris Webster

Professor of Urban Planning in the Department of City and Regional Planning, Cardiff University, UK

Lawrence Wai-Chung Lai

Professor of Economics, Planning and Law, Department of Real Estate and Construction, University of Hong Kong

Edward Elgar
Cheltenham, UK • Northampton, MA, USA

Published by
Edward Elgar Publishing Limited
Glensanda House
Montpellier Parade
Cheltenham
Glos GL50 1UA
UK

Edward Elgar Publishing, Inc.
136 West Street
Suite 202
Northampton
Massachusetts 01060
USA

A catalogue record for this book
is available from the British Library

Library of Congress Cataloguing in Publication Data

Webster, Christopher J.
    Property rights, planning and markets: managing spontaneous cities/
by Chris Webster and Lawrence Wai-Chung Lai.
      p. cm.
    1. City planning. 2. Markets. 3. Right of property. 4. Planning. I. Lai,
Lawrence Wai-Chung. II. Title.
HT166.W416   2003
307.1'216—dc21   2003040772

ISBN 1 84064 904 6 (cased)

Printed and bound in Great Britain by MPG Books Ltd, Bodmin, Cornwall

Contents

Figures and tables

FIGURES

TABLES

Foreword

The theory of property rights offers the following fundamental three-part proposition: 1. Subject to the costs of transacting, individuals will organise and allocate their rights so as to maximise their joint wealth. 2. The level of wealth is enhanced when economic rights are allocated such that individuals bear more of the effects of their actions; that is, they reap higher rewards from inducing gains for others and conversely suffer heavier penalties from inducing losses. 3. Because the costs of transacting are positive, the Pareto conditions are never met. This theory is also operational, capable of yielding predictions about circumstances under which particular wealth-enhancing arrangements will be used.

Economic rights may be allocated in any number of ways, some more desirable than others. Various institutional arrangements are available to allocate such rights. These include the private use of markets, of informal communities and of certain governmental actions. However, the cost of reaching a perfect match between the allocation of rights and gains from action precludes some outcomes that would otherwise be advantageous to all. In other words, some resources are inevitably left in the public domain. We expect, then, that on the one hand individuals will exploit opportunities in order to benefit at others' expense, and that on the other they will constantly seek ways to reduce the associated deadweight losses.

The elbow-rubbing living conditions in urban communities makes acute the externality problem that prevents the clear delineation of rights. As a result, people in cities are especially well positioned to gain at each other's expense. In considering this circumstance, Webster and Lai imaginatively apply the property rights framework to the economics of urban communities and to urban planning.

Many urban resources are shared. Webster and Lai ask both how rights and liabilities over shared resources are actually allocated within urban neighbourhoods and how they might be allocated to maximise the wealth of the community. The strength of their analysis is in recognising that whereas the available tools are general, these tools are to be applied under diverse conditions. Both investigators and city planners must take into account the special characteristics of each situation in the allocation of rights.

They convincingly argue that in many urban situations where resources are shared, private markets are best suited to handle the problems at hand. These include internalising devices such as the use of share contracts and the formation of restrictive covenants. Many cities have intimate, stable neighbourhoods that are characterised by long-term relationships among neighbours. Webster and Lai discuss how such communities take advantage of the long-term relations by forming local organisations that address problems of noise or aesthetics. Such organisations are likely to deal more effectively with local problems than would citywide regulations. Webster and Lai indicate that in larger, more mobile communities, a higher level of collective action may fit the bill. In such communities, public domain problems persist if left unattended. More centralised governmental institutions must play an active role to allocate economic rights and liabilities clearly. The clearer delineation of legal rights is one of the basic means for the clearer allocation of the economic rights.

Webster and Lai consider the nature of the public participation in implementing public policies. They point out that, in the decision making process, the better the representation of individuals affected by public policies, the fewer free rides will emerge. Many communities follow this principle, and the net wealth the city creates for them tends to be higher.

Webster and Lai offer a fresh and productive approach to urban problems in this book. It should prove useful to those seeking to understand how cities evolved and how they function. It should also furnish a powerful and constructive tool to policy makers who wish to improve urban life.

Yoram Barzel
Professor of Economics
University of Washington

Acknowledgements

The ideas in this book reflect our intellectual quest for theory that makes sense of cities – theory that describes urban processes simply but powerfully. We are both committed urbanists and urbanites and our experiences of living in, working in and studying some of the world's major cities have provided the insights and facts with which to develop theory. Our ideas have grown under the influence of the writers whose works we cite and discuss in this book. We are particularly indebted to the personal encouragement and ideas of certain individuals, including Yoram Barzel, Mike Batty, Steven N.S. Cheung, Alan Evans, Fred Foldvary, Walter Issard, Harry Richardson, Huw Williams and Ben Yu. Our students at Cardiff University and Hong Kong University have provided an additional layer of scrutiny and have influenced the level and structure of argumentation. At Edward Elgar, we are grateful for the support of Luke Adams, Nep Athwal and Caroline Cornish. At Cardiff University we need to acknowledge the help of Joek Roex and Alex Farr in preparing the final manuscript. Our families deserve the greatest thanks for patiently and cheerfully enduring yet another project.

Chris Webster
Lawrence Wai-Chung Lai
London and Hong Kong

1. Introduction

1.1 INTRODUCTION

Be fruitful and increase in number; fill the earth and subdue it (Genesis 1:28).

The task of subduing the Earth is, in the final analysis, a co-operative one. Whether individuals seek to maximise the benefits achievable from their resource endowments or are happy to settle for something less – to satisfice – they clearly need to co-operate with each other in doing so. But how is co-operation best co-ordinated? Two competing answers have shaped the history of human civilisation. Crudely, human endeavour may be co-ordinated by top-down, hierarchical planning or by a bottom-up and more spontaneous approach that relies upon symbiotic exchange. The tension between these two approaches is manifested whenever a government enacts a law that constrains market activity or when markets ignore government plans. It is also manifested when a production unit in a corporation differs with central management in its view of how labour is most productively deployed or which process should be axed under a rationalisation scheme. Markets are institutions that allow individuals to co-ordinate without central planning. But the issue is not one of planning versus markets, since top-down organisation happens within firms and within groups of firms in markets. The issue is one of imposed and centralised co-ordination via organisations, versus spontaneous and decentralised co-ordination. The former happens in governments, firms and families. The latter happens in systems of voluntary exchange such as bartering and modern markets.

This book is about the strengths and weaknesses of these two approaches. It is about alternative means for achieving order and about alternative orders. It is a theoretical book about the very pressing practical task of governing, administrating, managing and planning cities. Theoretical because, in our experience, there is a search amongst those undertaking these tasks (broadly referred to as urban managers from here on) for an intellectual foundation for their various interventions. Theoretical also because pragmatism has forced academic scholars and students of urban issues to advance beyond the poles of debate and the paradigms of the last century.

The debate about spontaneous versus planned urban order took a major turn in the last quarter of the twentieth century. The demise of the planned economies, ideological and practical challenges to the West's costly welfare states, and the failure of governments to provide adequate infrastructure and services in the developing countries have led to new forms of local governance that involve partnerships between private and public decision makers. Governments became enablers rather than suppliers, and partners of, not opponents to, markets. The changes have been driven not so much by the arguments of libertarian thinkers but more by hunger, poverty, threat of fiscal insolvency and the collapse of entire political edifices and old ideologies. Among the latter is the scientific paradigm and modernism, the demise of which has challenged the idea that society is 'mathematically manageable'. The scientific prescriptions of twentieth century governments were only the latest incarnation of the belief that society is manageable by design. Historically, the degree of state control has waxed and waned, influenced by economic prosperity, internal and external political conditions and by beliefs and values.

In this book we address the question of how order emerges in cities and systems of cities that are largely shaped by market forces – capitalist-led cities, frequently struggling with a culture of welfare statism and the sense that old forms of government no longer work.

One purpose of the book is to help bring discussions about markets and urban planning into greater balance. Academic discussion about urban governance is frequently polarised. Those espousing a public service ethic often demonise the market while some urban economists and radical libertarians fail to appreciate the need for strong state apparatus. Our position in this respect is that state and markets co-evolve, complementing each other and, by trial and error, discovering better ways of distributing responsibilities between private and public sector and between private and collective action.

In developing this position we offer explicit arguments that are amenable to formal and empirically refutable hypotheses about the respective strengths of planning and markets and of collective and private action in allocating urban resources. We draw these from various strands of what has collectively come to be known as the new institutional economics and develop the following interrelated themes.

Theme 1: Individuals and firms agglomerate in cities in order to benefit from exchange opportunities which in modern times are organised largely via capitalist-driven markets. Market-based exchange is usually beneficial for direct exchange partners and is beneficial to society to the extent that the interests of third parties are accounted for in private transactions.

Theme 2: Order emerges in cities as individuals seek to avoid the costs of private transaction, or more generally, the costs of voluntarily co-operating over production and consumption activities (transaction costs). Transaction costs explain the patterns that arise in market-driven cities. In particular, they explain organisational order; institutional order; proprietary (ownership) order; spatial order; and public domain order (public domain is defined below).

Theme 3: Institutions emerge to reduce transaction costs and more generally, the costs of voluntary co-operation. Markets are institutions that reduce the costs of organising a multitude of individual transactions. Government edicts, policy and regulations are institutions that reduce the costs of collective transactions.

Theme 4: Institutions reduce transaction costs by assigning property rights over scarce resources. A property right is defined in this context as the right to benefit from a resource by use, income or disposal and an institution is defined as a system of rules and sanctions.

Theme 5: Institutions that protect private property are essential for market activity and economic growth. Institutions that create and protect rights of third parties (those that are affected by but not party to a private transaction) are essential for sustainable and ethical market-driven growth – markets governed by broadly accepted values.

Theme 6: Resources with unclear property rights are said to be in the public domain and are subject to wasteful competitive consumption (congestion).

Theme 7: When the value of a resource changes significantly, there will be a corresponding change in assignment of property rights. This happens when privately owned and public domain resources increase in value through changes in preference and scarcity and when public domain resources decrease in value through overuse and congestion. Whether or not property rights are reassigned depends on the organisational and political costs of creating and sustaining appropriate institutions and the technology costs of assigning individual property rights (including the costs of making a public domain resource excludable).

Theme 8: Resource values, transaction cost, exclusion costs, institutions, property rights and public domain–private domain boundaries constantly shift within cities. They are all interrelated and spontaneously co-evolve. They do so with local interactions (for example, a plot of land changes use because a neighbouring plot has changed use); and global interactions (for example, government or an entire industry adapts its behaviour and rules). Interactions happen in space and in time, thus making cities complex systems in which the outcome of any planned action is largely unpredictable.

Theme 9: Limitations in the cognitive ability of individuals and groups and the costs of acquiring information mean that any system of co-ordination is imperfect. The information problem is more serious for government because markets rely on prices – decentralised measures of resource value. Markets, governments and more generally institutions, adapt over time however, in pursuit of a more efficient distribution of property rights. Adaptation is more rapid and more responsive the more open the competition, the lower the transaction costs and the better the information. Governments as well as markets can deliver a kind of spontaneous order, although the difficulties facing government in doing so are generally greater.

Theme 10: The efficiency with which an institution allocates property rights to individuals and groups is a function of the distribution of knowledge, resources and transaction costs. We develop positive propositions about these relationships and apply them to an explanation of the way cities, markets and urban governance evolve. We develop normative propositions and use them to evaluate and compare different kinds of institution.

These themes form an underlying argument that we develop in different ways and with different emphasis in each chapter. In the remainder of this chapter we introduce the themes more fully and start to elaborate the connections between them, starting with a review of key theoretical ideas.

1.2   TRANSACTION COSTS, PROPERTY RIGHTS, INSTITUTIONS AND THE NEW INSTITUTIONAL ECONOMICS

Spontaneity, Markets and Political Markets

The overarching theme of this book is 'constrained spontaneity' or spontaneity shaped by institutions that evolve to reduce the costs of human interaction. Adam Smith demonstrated the beneficial social outcome that emerges through many individuals acting in their own self-interest. Hayek (for example 1967, 1978) elaborated the idea of spontaneous creativity. In a state of constrained spontaneity, the good outcomes of selfish behaviour overwhelm the bad outcomes of the same behaviour. Competition, law and shared values promote socially beneficial selfish behaviour and sanction and limit harmful behaviour.

We apply the term *spontaneous* to two distinct processes. First, following Adam Smith, Hayek and evolutionary economists (for example, Nelson and Winter, 1982; Witt, 1991; Nelson, 1995) we mean the ability of markets to adapt to changes in demand and supply without central planning. This includes the market's ability to reassign property rights in response to changes in resource value. For example, when land is subdivided; when a redundant building is converted into multiple uses; when a bus company is broken up into more efficient smaller companies; or when a private development scheme combines many small plots of land.

Second, we mean the political market's ability to adapt to changes in demand for collective action. Well functioning liberal democracies are responsive to voter demands and there can be a spontaneity in the way that policy follows demand that is analogous to the spontaneity of markets. This is the perspective of public choice (social choice) writers such as James Buchanan and Gordon Tullock – see Dennis Mueller (1989) for a review of public choice literature.

We chose to refer to responsiveness in political markets as well as economic markets as *spontaneous* to make the point that governments are just one kind of supplier of collective goods and services. Like entrepreneurial firms and non-profit organisations they supply to a demand and operate in a competitive environment that tends over time to tease out the better public policy interventions (a thesis developed in another context by Karl Popper, 1974).

As groups and individuals seek their own respective interests, certain government interventions will succeed in delivering acceptable distributions of benefits – those that protect property rights, preserve private benefits, but also deliver broadly acceptable constraints on private action. Other government solutions will be frustrated and eventually fail, either because they pay too little attention to constraints, making market-based co-operation too costly, or because they over-constrain, making it too unprofitable.

Other policies are successful, not because they deliver this balance in a way that pleases most of the people most of the time, but because they confer benefits (yield economic 'rent') to groups that hold power. A powerful industry might benefit from a regulation or tax regime, for example, or groups within a municipal administration may benefit from the expansion of responsibility. The rent-seeking thesis is another emphasis of the public choice school (Tollison, 1982). It also relates to the literature on asymmetrical information and so-called principal-agent problems (Stigler, 1971; Molho, 1997). Many government policies or management policies within firms, are taken advantage of by agents (workers, managers, administrators, professionals and politicians), who have information advantages over those they serve – their 'principals' (supervisors, board members, senior administrators, politicians and public). Self-regarding endeavours can lead to zero-sum results: rent-seeking groups using their position to create artificial income for themselves at the expense of other groups; corrupt officials, workers and politicians overtly stealing the principal's resources; indolent managers, politicians, professionals and workers free riding on others' labour.

Interventions that 'leak' economic wealth in these ways are sustainable only for as long as the power relations that protect the beneficiaries remain intact. It should be understood, however, that there are principal-agent problems, information asymmetries and rent seeking in all but utopian acts of co-operation (and about the latter, we offer an opinion at the end of this chapter). Indeed, to be efficient, organisations need to offer agents (employees, production units, subsidiary firms, government departments, sections and sub sections) incentives that allow them to retain a degree of the organisation's wealth in return for productive input. Efficient incentive structures (salaries, perks, allowances, bonus schemes) are also contractual boundaries to rent-seeking behaviour. In the long term it might be supposed that approaches to governance (in the firm as well as in public government) that leak too much wealth (redistribute consumer surplus) to powerful groups, will fail – as did the twentieth century planned economies.

Spontaneity in markets relies on the clarity of prices in signalling information about demand and supply. Spontaneity in political markets depends on the inherently more noisy signals of votes, press, lobbying and other forms of 'voice'. Governments are in this sense inherently inferior to markets as methods of organising exchange. There are some forms of co-operation that the market finds it difficult to organise efficiently, however – co-operation over goods for which property rights are unclear. Where society's institutions are responsive to failure, the boundaries between market-delivered order and planned order evolve over time in a spontaneous fashion.

Property Rights and Institutions

Hayek's optimistic view of spontaneity in markets and society does not address how the innate human capacity for wealth advancement can lead to anarchy and turmoil (the Great Terror in the French Revolution, the destruction by the red guards in the Cultural Revolution, urban decay and neighbourhood melt-down, or unrestrained industrial growth that dissipates its gains by despoiling the environment). Hayek assumes that a system of private property rights and the rule of law are already in place and offers no account of how these systems emerge in the first place. Property rights theory provides an explanation of how they come about – they emerge as a matter of social choice. Here, the two kinds of spontaneity interact – spontaneous markets and spontaneous political markets. Spontaneous markets require responsive governments to create legal environments that support innovation, competition and private wealth accumulation.

Whereas public choice theory applies economic analysis to political science, the economic theory of property rights applies it to, and learns from, law. For a review of the economic theory of property rights readers are referred to seminal contributions by Alchian and Demsetz (1973), Alchian and Allen (1977), Cheung (1969, 1983) and Barzel (1997). One of Barzel's great contributions is to develop a systematic normative as well as positive analysis of property rights. He gives us tools to describe the way property rights have been, are and are likely to be, allocated and also tools that suggest whether one allocation is more efficient than another. We use his normative analysis at various points in the book and introduce it here.

First we define several key terms. Property rights theory views commodities as having multiple attributes, the rights to which are, in principle, infinitely separable. A distinction can be made between *economic rights* (the ability to derive direct or indirect income or welfare from a resource or attribute of a resource) and *legal rights*; and between formal and informal rights. The relationship is not always straightforward: formal rights defined by ineffective legal instruments may give less protection to economic rights than informal customary rights. Where law and order breaks down, legal rights may not coincide with economic rights. Rights are exchanged by contracts, which may also be formal (legal) or informal. A home purchaser transacts with a vendor for a set of well-delineated rights over the home and the land on which it stands. The price paid, however, reflects the buyer's valuation of many neighbourhood attributes which are implicitly bundled in but which are not subject to formal contract. By comparison, rights to services and facilities are subject to more formal contractual attention in, for example, hotels, condominiums and privately managed science parks.

The degree to which ownership is established over a commodity's separate attributes depends on the cost of creating and policing contracts that establish that ownership – transaction costs. Attributes to which rights are not assigned by formal or informal contract are said to be in the *public domain* and are potentially the subject of competition. The public domain is therefore the domain (spatially or otherwise defined) within which competition occurs in the consumption of resources – or more generally, resource attributes. This leads to the idea that society allocates property rights in order to curtail resource waste (dissipation) resulting from competitive consumption of shared (public domain) goods. Since it is too costly, relative to value, to establish property rights over every attribute of a good or resource, some will inevitably be left in the public domain.

Which attributes are left in or removed from the public domain depends crucially on two values – the value of the attribute itself and the cost of assigning property rights over it. As attributes change in value due to shifts in preferences, degradation or enhancement and as the transaction costs of assigning property rights change through technology and price changes, so there will be a demand for reallocation of property rights. The change in value of a home's *security risk* attribute, for example, may lead to demands for greater rights to public policing; greater rights to engage in resident policing; or greater rights over who uses local streets. The UK's highest decision making body, the House of Lord's, is at the time of writing debating a further round of policy measures designed to give stronger powers over speed limits to local communities. The value of local roads has diminished through increased congestion, danger and so on, leading to the redistribution of rights over road space and transport externalities from individual road users to the community.

In the absence of clearly assigned rights, resources are likely to be expended in capturing or protecting scarce public domain attributes and this is assumed to be inefficient since such resources are likely to be dissipated, accruing to no one. Sitting in a traffic jam, for example, dissipates time, fuel and clean air – a result of competition for public domain road space. The dissipation costs in a particular property rights assignment is therefore a normative issue: an allocation of property rights with less dissipation is more efficient.

Where attributes are not scarce (where they are not congested), however, there may be no inefficiencies in leaving them in the public domain. Indeed, a community may consider it desirable to leave certain attributes of civic goods and services in the public domain for equity reasons as well as the efficiency reason that it is too costly to allocate individual rights to all citizens.

However, with few exceptions, public domain goods and services in cities have a habit of becoming congested, resulting in dynamic realignment of property rights over time. The right to an on-street parking space in most cities was once left unallocated – left in the public domain. This may be efficient below congestion levels but when the demand for spaces exceeds supply it incurs dissipation costs in the form of queuing, disputing, lobbying policy makers, and adopting inconvenient trip behaviour. A responsive local government will look for ways of assigning the right more efficiently – residents only permits (with various pricing regimes), closing a lane, closing the road to through traffic and so on.

This raises the question of how any particular assignment of property rights may be judged as being less or more efficient. This can only be answered in the context of allocating resources to some common purpose (such as maximising revenue, profit, votes, citizen satisfaction, neighbourhood quality, minimising an externality and so on). The technical answer to the question is founded on common sense: rights to a resource should be assigned to those in the strongest position to influence the resource's contribution to the desired outcome. This is a simple formula with remarkably wide application.

In the case of private transactions it means that rights and liabilities in a contract should be assigned in a way that maximises the value of the contract. Computers sold with a manufacturer's warranty over parts failure are more valuable – to producer and customer – than those that leave the customer liable to poor workmanship. Making manufacturers liable for an attribute (quality) that they have control over yields better products. On the other hand, consumers have control over the way the computer is used and it would be in no-one's interest to assign liability for accidental damage to the manufacturer. However, an insurer may be willing to buy this liability from the customer because the insurer has specialised knowledge that enables it to spread the risk across other customers. When manufacturers have liability for quality, they have the incentive to discover efficient processes – which deliver higher quality at less cost. When customers have the liability for accidents they have an incentive to take better care of their purchases (behave more efficiently, dissipating less of the wealth of manufacturers or insurers). When insurers assume liability for accidental loss they have an incentive to devise efficient risk-spreading formulae and contracts that maximise cover for minimum cost. Assigning property rights over a resource makes the resource owner a residual claimant of benefit (use and income) generated by that resource and encourages efficiency – increased efficiency means private gains.

In the case of collective action problems, such as solutions to externality and public goods problems, the same common-sense principle suggests that liabilities be assigned to agents most able to maximise the value of the collective action. If the action is directed at reducing externalities to some socially acceptable level, then rights over the various resource attributes involved should be assigned to those who have the greatest ability to influence the way those resource attributes contribute to externality reduction. If the objective is to moderate pollution from industrial workshops in residential areas (moderate not remove, accepting that a healthy economy has certain environmental costs) then giving urban planners powers to ban such uses entirely is an inefficient assignment of property rights. If the object is to conserve a threatened habitat it will be inefficient to assign unrestricted access rights to the public. Lai (1993) and Yu (2000), for example, show that privatising fishing rights in Taiwan and Hong Kong have led to reduced pollution and increased stock quantity, variety and quality.

In the case of choice of governance model, the same principle suggests assigning governance functions to levels of organisation and governance most able to deliver those functions in pursuit of accepted goals. In this context it is similar, if not the same as, the principle of *subsidiarity*. *Subsidiarity* is a legal principle much featured in discussion of the European Union (de Búrca, 1999), where it means the assignment of policy or legal jurisdiction to the level of government most able to deliver a particular government function effectively. The idea extends beyond the question of designing political systems, however. Political systems are just one approach to organising collective action in the provision of shared goods. The analysis of efficient assignment of property rights – of subsidiarity – helps evaluate alternative models of urban governance such as entrepreneurial clubs and public–private partnerships.

Transaction Costs and Urban Order

Ronald Coase (1937) proposed that transaction costs explain the existence of organised economic activity (firms). If the market is so efficient at ordering spontaneous transactions, he asked, why do firms exist? His answer was to point to the costs of making and policing contracts (see also Cheung, 1983). Transaction costs are saved when owners of labour, land and capital resources pool property rights and submit to planned economic co-operation. This observation prompted him to ask another question – why is the economy not one large firm? The answer to this, he suggested, is that at some point the costs of organising production within a firm exceed the costs of transacting in the market and a firm becomes too large.

This is an insight that can be generalised to apply to all forms of organised co-operation. The costs of a government programme or policy can exceed the benefits delivered. There may be alternative organisational arrangements that could deliver greater benefits at lower cost. Much of the current debates about public–private and public–voluntary partnerships in the supply of urban services are an exploration of these alternatives. This perspective has an obvious relationship to the questions of rent seeking and asymmetric information to which we have already referred. It also relates strongly to another line of inquiry – that of economic historians such as Douglass North (1990, 1992) who demonstrate the relationship between institutions, transaction costs and economic performance; and that of Eggertsson (1990), Kasper and Streit (1998) and others who have sought to synthesise an economic theory of institutions. The institutionalists emphasise the importance of rules in reducing transaction costs. Indeed, firms and governments economise on market-based transactions because they replace these transactions with systems of rules. If a system of rules becomes too costly to maintain – taking account of the costs of perverse responses to rules as well as the costs of administering and policing rules – then an organisation becomes inefficient. It will either change or fail. Property rights, organisations, institutions and transaction costs reorganise.

Our arguments in this book are structured to reflect this evolutionary dynamic. Specifically, we find it helpful to think of five kinds of order emerging as cities evolve. Each is driven by an aversion to transaction costs of various kinds.

Organisational order emerges as individuals pool property rights to form firms. *Institutional order* emerges as society invents systems of rules and sanctions that reduce the costs of competition. *Proprietary (ownership) order* emerges as those institutions allocate property rights over scarce resources. *Spatial order* emerges as individuals and firms seek locations that minimise both travel-related transaction costs and information search costs and that balance these against congestion costs of crowded cities. *Public domain order* emerges as individuals engage in collective action through governments and other agencies to clarify property rights over jointly consumed goods (externalities, public goods and natural resources) and thereby to reduce the costs of competition, and in the extreme, the costs of anarchy.

A General Urban Theory

Four key propositions arise from this brief discussion of institutional economic theory and are summarised below, respectively designated the *subdivision rule, combination rule, public domain rule* and *subsidiarity rule*. The first three are generalised positive statements about the evolution of property rights. The fourth is a generalised normative statement about the efficient division of ownership in pursuit of some collective goal. We view these as fundamental organising principles that apply equally to the evolution of cities, firms, markets and governments; to the evolution of public policy regarding externalities and public goods; and to the evolution of market and other voluntary solutions to urban problems.

Proposition 1: Subdivision rule
Any particular configuration of property rights over a resource is a function of the value of the resource and of the costs of assigning effective property rights. The latter includes the cost of technology required to make the resource excludable (to facilitate efficient pricing). If the value of a resource rises, or the cost of assigning property rights to a valued resource falls (due to technological or institutional innovation), then there will be a demand for a reassignment of property rights.

Proposition 2: Combination rule
Property rights will be combined if the transaction costs of co-ordinating resource use via organisation and planning is less than the costs of co-ordination via market transactions.

Proposition 3: Public domain rule
A resource will be left in the public domain if the costs of assigning property rights over it exceed the value thus created.

Proposition 4: Subsidiarity rule
The total value of a contract or of any collective action is maximised when agents with an ability to influence the value of the contract or the outcome of collective action bear the full effects of their actions. This will be achieved when agents have a residual claim on the benefits created by the resources that they influence. This way, they have an incentive to deploy their resources efficiently in the attainment of the contract of collective action goal.

We use the rules throughout the book to interpret the processes by which spatial concentration, knowledge specialisation, economic development and the evolution of markets and governments proceed.

1.3   PLANNED VERSUS SPONTANEOUS ORDER

Planned order is top-down, hierarchical, conceived of by experts, managers, administrators and political representatives and based on centralised information. It is attempted by governments and it is attempted by the hierarchical decision making systems within firms. Although it is appealing to those with power and responsibilities to fulfil, it has an inherent information disadvantage when compared with the spontaneous ordering power of the market. This is due to its dependence on the central collection and analysis of data about needs, demands and wants. Also inherent, and also related to information, are the dangers of opportunistic behaviour – rent seeking. Where experts process information they often have a monopoly advantage over decision makers and can use their power to influence decisions that benefit them one way or another. Decision makers too can act opportunistically to the degree that they are not held responsible for all of their decisions.

On the other hand, there are certain types of order that can only be, or are most efficiently, delivered by government and other hierarchical bodies. Governments owe their existence in the first place to the need for collective action in regard to the protection of property and personal liberty and the efficient supply of security. When considering what functions are best delivered by governments, by private firms and by new agencies with joint public–private liability, the costs and benefits of various patterns of liability should be considered. This entails understanding which agency can most efficiently control resources in pursuit of any particular set of goals.

Spontaneous order is the order in the work of Friedrich Hayek, *Guan Zi*, John Locke, Jeremy Bentham and Adam Smith. It is the order that emerges as individuals and organisations (notably firms in modern time) exchange rights and liabilities – those over land, labour, capital and other resources and over distinct attributes of these resources. It is the order that gives rise to families, households, clubs, firms and markets; to land and housing markets; to urban labour markets; to neighbourhoods within cities; to transport systems that link workers with work places; to cities themselves; and to systems of cities. In the words of Hayek:

> To understand our civilisation, one must appreciate that the extended order resulted not from human design or intention but spontaneously: it arose from unintentionally conforming to certain traditional and largely moral practices, many of which men tend to dislike, whose purpose they usually fail to understand, whose validity they cannot prove, and which have nonetheless fairly rapidly spread by means of an evolutionary selection – the comparative increase of population and wealth – of those groups that happened to follow them (Hayek, 1988: 6).

Hayek refers to the human civilisation in general, not just to the Western form. The *Book of Guan Zi*, written in or about the fourth century BC in China, offers in one place an Oriental version of the Austrian economist's idea of spontaneity. It is also an Eastern version of the English concepts of property and utilitarianism and the Scottish idea of the 'invisible hand':

> It is human nature to feel pleased on getting what one desires and to feel worried on meeting what one is averse to. This is something common to both the high and the low (Chapter 'Jin Zang' in *Guan Zi*, as quoted in Hu, 1988: 108).

> It is human nature not to refrain from going after profit and to keep away from danger when either of them is in sight. Where profit is anticipated, traders will quicken their pace day and night and make light of travelling over a thousand li (miles) to get it. When gain is expected from the water, fishermen will go out to the sea thousands of fathoms deep, sail against the tide and venture on a dangerous voyage of hundreds of li for nights on end.... They will go forward with nobody's push and come along with nobody's pull, and the ruler has no worries or troubles while the people get rich spontaneously. He will be like a bird hatching eggs, sitting there easily and silently, expecting fledglings to come out (Chapter 'Jin Zang' in *Guan Zi*, as quoted in Hu, 1988: 108).

'Profit' in *Guan Zi* refers generally to interest, benefit or the economist's general notion of welfare and is not limited to the accounting difference between revenue and cost. The point made is that the human drive to be fruitful is a reliable device for those vested with the responsibility of governing society towards greater prosperity.

1.4   CITIES, WEALTH AND INSTITUTIONS

Cities are the spatial manifestations of co-operative acts. They indicate a universal compelling advantage of spatial concentration, spatial differentiation and economic specialisation. They are systematic concentrations of individuals, each of whom possessing distinct capabilities and who are densely bound together by webs of institutions (informal and formal rules and sanctions). Institutions are the sinews of society. They reduce the costs that arise when people and firms co-operate with each other by informal agreements and formal contracts. This is true of all societies, ancient and modern, but modern urban economies require an unprecedented complexity of institutions because of the complexity of exchanges they are built upon.

The institutions that make cities attractive to individuals and keep urban society from the anarchy of uncontrolled competition have been evolving since the earliest stages of civilisation. These institutions are subject to relentless evolutionary changes as co-operative motivations (individual needs and demands) change and as the number of individuals co-operating steadily rises.

In 1994, approximately 2.5 billion individuals lived in the World's urban areas. This is set to double to around 5.1 billion in 2025 (United Nations, 1995). The same source estimated that in 1995 there were 3329 major cities or urban agglomerations in the World, including capital cities and cities with more than 100 000 population. In 1950, there were only two cities, namely London and New York, housing more than 10 million individuals. By 1994 this had risen to 14 and by 2015 there are likely to be 27 mega cities (Stubbs and Clarke, 1996). London will not be one of them because its population has dropped considerably since 1950. Seoul in South Korea will, being a city of over 10 million with ten nearby satellite cities holding populations of between 200 000 and a million. The constellations of interconnected cities in the Pearl River Delta and in the Shanghai region of Southern China constitute metropoles in excess of 40 million citizens each.

The rules needed for the productive cohabitation and co-operation of 1, 10 or 40 million individuals would seem to be quite different from the institutions governing the agrarian village or market town; the medieval city-states of Europe and Asia; the early industrial cities of America and Europe; or the pre-modern settlements in Africa and Australia. This is only partially true, however. It is true of the rules that govern planned *prescriptive* order (whether by government or within a firm or family) – attempts to allocate resources by design, edict, coercion, persuasion, directive and administrative fiat. Many of the modern welfare state functions attempt to impose this kind of order – prescribing who should have what in what quantities, at what times and under what conditions. This kind of planning requires enormously complex rules and costly information gathering, monitoring and policing.

This is not true of the spontaneous and unplanned order that emerges from the voluntary exchange among many individuals in the market place. A characteristic of the order arising from markets and more generally from voluntary exchange or decentralised resource decisions is that it can be achieved with a relatively simple rule – the institution of *private property*. Conversely, any erosion of this institution implies a weakening of society's ability to order itself spontaneously.

The institution of private property – a set of rules governing competition – achieves two significant functions. On the one hand, it transforms anarchy into a state of affairs in which the full benefits of the division of labour and the associated accumulation of wealth in society are possible by voluntary interaction. On the other hand, it also defines and protects an individual's liberties: the freedom to enjoy the use or exchange of possessions; the freedom from undue interference with the fruits of labour by theft, slavery, violence, or unreasonable government exaction; the freedom from opportunism in exchanges with partners in markets or government; the freedom from unreasonable levels of external costs arising from other individuals' production of exchanges of goods or services; and as an option, the freedom from interacting with others altogether.

Unlike the prescriptive rules that govern much of the planned order of the state, the rules necessary to ensure that individuals use their private property rights (including the right to their own labour) for the benefit of others are simpler and fewer, more abiding and more universal. They are the *proscriptive* rules of liberty and security; the rules that safeguard property, open-competition, creativity and innovation; the rules that safeguard individuals from third party costs; and the rules that hold collective decision makers (in private and public governance) accountable to those whose interests they serve. A crucial job of the state is to create and maintain the institutions that safeguard these public goods and thus to ensure a foundation for productive, economically healthy cities based on individual incentive.

Proscriptive rules ('freedom from') tend to have stronger organising power than prescriptive rules ('freedom to'). The former are less likely to be subverted by markets that are driven by more accurate information about society's valuation of the resources subject to rules. One of the themes in this book is that information scarcity and the cognitive capacity of decision makers severely limit the benefits of action planned by a few for the benefit of the majority, however well educated or well intended the former may be.

The greater the complexity of the system being planned, the greater the information burden; the greater the costs of information search; and the less likely it is that imposing planned solutions will successfully yield beneficial order.

Simple rules that guide decentralised exchange decisions made on the basis of freely formed local subjective individual information are capable of ordering highly complex systems. Cities are highly complex systems and it should be of no surprise that attempts by any authority to manage and plan by detailed prescription frequently fail. Where such attempts do succeed it is likely to be because the prescriptions – major infrastructure investments for example – have created conditions within which a spontaneous, decentralised order can flourish. The order that emerges from government plans is therefore capricious, and success in terms of a plan's stated objectives is a matter of chance.

1.5   'MARKET FAILURE'

The decentralised decisions that occur in markets are social and co-operative decisions. They are benevolent in a paradoxical way. In pursuit of by-and-large self-interested goals, individuals contract to exchange property rights with others and in so doing provide other individuals with goods and services that they need. Individuals compete in this self-regarding contracting process but the results of the competition are generally mutually beneficial rather than destructive or exploitative.

This is so to the extent that all resources that have a value also have a price. Many valued resources are not allocated by markets, however, giving rise to what has come to be termed *market failure*. Principal among the market failures used to justify government intervention are externalities (third party costs not taken into account in a transaction); public goods (collectively consumed goods); and monopoly behaviour. We treat the monopoly problem as a public good problem in the sense that the market tends not to deliver the public good of self-regulation against monopoly practices.

In Chapters 5–7 we critique the notion of market failure, preferring to view externalities and public goods as unpriced goods and resources – unpriced because of the high costs of assigning the property rights that would render them marketable. The shift in perspective is profoundly significant when it comes to considering solutions to externality problems.

Externalities and public goods cause distortions in the allocation of private resources because of the absence of accurate information about how they are valued. They are endemic in cities, however, and at the heart of most urban management issues.

Where people and firms crowd in close proximity, externalities are inevitably ubiquitous and dense. It is a perverse feature of modern development that the greater the spatial concentration and differentiation of individuals, the greater the total shared benefits and the greater and more complicated are the hidden social costs of consuming and producing. The social costs (congestion and other externality costs) of population agglomeration typically rise disproportionately to benefits within a given infrastructural and institutional framework. The net benefits of city living are therefore likely to decline at some point: the benefit curve in Figure 1.1 eventually peaks and then falls as net benefits of urban growth start to fall (benefits of urban-based co-operation minus the costs of co-operating).

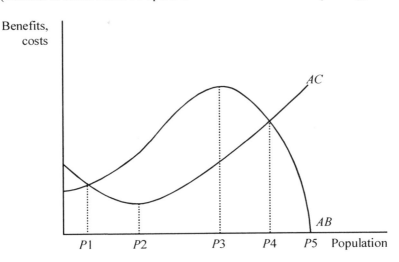

Notes:
P1 = minimum city size
P2 = lowest cost city size
P3 = city size giving maximum welfare to existing citizens
P4 = optimal city size
AB = average net benefits
AC = average costs

Source: Derived from Alonso (1971); Richardson (1978)

Figure 1.1   Urban efficiency and city size

If the net benefits of agglomeration fall below the costs of managing the city (to the right of point *P4* in Figure 1.1), then the city is theoretically too large in respect of the dimension taken into account in measuring costs and benefits. This will not, on its own, prevent a city from expanding since the marginal externality costs arising from an individual's actions are dispersed over many individuals and *marginal* disbenefits and marginal urban management costs are not easily perceived. *Average* net cost (quality of life) may be more easily judged, and if this is palpably diminished, a natural force for change may emerge.

Figure 1.1 is a simple model that demonstrates the ideas that congestion and other externalities tend to rise with city size. The reality is that there are many benefits gained from locating in cities and many social costs arising. The relationship between benefits and costs and population size is unique for each factor that contributes to a city's attractiveness. A city may be operating efficiently in one dimension, but may not have crossed thresholds in other dimensions such as market catchments for certain goods. Public transport may be operating efficiently but private transport-related externalities may be running at unacceptable levels. Adjustments to land policy to overcome land-use externalities (spillover effects) may throw transport systems out of equilibrium and generate yet more traffic externalities.

Planning for infrastructure, services and utilities with a view to optimising benefits and costs, including externality costs is an imprecise science. This is all the more so when these are supplied by the public sector without pricing information. Even if it were possible to gauge a set of optimal planned thresholds (each representing a discrete lumpy investment) of multiple infrastructural investments, they would not coincide: it is impossible to pin down population targets that satisfy all thresholds. Governments do not find it easy to deliver public goods efficiently, particularly when the criteria for efficient allocation are prescriptive rules (the right to clean water, uncongested streets, local schools, a certain amount of green space per person and so on). If methods can be devised that give private entrepreneurs adequate incentive to supply public goods and methods devised to encourage the internalisation of externalities (to price congested resources) then we may be surprised just how many of the costs of agglomeration yield to the spontaneous ordering power of markets. In Chapters 6 and 7 we evaluate and illustrate the different classes of approaches that may be used to assign property rights in the face of public goods and externality problems. In Chapter 8 we conclude the book with three substantial examples of public domain problems and consider how property rights might be optimally allocated using the subsidiarity rule.

1.6 SPONTANEOUS SOLUTIONS TO 'MARKET FAILURES'

The inability of markets to deliver certain kinds of goods and services is the assumption underlying many municipal government functions. If allowed, markets can be very creative, however, in filling in gaps left by government-delivered civic goods, and indeed can, under appropriate institutional constraints (such as laws governing public–private partnerships) help to deliver those services efficiently. The creative market supply of infrastructure and services is most flexible where decentralised private decisions are not artificially restrained by rigid central plans and regulations. The urban economies of the developing world thrive on creative improvisation and the use of substitutes for municipal-supplied public goods (such as LPG gas, bottled water, community para-transit, waste-collection, community policing and water boreholes).

The market can also deliver solutions to externality problems. Third party commercial disputes may be solved by private mediation. Voluntary negotiation between producer and consumer of an externality may lead to compensation and a reduction of output. Entrepreneurs may offer new forms of product that reduce externalities such as improved transport technology, neighbourhoods with privately managed community facilities, private policing, private street cleansing and shopping malls (private high streets).

Returning to the illustration of the congested city (Figure 1.1), we may reasonably claim that both governments and markets are responsible for the downturn in net benefits of city life by failing to supply adequate public goods and control externalities. However, the notions of market failure and government failure are both short-term. There are good practical reasons of course for identifying problems with either method of organising society's resources at any one point in time. From a longer-term perspective, markets and political markets tend to succeed by spontaneous adaptation. This is not an argument for doing nothing about short-term problems, rather an argument against short-termism and an argument for looking out for emergent spontaneous market and collective action solutions.

It is worth considering how markets and political markets might respond to a city suffering from over-congestion. Markets respond as individuals make decentralised decisions. Governments respond to voters and to their own needs, with centralised decisions.

First, there will be spatial readjustment in the land market. People and firms may leave the city, as happened in London and other congested cities in the last quarter of the twentieth century. This is the *exit* option of Hirschman (1970). Voluntary dispersion from the city, permitted by improved transport technology, is an example of spontaneous order. Individuals and firms exchange property rights in a congested city with someone for whom those rights are valuable, and purchase new rights in an alternative location. If purchasers of locational rights in the congested city impose fewer social costs, then the spontaneous order yields benefits for others beyond the two exchange partners (positive externalities). This happened when old industry and warehousing vacated vast tracts of land in western cities during the second half of the twentieth century.

Second, there will be a re-shuffling of property rights within the city, as people and firms move in search of locations and exchange partners that for them yield higher benefits and lower costs. The co-operative patterns in a city adjust in response to secular changes in congestion, crime, pollution and other social costs. Firms change suppliers, location, and market strategy. Individuals change shopping destinations, places of schooling, locations of work, outlets of leisure activities and modes of transport.

Third, there will be a demand for a reassignment of property rights in the political market. This is the *voice* option – Hirschman's alternative to *exit* (1970). Firms and individuals make demands for law and policy that better protect their private property and give greater security of rights over shared goods and services including neighbourhood facilities and environments – often at the expense of other groups. This accounts for the resilience of regulative land use planning as a government activity in advanced democratic states. Individuals will also demand the right or privileges to new and improved infrastructure and services – something that invariably involves reallocating the rights to tax revenues between competing groups and neighbourhoods and ultimately redistributing private property rights over personal income and wealth. Government decision makers and planners have both economic and professional incentive to take advantage of demands for new planned order and in this way they enter the fray in the competition for a cut in the benefit ('rent') as the city adjusts to its congestion. Professional urban planners, for example, espoused to their advantage the scientific cause of system efficiency in the modern era starting in the 1960s. They have done the same with the sustainability cause.

Fourth, innovations by individuals, firms and governments act to minimise the problems of over-concentration – by new building forms, notably high-rise property, mass transit infrastructure construction and various improvised means to tackle bottlenecks.

What can be said about the congestion and evolution of the city as a whole is true of parts of the city. Neighbourhoods change – rapidly or imperceptibly; by intrinsic or extrinsic influences; by market activity or government activity. Citizens standing to lose from the emerging order may react by *exit* or by *voice*. New spontaneous order emerges in response to exit, and new planned order emerges in response to voice.

1.7 GOVERNMENT FAILURE – WHEN PLANNED ORDER IS UNRESPONSIVE OR GOING WRONG

Much of the planned order attempted in cities (city planning, urban planning, neighbourhood planning, community planning, town and country planning) and systems of cities (regional planning, sub-national planning) has faltered, failed or been revised by the market. This is because the government planner has ignored the strength of spontaneous re-ordering on the one hand and the interaction between planned and spontaneous order on the other hand. The failure also occurs, as we have said, because the information and knowledge base that informs planned order solutions is more limited than it claims to be and in some cases is simply defective or even wilfully misleading. Mistakes in the planned order are often lumpy, and resistance to rectification is often stubborn. This is in sharp contrast to the more dispersed subjective knowledge that governs the host of decentralised decisions that produces spontaneous responses to secular changes in resource values and transaction costs and to more sudden exogenous shocks. Three examples are given to illustrate these assertions.

The first example is rent controls on housing, which redistribute property rights from landlords to tenants. They arise as a planned attempt to order housing markets in line with the social and political goals of dominant decision makers. Their stated intent is to expand the supply of cheap rental housing. Their effect, however is under-investment in private-rental sector housing and premature redevelopment of rent-capped property as a means of bypassing rent regulations. All this works to the longer-term detriment of low-income groups. The experience is universal (Hayek et.al., 1972). Thus, more people sleep under the stars than under roofs with protected rent (Cheung, 1975). The outcome of most rent control experiments has been jeopardised by inadequate information about the spontaneous ordering processes governing housing supply.

The second example is the large-scale socialisation of housing production that characterised the post-war years in Western and Eastern Europe. This has left a slum-clearance (or social re-engineering) legacy greater in scale than the one it was partly designed to address. This is not a criticism of social housing policy *per se* – housing subsidies appear to be necessary in most states; it is rather an observation that urban planners and politicians apparently lacked the information necessary to supply and manage housing in a way that matched demand. The diversification of uses and tastes in those former public housing estates that are now under new property rights regimes better reflects the diversity of demand that was latent under municipal socialism. Transfer of property rights to individuals has helped satisfy this demand but so too have new forms of collective ownership and administration, via estate management companies, community mutual societies, co-operatives and state-subsidised housing associations operating under some degree of competitive discipline.

The third example is provided by London's famous green belt policy – exported around the world for more than half a century. Initially intended to be both a growth control device and a recreation provision, it now largely serves the interests of a minority of privileged suburban and ex-urban town and village dwellers who lobby strongly and successfully for its protection (Hall et al., 1973). The green belt has failed to halt the growth of the metropolitan region, however, which is accommodated in towns beyond. It increases aggregate commute times and energy consumption in the capital region; protects much land that is of questionable recreational value; pushes the metropolitan population further away from the city where they consume more land per capita than they would further in; and artificially inflates property values to the detriment of lower-income citizens and to the detriment of economic prosperity (Pennington, 2002; Herington, 1984, 1990; Simmie, 1996). Spontaneous market order adjusts to unyielding planned order and property rights are reallocated through political markets as well as land markets. Higher income groups secure most of the recreational and amenity benefits of the greenbelt by colonising its fringes and villages and secure political support for this advantage in exchange for votes in municipal elections.

While spontaneous order may eventually subvert planned order as the true costs of the latter are realised by society, the process may take a long time. This will especially be the case where groups seek to protect vested interests. Hong Kong, with its massive public housing and urban renewal schemes and now theoretically under the 'constitutional capitalism' of the *Basic Law* (Lai, 2002) is a case in point. With more than half of the population living in public-rental or subsidised purchased housing it took almost 49 years for post-war rent control in Hong Kong to be diluted in favour of the landlord (Wong, 1998).

1.8   THE ALLURE OF UTOPIA

We close our introduction by indulging in literary licence to address the important issue of *prescriptive* versus *proscriptive* institutions and order. Few of those involved in urban management and planning are ardent utopians. Many, however, hold or learn values that have an optimistic view – an over-optimistic view we would say – of what planned order can achieve. At risk of being mistakenly labelled anti-government and anti-planning, we draw some insights for the discussion in the following chapters from the history of utopias.

> The authoritarian utopias have aimed at giving shepherds, captains and tyrants to the people.... These utopias were progressive in as much as they wished to abolish economic inequalities, but they replaced the old economic slavery by a new one: men ceased to be the slaves of their masters or employers, to become the slaves of the Nation and the State.... The builders of utopias claimed to give freedom to the people, but freedom which is given ceases to be freedom (Berneri, 1950: 3).

Archaeological evidence and historical documentation show that settlements were always planned whenever the state, be it personified by the shepherd, captain or tyrant, marshalled sufficient resources and power. Ancient Alexandria as seen by Caesar was planned. Babylon, before the eyes of its Hebrew captives, was planned. Chinese imperial cities Chang'an (now Xi'an) and Luoyang, faithfully imitated by the Japanese in their planning of Kyoto, were planned by the state. In these examples, the association of imposed order with military and dictatorial political power, or despotism, is striking.

The power to regimentalise individual property rights into collective organisations such as legions, firms, cities and even states, lies with the owners of the rights that are most scarce (Barzel, 1997). Where security is the bottleneck to material progress, economic organisation is led by experts in the monopoly control of violence. Following the retreat of the Roman Empire, Europe's nation states emerged through wars between powerful tribal leaders. Economic order currently emerges in post-socialist Russia and other lawless places under the leadership of men with access to violence. Economic organisation in feudal China and Europe was led by those able to provide collective security to those with land, labour and capital. In the marshal cities of history and the early pioneer settlements of the new worlds, local governors, who held the power of life and death, took the lead and planned new settlements, new laws and new forms of government. In times of modern war, or other natural or economic catastrophe, martial laws are enacted and marshal plans made by governments, who alone have the right to use force in the achievement of national defence, physical and economic restructuring.

If violence is defined as the taking of individual property rights, then the nationalisation of the right to develop land by a government, as the British government did so effectively immediately after the World War II, may be interpreted in this light. That drastic constitutional revision was carried because of the compelling requirement for organised reconstruction after the war, helped by the economic crisis besetting the world before the war.

When stable institutions provide security from internal and external threats, other factors of production become the bottleneck to prosperity. Where labour is scarce, labour representatives can wield organising power. Where licences and official sanctions are a limiting factor in economic endeavour – as is still the case in 'two-system' China and as is the case under all centrally planned and bureaucratic regimes – economic activity is organised by entrepreneurs with access to political decision makers and to powerful bureaucrats. Or it is organised by the politicians and administrators themselves.

Where capital is the scarce factor, organisation of the economy is by those with property rights over capital. Most cities at the present time are organised under the leadership of capitalists – small domestic households investing in their own homes and their own human capital as well as small and medium sized businesses and large capitalists operating in global markets.

Utopias are romantic visions of alternative orders – literary or experimental reactions to existing orders. Perhaps they are a dialectical necessity – statements of what could be dreamed of, what could be worked for. They may inspire activism and political reforms. Of themselves, however, they tend to share a common set of fallacies including a belief in human perfectibility by reason if not innate selflessness; a belief in the ability of a select few to impose sustainable planned order; and a belief that private property rights may be, can be and should be beneficially transferred to the 'collective'.

In making these kinds of assumptions, they fail to understand or accept the realities of economic co-operation and organisation that we have started to discuss. Modern utopian voices often seem not to understand that capitalist-led development is a result of capital scarcity – that is, demand for capital – and that the demand for capital arises from individual preferences for consumption goods – including the demands of most utopians. However, the fatal mistake of most champions of utopias is that their plans require the rest of society to accept their ideals and disallow the option of *voice* or *exit*. The *practice* of utopian thinking reveals that only voluntary association with the option of exit, as evidenced in the persistence of religious orders, has any chance of long-term success. The experimental utopian communities of nineteenth century industrial Europe and America eventually succumbed to the dominance of capital-dominated order. The imposed utopian experiments of Eastern Europe, Russia, Cambodia and Vietnam are over. China's is in a planned decline in which spontaneous order is allowed to compete openly with imposed planned order and the processes of government are learning, themselves, to develop more of a spontaneity.

The utopian theme was dominant in the discourses of professional urban planners during much of the twentieth century. The influence of the early Twentieth Century Garden City Movement went deep and still does, in places where the education of planners and urban designers has not come to terms with market reality. Many urban planners throughout the world are still deeply wedded to a belief that 'utopias' can be planned, be it at the regional, city or neighbourhood scale. There is a role for urban plans and planning in a market economy, as we shall discuss in later chapters, but it is not the role of imposing order by the design of a few – albeit carefully constructed designs produced by collaborative engagement with stakeholders. It is a dangerous temptation for planners today to imagine themselves as modern Michelangelos or De Vincis who can impose an order of functional beauty for everyone.

Urban planners in many countries have professional jurisdiction over the strategically important factor of production – land. Land is usually developed site by site and the buildings on individual sites are usually designed. It was a natural step therefore for architects and engineers who found themselves asked to plan whole towns, to think in terms of physical design and planned order – utopia by physical design. The illusion started to crumble in many western countries as early as the 1960s when it became clear that master plans with their architectural orientation were not effective urban development or management tools in a mixed economy. The belief in utopia by physical planners typically lives on, however, even in the more market-sensitive planning tools that have replaced blueprint land-use planning. It is the belief that the planner with his or her long-term, synoptic analysis of stakeholder interests, market trends and constraints can create a plan that will beneficially co-ordinate and guide the exchange of and redistribution of property rights. There is a place for master planning – in designing private estates subject to market discipline and designing shared infrastructure in partnership with markets.

Urban planners, guardians of the least mobile factor of production, tend to think in terms of spatial, physical or graphical utopias. There is a sense in which public administrators and professionals who manage other sectors of the urban economy have also been influenced by their own aspatial versions of utopia. By this we refer to the ideal of the perfect market and the Pigovian economic notion of market failure and precise correctives. It was the market failure ideology, and its macro manifestation Keynesianism, that provided the intellectual underpinning for the massive expansion of the welfare state and municipal government in the second half of the twentieth century. The idea that governments should intervene in labour, land, education, transport and health markets by taxation, subsidy, regulation and direct investment may be defensible using public goods and externalities arguments. The idea that markets can be adjusted to some notional perfect-market allocation is a fiction, however. Some would say it is a useful fiction and better than not intervening at all.

The response to this, however, is that the judgement should be an empirical call. The textbook perfect market situation by which failures are notionally identified and correctives are designed does not hold because information is not perfect in the real world. Nor do the zero transaction costs of market exchange assumed by neo-classical market failure models exist in reality. Transaction costs of information search are positive because information is not perfect (the two simplifying assumptions of market correcting models are essentially one and the same). By the same token, the internal costs of decision making within firms (organisational costs) and the costs of government policy making (also organisational costs and sometimes referred to as agency costs) are also non-zero because information is not perfect.

The spatial utopias of urban planners, architects and urban visionaries and the sectoral or aspatial utopias of those schooled on traditional welfare economics are equally fictional. With their intellectual springs in Plato's class-based Republic, the most famous modern versions of utopia were the Marxist classless utopia on the one hand and the Keynesian macro-econtopia and Pigovian micro-econtopia on the other. Equally influential is the 100 per cent land tax utopia of the nineteenth century thinker Henry George, who found more support in Russia and China than in the USA.

Instrumental utopias may be, but cities should not be managed on the erroneous belief that planned order is the best guide to prosperity – or even to justice and equity, although we leave this argument to later. A preoccupation with planned order tends to lead to over-regulation; over-taxation; an undermining of government authority; undermining of professional managerial credibility; reduced individual independence and enterprise; and to societal cynicism (because it can never deliver). It is no surprise that the urban planning profession worldwide has lurched from one crisis of identity to another. That it survives is testimony to the social necessity of some of the functions it performs. Regulating land use externalities, protecting land and building property rights, co-ordinating infrastructure investment, and providing land markets with subsidised strategic intelligence are all valued functions. Prescribing big designs that are ignored by the market or that reduce wealth and welfare are not.

Consider Figure 1.1 again. The points at which cost and benefit curves intersect illustrate potential design criteria for utopia. Population $P1$ is the minimum viable city size for a cost minimising utopia. Point $P2$ is the size of utopia that residents would choose if consulted about expansion plans, maximising the gap between costs and benefits. *P*3 sizes utopia for the national or regional planner – the residents' utopia can accommodate *P*3 minus *P*2 more people before net costs kick in. If residents are not consulted then they may not notice the transfer of a portion of their consumer surplus to the newcomers. In reality, the chances are that utopia will grow beyond the planned population target, whichever one is selected. When Metroplan of Hong Kong was first conceived in 1988, the population estimated for the year 2011 was 6.8 million people. The 1996 census revealed a population (6.4 million) that had almost reached the 'long term' population target. This has been the experience of China's southern cities in spite of the tightest controls on population movements in modern history. It is certainly the case with most new towns and planned town expansion schemes in market economies. Does this mean that towns (and neighbourhoods and regions) that have outgrown their planned-for capacities are inefficient? The answer is no for two reasons, and here we return to our opening discussion of spontaneity.

First, the utopian design parameters are based on imperfect information. Planners cannot possibly understand or estimate the multitude of individual subjective valuations that in reality determine the maximum capacities of a neighbourhood, city or region. They can at best guess at targets – or most other design parameters including acceptable quantities and locations of urban services. Second, as discussed earlier, cities have more than one market or utility threshold and are very adaptive. Producers and consumers under the discipline of competition constantly search for new ways of using their property rights – new exchange partners in consumption, new combinations with the rights of others in production.

The curves in Figure 1.1 define comparative static equilibria. The reality of urban markets is dynamic and the curves constantly move upwards and to the right. Market-driven cities constantly innovate, producing new styles of living, new products, new technologies for overcoming the constraints of distance, congestion and resource management. Notwithstanding its 20 million inhabitants, South Korea's capital region – Greater Seoul – appears to function remarkably well around an efficient transit system. Mega cities avoid death by monocentric congestion by becoming polycentric. The actions of local governments help to shape systems of subcentres but by and large government plans channel a spontaneously decentralising population. Subcentres form naturally without planning. The log-jammed streets of downtown Bangkok cleared when a joint venture organisation linking capital market, engineering and government knowledge and resources filled in the canyon-like streets with two- and even three-tiered elevated highway and transit systems. The new transport system had the effect of strengthening some of the subcentres that formed in response to road congestion and made downtown areas more attractive as places to live.

A term that has come into usage to describe the dynamic evolution of markets is *catallaxis*, popularised by Von Mises (1949), from the Greek *katallatein* – to convert an enemy into a friend by mutually beneficial exchange. We return to the idea of urban catallaxis in the next chapter. Catallactic evolution of markets and of the institutions that govern them mean that urban planners and managers live in a perpetual state of surprise. Where institutions permit, innovation and creativity colonise plans and have a habit of subverting them.

2. The benefits and costs of co-operating in cities

2.1 THE BENEFITS OF CO-OPERATING

To overcome the rivalry between the States of Victoria and New South Wales, Canberra, being located equal distance from Melbourne and Sydney was chosen as the site for the federal capital of the Commonwealth of Australia. The location and layout of this city were both carefully planned; its shape, infrastructure and functional spaces being designed by Walter Griffin and Marion Mahoney were selected through a high profile international competition. It is, for many, a masterpiece of urban planning. Today, it is a perfectly clean and orderly city, but its exports are predominantly invisible federal government services. It is clean, as there are no hectic commercial, recreational or industrial activities. There are no problems of urban poverty as the population consists predominantly of civil servants, foreign delegates and ambassadors. The location was chosen for its political geometry with little attention paid to market preferences. For all but a very specialised set of individuals and firms, the costs of transacting in Canberra are too high. To those who admire the romantic chaos of Rome the Eternal City, Canberra is a sterile administrative settlement with a vulnerability shared by other mono-functional settlements. If the costs of market-based co-operation are too high to sustain spontaneous urban growth at this location, one suspects that the costs of government-based co-operation are inefficiently high too. Strong and economically sustainable cities succeed because they effectively reduce the costs of co-operative acts of all kinds, but especially of market-based transactions.

Urbanisation as Knowledge Diversification and Deepening Interdependence

Urbanisation is a process of concentration of spatially differentiated uses that corresponds to economic specialisation. More precisely, it is a process of knowledge diversification and deepening interdependence between individuals. Cities grow as people and firms with specialised knowledge locate themselves near to others who have complementary knowledge.

29

Urbanisation is a type of social order that reduces distance-related and other transaction costs. In particular, urban spatial order reduces the costs of searching for partners with which to exchange property rights over knowledge and the resources that knowledge yields. Rural migrants travel to cities with little more wealth than the right to their own labour. They seek others who value their labouring, petty-trading and other skills and who can combine these with managerial, entrepreneurial and capital management know-how. Farmers and fishermen negotiate contracts with urban firms that can combine agricultural knowledge with the knowledge of other individuals who know how to process, to package, to market, to retail food. Individuals trained as teachers sell their knowledge to schools which also purchase the knowledge of those who can construct buildings, provide electricity, write books, manufacture pencils.

Even something as simple as a pencil requires the combination of knowledge from millions of individuals spread across the globe, from graphite workers in Asia to foresters in North America. A team of the best scientists in the world, using their efforts alone without the assistance of others, may not be able to make a single pencil in their lifetime.

Actually, millions of human beings have a hand in my creation, no one of whom even knows more than a very few of the others. Now, you may say that I go too far in relating the picker of a coffee berry in far-off Brazil and food growers elsewhere to my creation; that this is an extreme position. I shall stand by my claim. There isn't a single person in all these millions, including the president of the pencil company, who contributes more than a tiny, infinitesimal bit of knowledge. From the standpoint of know-how, the only difference between the miner of graphite in Ceylon and the logger in Oregon is in the type of know-how. Neither the miner not the logger can be dispensed with, any more than the chemist at the factory or the worker in the oil field – paraffin being a by-product of petroleum.

Here is an astounding fact: Neither the worker in the oil field nor the chemist nor the digger of graphite or clay nor anyone who mans or makes the ships or trains or trucks nor the one who runs the machine that does the knurling on my bit of metal nor the president of the company performs his singular task because he wants me. Each one wants me less, perhaps, than does a child in the first grade. Indeed, there are some among this vast multitude who never saw a pencil nor would they know how to use one. Their motivation is other than me. Perhaps it is something like this: Each of these millions sees that he can thus exchange his tiny know-how for the goods and services he needs or wants. I may or may not be among these items (Read 1958, quoted Friedman and Friedman, 1990: 11–13).

Leonard Read's story has become as well known as Adam Smith's story of the pin. The complexity of making a pencil is much lower than making a house or factory or building a bus, a bus service or retail chain; but the idea is the same. Without co-operation, almost no object of consumption we take for granted can ever come into existence. The market is an arena in which spontaneously co-ordinated co-operation is possible.

Co-operation and Markets

The ordering of interaction between individuals or groups may range from maximal interdependence, as in the case of co-consumers of common lands, to maximal independence, as in the case of an owner of a private property living in complete self-sufficiency.

For the former, the 'value of the share in the jointly produced good that is secured depends on the behaviour of all members of the sharing group; and this value is influenced by the behaviour of the individual only in proportionate relationship to the size of the group' (Buchanan, 1993:1). For the latter, there is no trade or exchange. In the former, there is maximal co-operation, and in the latter, there is no need for co-operation.

In reality, men and women do not exist exclusively as sharers of commons or in perfect autarchy but in most instances as individuals and groups interacting in a co-operative manner through the market. In modern times, it is voluntary exchange through markets, as opposed to passively waiting for windfall redistribution from colonisation, war or capricious rulers that is the principal active means of acquiring greater wealth. Market co-operation grows hand-in-hand with the processes of knowledge specialisation and labour division. It is driven from one perspective by the limitation of any single individual's or group's knowledge and from another, by the comparative knowledge advantages between interacting individuals and groups. When private property rights exist, however compromised or deficient they may be, an incentive is established to co-operate for mutual gain. The story of humanity is not one of isolated homesteads (where each piece of land is one household's castle) or nomadic groups perpetually wandering in the margins of deserts and steppes. It is, by and large, one that describes the rise and fall of spatial concentrations of households in settlements (the process of urbanisation). Settlements, by their nature, have always been founded upon systems of exchange since they arise from, and foster, labour specialisation. Modern urbanisation is distinguished from its antecedents, however, by the sophistication of its underlying market exchange systems and more specifically, their capitalistic nature.

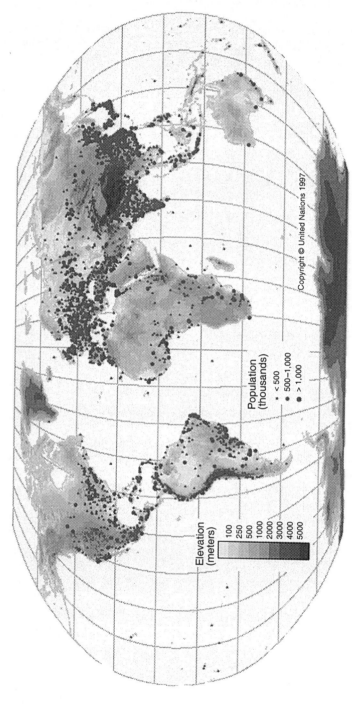

Source: United Nations (1998)

Figure 2.1 World population distribution

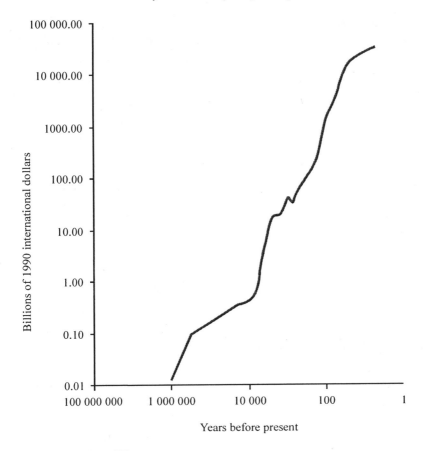

Source: De Long (1998)

Figure 2.2a   Growth of world GDP from past to present

Figure 2.1 shows the worldwide distribution of cities with 100 000 or more population in the last decade of the twentieth century. It is clearly not a random distribution across the earth's landmass and there are strong underlying ordering influences. Two influences evident from the map are elevation and proximity to the ocean. What cannot be seen from the map are the forces that entice people to live not just on the same coastal plains but within realistic co-operating distance of each other – in the clusters that we call cities. For obvious reasons people have always congregated on coastal lowlands. They have not always concentrated within those lowlands to the degree that they now do, however. Three hundred years ago the spread of population over the cultivable portion of the earth would have been noticeably more diffuse. Modern urbanisation is driven by the apparently irresistible benefits of market-based co-operation – trade on a local, city, regional and global scale.

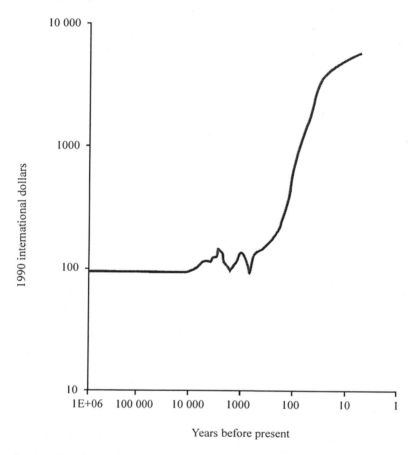

Source: De Long (1998)

Figure 2.2b   Growth of world GDP per capita from past to present

Figure 2.2 (a and b) indicates of the size of these benefits. From the start of the industrial era, average GDP per capita is estimated by De Long to have increased by a factor of about 30 from $195 (1990 international dollars) in the year 1800 to $6539 in the year 2000 (DeLong, 1998).

Catallaxis

The creative order that emerges as individuals interact to discover, test and exchange new knowledge has been termed *catallaxis*. Catallaxis involves innovation. It happens when resource owners, however meagre their assets, find others who want something that they possess and discover how to process their assets to supply that need in return for remuneration. Catallaxis as an economic model contrasts to the traditional neo-classical maximisation model by being open ended and relatively unconstrained. In the comparative static neo-classical world, profit and utility maximisation is limited by endowment constraints including production technology. In the catallactic world, knowledge evolution, innovation and adaptation guarantees a constant supply of new wealth-enhancing opportunities for those willing and able to use their resources productively in exchange or in combination.

Catallaxis gives Bombay's squalid pavement communities a simple order, making them bearable and for some, creating chances to prosper. It turns the developing world's informal sector economies and declining commercial areas in prosperous cities into incubators of adaptable labour and innovative processes and products. Catallaxis created the new markets for central area living currently changing the face of many European cities; it gentrified historical urban quarters throughout the world during the latter part of the twentieth century; it is driving the growth of so-called edge cities in dynamic urban regions. It creates regions of industrial specialisation and prosperity; it sustains the advantages of world cities like Tokyo, New York and London in the global economy; it creates gateway cities and regions like Hong Kong. It confers local, regional and national economic advantages.

Urban and economic phenomena such as these seem complex when viewed in their totality. At a global and city-wide scale they are difficult, if not impossible to understand, to predict, to control or to copy. This is because urban order unfolds by path-dependent evolutionary sequences of a multitude of individual exchanges; many of them creative, innovative and unpredictable. In the nexus of these exchanges, cities and systems of cities take shape as individuals seeking to overcome personal knowledge constraints make contracts; combine and exchange property rights with others in formal and informal organisations; organise themselves in space; and collectively develop norms, customs, rules, sanctions, laws and constitutions that facilitate exchange by reducing the costs of knowledge transaction. An understanding of the creative, evolutionary and unbounded catallactic economy has profound consequences for the way governments seek to manage and plan cities.

Market-driven Competition

The constraint of competition is essential to catallaxis and to the spontaneous generation and distribution of wealth in cities. The constraints must, however, be conducive to voluntary exchange and capital accumulation. A strong redistributional professional ethic among municipal administrators and planners – a reaction against some of the social costs of urbanisation – has tended to obscure the creative role that market-driven competition plays in ordering cities. Competition creates wealth that can be redistributed to those in need, however, and it also creates new opportunities for business, which helps the spread of wealth throughout society. Von Mises noted that, unlike other economic systems, personal wealth in a competitive market economy comes by providing others with what they want (1943).

Competition between individuals and firms supplying goods and services forces them to outlay costs in the search for new information about the wants of others. Competing suppliers search for new ways of combining and exchanging property rights in production, including new and more efficient processes and new products. Competition among consuming individuals and firms causes them to outlay costs in seeking products that better satisfy their preferences. Without competing consumers, suppliers would not incur costs in process or product innovation. Without competing suppliers, consumers would not incur costs in seeking the best supply partners. Competition among suppliers acts as a self-imposed discipline therefore, keeping them active in the search for combinations of property rights that will best meet consumers' wants. The discipline is good for consumers but costly to suppliers who, in a competitive market, have to bear a share of the costs of seeking buyers. Conversely, competition among consumers is costly for them but good for suppliers since it saves suppliers search costs.

Competition therefore has the effect of distributing search costs between suppliers and consumers. Where demand is slack, sellers incur a greater share of the search costs in seeking buyers. When it is strong, sellers can rely on buyers to assume more of the costs of discovering goods.

It follows from this that another benefit of competition is that it deals with the problem of testing new knowledge. Without competition among suppliers, the task of testing how well new products or processes meet the wants of consumers becomes problematic. In a competitive urban property market, regional labour market, or national educational market, new and old products that do not meet the wants of others soon fail.

The benefits of competition in one market do not remain there – they spill over to others. A competitive labour market requires a competitive educational and property market. Conversely, lack of competition in one market inhibits growth in others. Strong controls on property and land transactions create serious problems for labour markets in congested cities like London. An uncompetitive and over-centralised higher education sector will impose inefficiencies on national and regional labour markets and ultimately on the competitive distribution of the population throughout the country. The classical Confucian intellectual class, having obtained imperial patronage to the exclusion of other schools of thoughts in 136 BC, developed a public examination and bureaucratic system that century after century ignored scientific inquiry. Confucian ethics supports a hierarchical social system based on status rather than the rule of law and equal human rights – an ethos that prevented imperial China, the early inventor of compass, rudder, explosives, manual calculators (the abacus), paper, paper money and open market operations (the grain market), from developing the necessary institutions, theories and techniques to compete with the Western nations on an equal footing in the early nineteenth century.

The evolutionary success of the urban capitalist system of co-operation lies partly in the mutually beneficial exchanges facilitated by competition. More specifically it lies in competitive markets in which money is an intermediate medium of exchange. In a competitive market, money-price accurately signals the value of a transaction to consumers and suppliers, permitting well-informed and satisfying exchange decisions. In a well-functioning competitive market, price equates marginal benefit of consuming a resource to the marginal cost of producing it. In terms of property rights, market price equates the marginal benefit to a consumer of acquiring the right to an extra unit of a resource (acquiring an extra unit of entitlement) with the marginal cost of combining property rights in the process of production.

Competitive markets in these ways increase the individual and total value from exchange. They make cities irrepressibly attractive to firms and individuals and irrepressibly productive, creative and adaptive.

Property Rights and the Benefits of Co-operation

We shall elaborate the relationship between property rights, institutions and urban development in the next chapter. Here we illustrate the importance of private property rights to the enrichment of individuals and wider society.

When a tenant in a public housing estate illegally sub-lets in the face of rigid allocation rules and a local shortage of affordable homes, at least two households gain from the traded property right. When British politicians in the 1980s legislated to make the right alienable by permitting sub-letting or giving public housing tenants the right to buy, the exchanges that followed created wealth-enhancing adjustments in the organisational and spatial pattern of property rights (ignoring the very real disaster of negative equity that ruined some households during the ensuing economic recession). The same thing happened on a much greater scale in China during the 1990s after first land, and then the housing market reforms. In both cases rights over homes became decentralised and with the advantage of decentralised knowledge, the combination of other property rights at the same location changed. With their newly acquired rights, residents started to invest private capital to improve their homes (giving up rights to other capital in order to raise the value of their homeowner rights). Homes were sold or rented to others who valued them more highly than their previous home. Some individuals temporarily transferred their new rights to a bank as collateral for a loan to purchase another home (common in China), a car, or to borrow for business investment. Some of these loans will have resulted in successful enterprises that bring employment and wealth to others. Those enterprises combine capital from investors with the labour of workers, the expertise of accountants, marketing consultants and so on. Many may ultimately benefit through the process of production organised by the enterprise and those benefits are matched, at the margin, by the benefits to consumers of the firm's products or services.

When the Peruvian Commission for the Official Registration of Informal Property (COFOPRI) awarded land title deeds to 70 725 Lima squatter households in 1998, about 24 000 of the households gained access to finance from banks, lending agencies and informal sources (Calderon Cockburn, 2002). In time, as local land markets mature, some of the new home owners may sell their land rights to developers who combine them with others in redevelopment schemes that may have long-term effects on the evolution of urban structure and the competitiveness of the neighbourhood, city and region. Then shortly after the government of China created a land market in the early 1990s by denationalising land ownership, GDP growth rose dramatically from about 4 per cent to about 12 per cent. The year after home owners were given the right to sell in 1998, creating a housing market, GDP was reported to have shot up to an extraordinary 17 per cent. Foreign economists were suspicious of the figure, noting that it exceeded the growth of power supply in the same period and could not, therefore, be an accurate reflection of economic growth. They may have ignored, however, the effect of redistributing a vast amount of wealth to millions of low-income individuals.

Assignment of property rights leads to spontaneous knock-on effects in the way individuals co-operate with each other. This is so whether it is an initial assignment of rights by government edict as in the examples, or via voluntary exchange – also in the examples. The effects can be far reaching, all the more so in cities, where knowledge specialisation and spatial ordering is so finely balanced. Each additional voluntary exchange of rights accrues net benefits to transacting partners and to other individuals involved in the contract.

Of course, there is a cost in the tale of privatised social housing and regularised squatter land – the loss of stock of affordable housing, and the opportunity costs of using squatter land for other public benefits. The welfare losses should be set against welfare gains, however. These include gains made by transferring property rights from the public domain to low-income households. And in the case of the right-to-buy policy, efficiency gains from the new and innovative forms of affordable housing supply that emerge with the demise of public-sector housing stocks (Walker and Jeanes, 2001).

By similar reasoning, where a change in a property right is *removed*, there is a reduction in the scope and depth of voluntary co-operation and a curtailment of mutually beneficial exchanges. This is less likely to happen by voluntary exchange than by government edict – unless the voluntary exchange is made under conditions of imperfect information. A home-mover unwittingly investing in a down-turning neighbourhood, for example, faces an attenuation of its property rights – deterioration in services and facilities and a fall in the re-sale value of its home-ownership rights.

Removal or attenuation of property rights by *governments* is very common however. In the 1980s and 1990s the French government banned retail stores above a certain size in order to protect city centres and the existing retail market from American-style out-of-centre shopping (Metton, 1995). Landowners could not exchange with developers for mutual gain; retailers could not exchange with banks and through banks with investors; shoppers could not refine shopping behaviour in line with international best practice; and innovations developed elsewhere could not be adopted by domestic retailers due to inadequate space. French supermarkets remained trapped in a time warp offering, on the whole, an inferior service. Shops in city centres may have been protected but they were also protected from the creative experience of having to innovate to survive. By contrast, Britain, the homeland of laissez faire economics, generally bowed to the market, liberalising regulations over opening hours, prices, store size and location (Guy, 1998). As a result it has developed some of the most sophisticated and consumer-sensitive retailing knowledge in the world. Perhaps mindful of this comparison between its two neighbours, the Dutch government recently relaxed a minimum shop size rule, concluding that it prevented competition in the supermarket industry to the detriment of customers.

The attenuation of property rights leads some individuals to adjust their behaviour illegally, for example by evading regulation, bribing and smuggling. The high cost of illegal activities eats into wealth – which may not be thought of as a problem if the attenuation is well conceived. If, however, the regulation is poorly justified or insensitively designed through inadequate information and the imposition of minority and unpopular values, then avoidance costs and the costs of policing unnecessarily subtract from individual and social wealth. The American prohibition of alcohol in the 1920s and 1930s may be a case in point.

2.2   THE COSTS OF CO-OPERATING

The exchanges that drive city growth and urban transformation are not without costs. These include costs expended before a productive exchange can occur; costs of making a transaction; and costs of policing contracts. More broadly they are the costs of co-operation – which include costs to third parties not considered when contracting parties weigh up the costs and benefits of a private exchange.

Individuals and groups of individuals seek ways of reducing all kinds of co-operation costs but will be more persistent and inventive in seeking to reduce private transaction costs than third party costs since they have more incentive to do so and more choice in doing so. Indeed, they are as creative in seeking ways of reducing the costs of exchange as they are in seeking new gains in exchange. They may stand to benefit from a reduction in third party costs but are generally unable to do so without collective action. We leave a detailed discussion of third party costs to Chapters 5 and 7. Our focus here is on the costs of participating in voluntary private transactions.

Co-operating costs have traditionally been excluded from mainstream economic analysis. This is strange given their importance in determining the allocation of resources within society. Krugman (1995), in considering why economists have tended to ignore the spatial allocation of resources, put the reason down to scale economies. Essential to an understanding of why households and firms cluster in space is the idea that unit costs of organising the production of goods and services fall as the productive capacity of a firm, industry or city rises. Without scale economies, Krugman notes, production of every commodity would be scattered across the spatial theorist's featureless plain, so that transportation becomes unnecessary. 'In the literal absence of any scale economies we would not even see a world of small villages – we would see one of self-sufficient family farms' (Krugman, 1995: 36).

Neo-classical models cannot easily cope with increasing returns to scale, and economists have therefore ignored spatial issues.

Scale economies are closely related to co-operation costs. In the next chapter we argue that organisations emerge to lower the costs of transacting in the market place. The costs saved by combing property rights into larger productive units contribute to the economies of scale that explain both organisational and spatial concentration. The economies of scale explanation of spatial concentration can therefore also become a cost-avoidance explanation. Individuals combine their productive knowledge by forming firms. They combine their knowledge about consuming by forming neighbourhoods. Firms combine their knowledge about suppliers and customers by creating industrial and commercial agglomerations. Municipal governments and entrepreneurial firms combine knowledge about building, maintaining and operating urban infrastructure and service by forming public–private partnerships. Together, individuals and firms form towns and cities and they do so largely to lower the costs of co-operation.

Table 2.1   A typology of co-operation costs

Type of co-operation cost		Definition	Includes costs of:
Exclusion costs		Costs of protecting property from third party opportunism	• Physically demarcating resources • Reaching agreements • Policing agreements
Co-ordination costs	Transaction costs	Costs of exchange and combination when markets co-ordinate co-operative acts	• Searching for exchange or combination partners • Creating contracts • Policing contracts • Third party costs • Compliance and clarification costs
	Organisation costs	Costs of exchange and combination when an organisation such as a firm or club co-ordinates	• Gathering centralised information • Making rules and decision about resource allocation • Policing rules and decisions
	Organisation costs (government)	Costs of creating and operating rules that govern the behaviour of individuals, markets and organisations	• Gathering centralised information • Making rules and decisions about resource allocation • Policing rules and decisions

Table 2.1 identifies different types of cost that individuals and groups of individuals incur when they co-operate in various ways. Costs of co-operation arise when individuals possess rights over resources. The various categories of costs in the table may therefore be thought of as the costs of owning and using resources.

Exclusion Costs

In a world of isolated farmsteads or primitive hunter-gatherer family groups the only cost of resource ownership is the cost of excluding others. This is a type of co-operative cost in the sense that to be effective, resource boundaries have to arise from agreements – even if individual acts of policing infringements may not always be amicable. If owners put their resources to productive use, however, they face certain co-ordination costs in addition to the costs of exclusion. These are the costs that arise in *exchanging* resources with those of others, *combining* resources with those of others, and *de-combining* resources. The type of costs faced depends on the institutional system that organises the co-ordination.

Transaction Costs

When exchanges, combinations and de-combinations are co-ordinated in markets, we speak of transaction costs. Transaction costs are, broadly stated, the costs of searching for partners with which to transact and the costs of making and enforcing contracts that govern transactions.

Transaction costs may include some *exclusion costs* if a transaction involves defining, verifying or securing the boundaries of a resource being exchanged. For example, a rural land holding may have unclear or contested boundaries that need to be legally defined before it can be sold. Lawyers and surveyors usually verify the extent of urban land holdings before they change hands. The owners of a building that is not well enough protected from illegal entry are likely to have to outlay costs to make the property secure before selling it. Alternatively, the financier of the transaction may require the purchaser to outlay the costs. The delineation, verification and physical protection of property rights is a *sine qua non* for market transactions. They give rise to the transaction costs of measuring the non-monetary considerations of the transaction. Where this is a complex process, market exchange may be inhibited or prevented. One of the reasons why there is so much vacant floor space above ground level in the shopping streets of many cities is that there are technical and legal problems in defining property boundaries. Residential and other uses are viable in principle in these locations but there are often insuperable difficulties in designing access, soundproofing and security solutions – problems that ultimately relate to the costs of physically creating excludable subdivisions of rights over redundant urban space.

The high transaction costs of delineating resource entitlements (property rights) is also a way of understanding externality and public goods problems as we shall see in Chapters 5–7.

A second type of transaction cost is *search costs*. Sellers need to find buyers who want their products and services, and buyers need to find sellers. We have already discussed the role that competition plays in apportioning the costs of search between buyers and sellers. Search costs vary considerably between products. For non-standard products or 'experience goods' – goods such as package holidays and homes, the true value of which is only learnt through consumption – the information costs to buyers are potentially high. This is because the product is actually a complex bundle of attributes, each one of which may contribute independently or interactively to a buyer's enjoyment. Comparing two homes, office buildings or holidays is a non-trivial multi-criteria evaluation problem because there are many points for and against each option. By contrast, standardised goods, such as groceries, hi-fi and new cars, require much less information before a buyer is able to form a view about value. It is more likely that buyers will outlay most of the search costs for these 'search goods'. Sellers of 'experience goods', however, have, for a variety of reasons, more of an incentive to bear some of the search costs. They can generally produce information about their products at lower cost than can buyers. They can subsidise buyers' search costs as a competitive strategy. With some products the information costs to buyers may be too great and a market may not develop without producers investing heavily in advertising, product packaging and branding – all strategies that lower buyers' search costs.

Search costs are therefore a function of standardisation and familiarity. They are also a function of distance and density of exchange partners – something we pick up in Chapter 4 in discussing spatial order. In fact it is *familiarity* that lowers search costs. Familiarity increases with standardisation – hence the success of franchised burger businesses, package holiday operators, branded high-street fashion, and branded cities. Familiarity also increases with advertising and with spatial proximity. The information costs of moving home or business within a familiar neighbourhood are much less than those incurred when moving city, region or country. Businesses in which frequent deals have to be struck on the basis of trust and tacit knowledge tend to cluster to avoid search as well as contract costs.

A third type of transaction cost is the *costs of contract creation*. This involves negotiations concerning the terms of exchange – price, timing, conditions, caveats, distribution of liabilities after exchange and so on. These are trivial for most small consumer purchases. Buying a consumer durable item, a car, home or investment may take longer to contract, however, and the information costs may warrant the employment of an expert lawyer or broker. Producer purchases tend to be higher value and repetitive, and contracts are therefore more complex.

Once transacting partners have contracted to exchange, there will usually be a requirement to monitor, police and enforce contracts against post-contractual strategic behaviour. Information will typically be asymmetrical, which creates opportunities for cheating (or *moral hazards*) and over time, contracts will become more detailed to reduce monitoring and enforcement costs.

Contract creation and policing costs include the costs of combining property rights to create organisations. A transaction between two individuals or two firms to form a new firm, or between governments to form a higher tier government involves the exchange of certain rights for certain benefits. The costs of such transactions rise with the numbers of individuals involved and with the complexity and value of the rights being exchanged. The cost of setting up a small firm may amount to the cost of buying a company off-the-shelf and hiring an accountant once a year. The cost of creating a home owners association in a local neighbourhood might include hiring specialist advice, organising meetings amongst residents and contracting a lawyer to draw up legal documents. The costs of creating and policing an expanded European Union and introducing a new currency will run to billions of Euros – including organisational costs within government and transaction costs of using markets to create the institutions of the EU.

An additional source of transaction costs relates to third parties to a contract. Where informal or formal institutions have developed to allow third parties to negotiate with contracting parties about the level of social costs and benefits, then contracting parties face additional costs – transaction costs of engaging with third parties. Where the third party is successful in changing the terms of the contract – for example, when a residential community successfully lobbies to reduce the scale of a commercial development that will increase traffic volumes – then there is an additional cost of lost wealth.

Compliance costs arise when consumption or production behaviour is modified as a result of government rules, informal social rules or formal non-government rules. Where third parties successfully negotiate modification of a contract (via regulation, persuasion, litigation or compensation), compliance costs become part of the third party costs of the private transaction.

Organisational Costs

When transactions are co-ordinated within an organisation – firms, informal groups and governments – many market transaction costs are avoided. Indeed, as we show when discussing *organisational order* in the next chapter, this is a powerful explanation for the existence of organisations. Search costs are lowered by the existence of job descriptions, centralised knowledge and organisational structures. Contract costs between individual transacting parties within an organisation are reduced or avoided altogether since both parties belong to the same legal entity. Organisations are not costless to create and run, however. Costs are incurred in creating centralised information; in contracting with employees for their labour; in decision-making processes; in monitoring and policing decisions; and in wasteful practices that arise through unequal access to information and rent seeking. We elaborate the costs of government organisation when looking at *institutional order* in Chapter 3.

Transaction Costs and the Land Market

In the next three chapters we develop the argument that urban order can be interpreted as a response to transaction costs. Here we use the example of the land market to illustrate how specific resource-ordering strategies emerge in response to particular types of co-operation cost.

Land changes hands via informal understandings based on relationships and via formal contracts enforceable by the state. Land markets develop where institutions exist to create and protect private property rights in land; where there are sufficient buyers and sellers of such rights; and where institutions exist to support formal contractual-based exchange. The typical costs involved in exchanges of land rights based on formal contracts include the following:

a. The transaction costs of *delineating the physical dimensions of land rights*. These include the costs of land surveying, valuation and conveyancing. The measurement tasks are complex and the transaction costs are therefore high; too high generally to be borne directly by sellers and buyers. Specialist knowledge, in the form of lawyers and surveyors, develops as a response, and institutions emerge to govern the role of these third party market participants.

b. The transaction costs of *identifying parties to the contract*. Given the uniqueness of any particular plot of land or building, search costs are high in the land market. The information costs facing buyers include the costs of valuing the multiple attributes – on-site and off-site attributes that give land its value. As with the costs of delineating property, institutions and specialist knowledge emerge to lower search costs. Real estate agencies, land agencies, development firms specialising in bringing together investors, landowners and other interested parties, all reduce search-related transaction costs.

c. The transaction costs of *making and enforcing land contracts* are reduced by estate agents who initiate contracts; lawyers who draft them; firms that advise on self-conveyancing; institutions that certify the standards of such professionals; and institutions that protect contracting parties from opportunism by other parties (including rent-seeking professionals).

d.   Transaction costs of *resolving third party interests in land* may arise from government action, litigation, mediation or from more informal negotiations. Planning regulations may, for example, require contracting parties to compensate the community in cash or in kind as a condition of sale. A sufficiently organised community may achieve the same result through tough bargaining sanctioned by community action. The cost to transacting parties of negotiating with, compensating or being compensated by third parties may be reduced by designing more efficient forms of government intervention; by leaving the market to resolve its own third party costs where it can do so more cheaply than government; and by creating property rights that permit market-based resolution of third party problems. These strategies are considered in detail in Chapters 6–8.

2.3   ARGUMENTS AGAINST FREE TRADE AND SPONTANEOUSLY ORDERED HUMAN CO-OPERATION

In this book we view markets as yielding net benefits to individuals and to society. This does not have to be an ideological statement, though it may be construed as such. It may simply be a pragmatic one. There are few critics of free trade who would not accept some kind of role for markets and most who support strong government intervention enjoy the personal benefits of markets. At all but the extreme points of the debate, the contention is about the *limits* of spontaneous order – the boundary between market order and planned order. We address this issue in detail in Chapters 5–7, which consider the social costs arising from private *co-operation* as distinct from the private costs of *co-operating* as discussed already. However, it is appropriate at this stage of the argument to recognise positions that take a contrasting standpoint to ours. Many people are uncomfortable with the view of markets as benevolent institutions conferring mutual gains on trading partners and wealth to society as a whole, preferring to stress the grounds for government regulations or control of spontaneous market order. The arguments they commonly posit are summarised as follows (following Lai and Yu, 2002).

a.   The *weak consumer/producer* or *protectionist* argument – some consumers and producers are unable to *enter* or *stay* in certain markets. Equity or indeed efficiency arguments may be made for protecting weak consumers and producers by protectionist interventions. For example, new industries or established local industries vulnerable to external competition may be non-viable in an unprotected regional or national market. Such industries are described as 'infant industries' or 'strategic industries' and, it is argued, require assistance from the tax-paying public. By similar reasoning, low-income households in certain locations may not be able to afford to rent units in the uncontrolled rental market and therefore have an imputed 'need' for subsidised housing. Sometimes favoured or vulnerable groups are protected by exclusionary zoning that prohibits the intrusion of another group (Lai and Yu, 2001a; Frantz, 2000a).

b. The *immoral trade* argument – some trades are in themselves immoral and either one or both parties to the contract is, or are, blameworthy. Examples include slave and baby trading; loan sharking; drugs trafficking; prostitution; gambling; and trading in goods seized from or produced by slaves, children or prisoners. In urban planning, sex and gambling industry establishments are typically considered uses incompatible with residential, educational or religious institutions and are ousted by zoning or development control. Kowloon Tong in Hong Kong, once an exclusive housing area developed according to the Garden City concept and now a major mass transit interchange, has witnessed the proliferation of such uses. Sordid motels are now back to back with seminaries, elderly persons homes, kindergartens, a university and a major shopping complex. Societies vary considerably in the degree to which they permit market activity and personal and national prosperity to be constrained by moral absolutes.

c. The *non-tradable* argument – some objects, services or transactions should not be priced, or if they are, should be taken out of the market. Examples include the transfusion of blood; the sale of human organs or tissues; the sale of antiques, monuments and land of special national value; the sale of genetically modified (GM) food.

d. The needs or *inalienable* argument – some objects cannot be or should not be traded as goods at all. Examples include the natural environment, life necessities and human freedom. London Bridge, the Eiffel Tower and the Great Wall of China are classic examples, though as tourist assets they are also sources of income for tourist activities. The Berlin Wall almost completely sold out in parts, testifying to the inverse of this argument.

e. The *retaliation* or *self-defence* argument – local producers need to be protected from trading partners who use non-legitimate practices such as 'dumping' or using 'unreasonably cheap' labour.

f. The *externality* or *third party cost* argument – some voluntary transactions if completely free from regulation, would affect an innocent third party such that the welfare benefit from the contract is partially, fully, or more than offset by the damage inflicted on the third party. In the land market, this argument is now the basis for zoning control and many other types of restrictions and standards.

g. The *monopoly exploitation* or *unequal trade* argument. In some circumstances the 'surplus' (consumer or seller surplus) obtained by one party to the contract is or could be substantially appropriated or reduced by another with greater bargaining or market power. The legal proceeding against Microsoft using Antitrust laws and the accusation of developers by the Consumer Council in Hong Kong for being oligarchic are examples of this line of thought.

h. The *public goods* argument – there are some goods which for technical and transaction cost reasons will not be produced by entrepreneurs and for which markets will not therefore develop. The classic example is national defence, but many civic goods and services have public goods attributes. The state provision of national parks and nature reserves are examples in the land market.

i. The *future generation* or *sustainable development* argument – this argument embodies all the above arguments under a belief that unfettered markets that allocate resources according to short-term cost–benefits evaluation will ruin the world and deprive future generations of their deserved inheritance. The Ramsar Convention that protects wetland habitats, for instance, is a major force in environmental legislation.

The last five arguments – (e), (f), (g), (h) and (i) – invoke concepts of 'efficiency' due to 'market failure'. The first four arguments – (a), (b), (c) and (d) – involve normative judgement about the nature of the voluntary contract itself. The concept of the incompetent consumer or producer is the standard policy ground for government subsidy of various kinds: public housing, rent control, low-interest loans, nationalisation of certain industries. The concept of immoral trades and the indignation against commercial exchange for some goods cannot be discussed further without resort to a much wider debate about ethics. Argument (d) relates to the issue of 'need', which again involves ethical controversies. The fifth argument (e) is usually advanced by international trade protectionists for erecting trade barriers against foreign imports. This is a modern version of Mercantilism (promotion of export and discouraging imports to maximise trade surplus and foreign reserves) in the name of free trade (on such grounds as the trade partner has suppressed trade unions or refrained from imposing environmental or wage controls) or 'fair play' (say the trade partner has been wrongful in using state subsidy).

Consensus about normative issues among people holding different ethical beliefs is impossible without some of those beliefs changing. However, irrespective of one's moral judgements about economic phenomena, the market as a human institution is shaped by the material values of the participants, not directly by the moral beliefs or intentions of commentators or market participants. We may wish that the activities of individuals and firms were guided by a different ethic or morality; that there was less individual and corporate greed; more individual and organised giving to the underprivileged; and more private investment in community infrastructure and services. To move from such a wish to a call for prescription and policy is a dangerous step, however, on two counts that we note here.

First, the centralised information required to create and police mechanisms that efficiently modify the behaviour of market participants is vast, costly and inherently problematic. Second, the coercion of individuals into conformity to a set of beliefs and values begs the question, which – or who's – values? History shows that the democratic principle is not a sufficient safeguard against harmful and potentially catastrophic drift towards ethical agendas that end up infringing basic human rights. Everyday reading of the newspapers shows that the democratic principle does not safeguard against powerful groups steering government intervention towards their own values, standards and wants. Indeed, democratic institutions often facilitate this process. The claims for 'social justice' or 'meeting social needs' or 'equity' are not always unselfish pleas to join personal sacrifice in helping the needy. They can also be pleas for helping others to use others' money; and they may bring immediate or more general benefits to proponents. In lobbying for redistributive policies that benefit others, one may become a beneficiary. Gordon Tullock (1993) advanced his rent-seeking thesis to describe and explain the strategies by which individuals seek direct personal gains in such circumstances. Politicians, professional bodies and organised groups of all kinds are competent rent seekers. Where the benefit sought is more distant or constructive, it reminds us of John Rawls (1971) who sought to justify tax expenditure on welfare services using an insurance concept. Everyone, even the wealthiest, Rawls argues, may become poor tomorrow. Thus, it pays everyone to pay tax now. Many normative issues, often dressed up in black letter laws, have fundamentally self-serving economic considerations.

We are not arguing that normative issues should not be used to curtail markets. Indeed, we started this chapter by saying that competition needs to be constrained in order to create social and individual wealth. The constraint of competition – by the laws of property and other market and regulatory institutions – is acceptable only if there is agreement that wealth creation (economic growth) is good – a normative proposition. Societies may have widely held shared values about ethical issues that translate into broadly acceptable constraints on markets. Our point of caution is that normative arguments for curtailing markets can unwittingly and unjustly infringe more basic human rights and be used to impose the redistributional preferences of a few on the majority. If the vast majority of individuals in a state are willing voluntarily to give up rights over personal wealth in order to maintain a free-at-point-of-use national health system (as appears to be the case in Britain where a new health tax was introduced in 2002 by popular demand) then we need not worry about human rights violation. If the wealthy, propertied, motivated and articulate, lobby against a social housing development in a green belt site of little recreational or agricultural value using sustainability arguments, we should be concerned at their use of state-funded regulation to secure a redistribution in their own favour. We continue this discussion in Chapters 5 and 6 by viewing shared ethical preferences as public goods.

2.4   KEY ARGUMENTS OF CHAPTER 2

• Urbanisation is a co-operative and spontaneous process of knowledge diversification, deepening interdependence between individuals and individual and social wealth creation. Cities expand as individual decision makers with specialised knowledge locate themselves near to others who have complementary knowledge, thus reducing distance-related and other transaction costs.

• The ordering of interaction between individuals or groups may range from maximal interdependence, as in the case of co-consumers of common lands, to maximal independence, as in the case of an owner of a private property living in complete autarchy. Most interactions, however, involve the voluntary transaction of private rights over resources through markets.

• Transacting through markets, or any other type of institution, is not costless. Co-operative approaches to individuals and social wealth creation come at a price. The key types of institutional costs in using the private property rights system in cities include costs that may be described as exclusion costs, transaction costs and organisation costs. Exclusion costs include the costs of surveying or physically demarcating resources, the costs of reaching agreements as regards exclusion or inclusion, and policing agreements. Transaction costs include the costs of searching for exchange or combination partners; making contracts; policing contracts; handling third-party interest and compliance with and clarification of contracts. They may be defined narrowly as the cost of co-ordinating exchange through markets. Organisation costs are those of gathering centralised information, making rules, and policing rules. They are the costs of co-ordinating exchange through organisations and planning. The co-operation costs of exclusion, transaction and organisation are sometimes referred to generally as transaction costs in the literature.

• The typical arguments against voluntary exchanges in cities include the weak consumer/producer, immoral trade, non-tradable good, inalienable good, self-preservation, externality, monopoly, public good and future generation arguments. Application of such arguments to constrain specific manifestations of spontaneous order inevitably benefit particular groups at the expense of others. The redistributional consequences (including invisible transfers to rent-seeking groups) and the accuracy of information guiding the intervention should be understood, as should the welfare losses incurred by restraining voluntary exchange.

3. Organisational, institutional and proprietary order

3.1 MARKETS NEED THE STATE

Hong Kong's once famous Kowloon Walled City had its origins as a fort, built by the Chinese in the area now called Kowloon City as a defence against the British who were busily developing the Island of Hong Kong. The British took over Kowloon and regarding the fort as a threat, later leased the part of China they called the New Territories. In the lease, the Walled City remained expressly a Chinese enclave under Imperial Chinese jurisdiction and in the years that followed, its status remained ambiguous, with successive governments of China maintaining that it belonged to them. As a result, the property laws and regulations of Hong Kong were haphazardly applied or not applied at all. A chaotic pattern of building construction emerged after World War II, leading to the removal of the remnants of the original wall, over-development, under-provision of infrastructure and services and unhealthy living conditions not dissimilar to medieval walled cities – apart from modern levels of density. Builders did not submit building plans and properties had no title as there were no Crown leases for the area. With a lack of state policing, the Walled City famously became a concentration of vice dens. It was also home to many decent and hard-working people, whose industry benefited from the lack of state regulations over labour markets, health and safety and so on. Market-based exchange within the Walled City clearly had many inefficiencies in the market-failure sense. The source of the problems, however, lay principally with the uncertainty in institutional jurisdiction and resultant ill-defined property rights.

A certain kind of order prevailed within the Walls, however. Builders, for example, respected the airport height restrictions for the nearby Kai Tak Airport, voluntarily agreeing not to build taller than was regarded safe for aviation. Internal methods of maintaining law and order developed and informal customs evolved to cope with the problems of crowding. Though many physical standards, such as means of escape and open space for buildings, were inferior in this *city within a city*, it was not socially stigmatised as a ghetto. The rates of reported crime and suicide for the city were not higher than the territory average and were lower than for some of Hong Kong's infamous public and private housing developments. Politically, it may have been among the most tolerant of areas as people with hostile political stands lived together peacefully without major violent confrontation between factions or with the government, which from time to time was called upon to 'clean up' the vice dens.

The British and Chinese governments had an interest in resolving the problem since the Walled City was an eyesore and a reminder of old wounds. It took until 1984, however, with the signing of the Sino-British Agreement concerning 'the Future of Hong Kong', to seal the City's fate. Before the return of Hong Kong to China, all post-war high-rise buildings in the Walled City were demolished and only a few 'indigenous' structures, including a chapel, were retained as part of a Chinese landscape garden open to the public. Displaced residents were all well compensated and/or re-housed in public housing estates.

It was the State's inability to confer effective property rights that led to such a disorganised settlement. By the time China and Britain had negotiated a solution to their territorial dispute, property rights within the Walled City had fragmented to an irretrievable state of complexity. Owners and users of land and buildings had, over time, asserted their own economic rights, largely in disregard of third party interests; and a certain kind of informal property rights equilibrium spontaneously developed. The only solution open to the State at this stage was to reorganise rights forcibly – re-combining and expropriating the fragmented rights in return for new rights to alternative housing and monetary compensation.

The lesson we wish to draw from Hong Kong's Walled City is not that the market fails, or that the state's role is to clear up the mess of market-led urban development. It is that the leasehold-based 'planning by contract' system (Lai, 1998) that prevails in the rest of Hong Kong could not work due to ambiguity of governance. The lesson is that the market requires the state, in particular the institutional frameworks it creates, in order to operate efficiently. Modern Hong Kong is famously market-led, but it has avoided the inefficiencies of its former Walled enclave. Markets and prosperity flourish under freedom of action but, without rules, the costs of co-operating inevitably become too high.

The next five chapters consider five kinds of order that emerge to reduce co-operation costs. Institutional order, proprietary order and organisational order are discussed in this chapter. Spatial order is addressed in Chapter 4 and public domain order in Chapters 5, 6 and 7. Central to our argument is the idea that individuals and firms seek co-operative opportunities with lower rather than higher transaction costs; and that as they seek exchange partners, these orders emerge spontaneously from their cost-minimising behaviour.

Organisational order (patterns of planned co-operation) emerges as individuals combine property rights with those of others in order to reduce the costs of co-operating in the market. Households, firms, clubs and governments are the result and these set about replacing market co-operation with exchange based on rules governed by consensus, agreement and hierarchical decision making.

Institutional order (patterns of rules and sanctions) emerges from agreements made in organisations. Institutions are formed in order to reduce competition costs within markets and within organisations. They do this by assigning exclusive property rights over private goods and attempting to assign rights over contested public domain goods.

Proprietary order (patterns of exclusive property rights) is produced by institutional order. We make a distinction between institutional and proprietary order because it is possible to have the former without the latter – when institutions are poorly designed or otherwise ineffective.

Spatial order (patterns of activities over space) emerges as individual property rights owners and organisations of combined property rights seek to minimise the distance-related costs of co-operating with other individuals and organisations.

Public domain order (patterns of rights imposed upon common resources) emerges as organisations – governments and communities of firms and individuals – create institutions to govern the consumption of resources with incompletely assigned property rights. We make a distinction between public domain and proprietary order because the property rights that govern the consumption of shared resources are more contestable, less easily protected by law and consequently more fluid.

Markets, institutions, property rights, organisations and spatial order evolve hand in hand. Voluntary exchange cannot flourish and develop into firms, markets and governments without rules (institutions) to assign, arbitrate and protect private property rights. Without such rules, exchange becomes too costly. Responding to the same cost-sensitivity, organisations and spatial specialisation also emerge. As they do, however, there will be demands to adjust the rules of exchange. All kinds of order evolve interdependently and cities, being the manifestation of these intertwined processes, evolve with persistent and awesome self-determination.

3.2   ORGANISATIONAL ORDER

Organisation and planning naturally emerge as individuals seek to maximise the value of their property rights and knowledge – in consumption and exchange. Firms, clubs, neighbourhoods and governments emerge to lower the costs of catallactic interaction.

A distinction is often made between planned and market-oriented cities. In a planned city, strategic and maybe detailed allocations of land, infrastructure and services are made by administrative fiat. In a market city they are said to be made by market transactions. Both types of resource allocation require organisation, however. In the former, organisation takes place within the machinery of government and its bureaucracy. In the latter, organisation takes place within and between firms and other voluntary associations of individuals. Municipal governments themselves are organisations that emerge to implement institutions and deliver order. In this, they are homologous and analogous to firms, which also emerge to implement rules and deliver order. We return to the role of governments in supplying public goods in Chapter 6. Here we focus on the voluntary (private) organisations that emerge spontaneously within markets.

When the focus is on organisation, the distinction between planned and market resource-allocation greys (Alexander, 2001). Allocations within firms and voluntary organisations are also made by administrative fiat; decisions are taken by a governing body and implemented by some kind of bureaucracy. Allocations within a firm between departments and projects may, as with government, involve voting, agreed rules, budgetary formulae or pseudo-market pricing mechanisms and be governed by a constitution. The comparison between a large, entrepreneurial community constituted as a firm and a traditional town of equivalent size constituted as a polity is poignant in this respect. The underlying processes and issues of civic governance are broadly similar (Webster, 2001a). Firms and other voluntary organisations like co-operatives, home owners' associations, collectives, clubs, charities and non-profit associations are like mini-states therefore.

It is not just within-firm resource allocation that requires organisation by management and administration, however. Firms require organisation in order to transact with each other. Consider what is meant by the term *market transaction*. If it means a transaction in which buyer and seller are no longer contractually obliged after exchange (*caveat emptor* sales) then few transactions are in the market, since most of any value have conditions attached (Barzel, 1997). Conditions are a result of transactors organising between themselves the allocation of the expected value of their transaction. If the value can be expected to vary under different circumstances then a contract will be sought that assigns the variation in value to respective parties. Barzel (1997) observes that the pattern of ownership rights and responsibilities assigned by the contract will tend, at optimum, to maximise the total value of the exchange. Thus suppliers of goods and services retain, or sell to third parties, warranty rights and impose constraints on purchasers as a condition of warranty or as a condition of exchange (if warranty is not optional, as is the case for example in a lease transaction). Contractual conditions require monitoring and policing and in this sense most non-trivial market transactions are governed by organisation. The parties who effect such organisation may be those involved in the transaction; those employed by the transactors; or independent arbitrators. Thus the boundaries between market transactions and firm transactions, within-firm organisation and between-firm organisation are blurred boundaries.

Without organisation, the costs of searching for information about other individuals and firms with which to transact (*exchange partners*), would be prohibitive. Coase (1937) explained the existence and the size of firms in terms of these costs. On the existence of firms (voluntary combinations of individual property rights), he proposed that individuals choose to cede some of their sovereignty to a higher power in order to reduce the costs of transacting in the market place. It is generally a lower-cost option for a university lecturer, for example, to contract to supply her labour to a university than to organise a self-employed portfolio of teaching and research jobs in various institutions. Imagine the costs of search if an individual with newly acquired medical skills had to find his own customers or if he had to search for specialists each time he was presented with a new problem case. Imagine the costs to a lone engineer seeking partners to finance, manage and market a new production process; to a builder searching for labourers, suppliers, specialist contractors for each new job; or to a labourer searching for someone to employ him after each job – or each day's work – is finished.

Of course, certain industries rely on casual labour, piecework contracts and short-term sub-contracting. Reasons for these methods of co-operation can generally be related to the distribution of liability and the apportioning of costs in a contract. Gangs of labourers may be better placed than large construction firms to search for appropriate skills, organise them, motivate them and seek a regular supply of jobs (Chau et al., 1993). From the building contractor's perspective, it may make sense not to have to retain specialists like plumbers and electricians who become a liability in slack times. Specialists also tend to have a local monopoly on knowledge and in an industry such as building construction, where each application of knowledge has many unique features, it makes sense to give the specialist the residual claim on his own labour. Thus specialist sub-contractors quote a price for a job on the basis of their expert knowledge and have the incentive to deliver to that price. If they economise on effort they save money. This may be cheaper than combining specialists into a bigger organisation (firm) and having to hire supervisors to monitor their performance.

In other situations it will be less costly to combine individuals into a single firm. Manufacturers hire production workers, managers, accountants, IT specialists, a sales-force and so on because it is less costly to do so than to search for these skills for each new task. Where tasks are not easily specified and monitored it is more likely that permanent employment contracts will emerge. For example, it would not be easy for a shop owner to sub-contract a list of daily tasks to a sales-person or for an owner of a bank to sub-contract a list of deliverables to a manager. The monitoring costs would be too high. Instead, retail sales expertise and managerial knowledge is hired on a less specific basis – weekly or monthly payment is given for fulfilling a general job description rather than for achieving certain specific outputs or outcomes.

Guided by this kind of observation, modern theories of the firm focus on contracts rather than purely on production relationships and some have gone so far as to define the firm as a *nexus of contracts* (Barzel, 1982; Cheung, 1983; Hart and Moore, 1990; Coase, 1937). Coase posited that optimal firm size is determined at the margin by contract transaction costs – following naturally from the idea that firms exist to reduce the costs of contract. Extending the Coasian logic, Barzel (1997) proposed that the ultimate reason why firms exist is to guarantee the respective responsibilities for variation in transaction value written into contracts. Few resource owners are sufficiently capitalised to guarantee the outcome of their contribution to a transaction. Firms therefore may be understood to be partnerships between equity capital, debt-financed capital and individual resource owners (including owners of labour, land, ideas and other productive inputs). The cost of guaranteeing the outcome of a transaction is a transaction cost similar to contract monitoring and policing and the scale economies of equity capital therefore contribute, following Coase, to the determination of efficient firm size.

Private property rights therefore voluntarily combine, de-combine and re-combine as firms form and reorganise. Within firms, the management and planning of a city's private goods, services and spaces takes place. The production and consumption decisions taken by each organisation are co-ordinated by the market and by specialists who supply co-ordinative and brokerage knowledge privately. Firm and market, and indeed the interconnected urban markets that constitute the privately owned and managed city, form one great nexus of contracts. Within it, the boundaries between different groupings of property rights, between firm and firm, or firm and market blur on closer inspection.

There is also a sense in which the boundaries with the publicly owned and managed city blur. We shall leave this argument for Chapters 5–7 where we discuss public domain goods and third party effects. For now it will be sufficient to introduce the idea of the city as an organisation; a nexus of contracts; the city as a 'firm'.

Most public domain goods supplied by municipal governments are distance-attenuated and capitalised in land values. This means that they are experienced differentially by individuals and valued in markets, particularly the land market, as tie-in attributes of private property. The consequence of this is that a city's neighbourhoods – residential, industrial and commercial clusters – are, like firms, nexuses of agreements and understandings about entitlements to shared and pooled resources. They differ from firms in that they are spatial clusterings and in that they cluster around resources that remain to varying extents in the public domain. They are like spatial clubs. Members co-operate by various forms of informal and formal rules and agreements in order to ensure the continued supply and enhancement of shared public domain goods. Municipal government is itself a type of club, delivering collectively consumed infrastructure and regulations from a tax on its citizens, firms and visitors. Communities, in the social sense, are also clubs – delivering collectively consumed benefits such as a sense of belonging, security and culture. 'Payment' in this case is made in terms of loyalty, investment and other forms of commitment from individuals and firms. An elaborated discussion of this idea is given in the concluding chapter.

Firms may be thought of as organisations delivering private (excludable) goods; clubs as organisations delivering public (jointly consumed) goods. Whatever kind of goods or services an organisation produces, it does so using its own internal system of rules and sanctions (the institutions of corporate management). Organisations also owe their *existence* to institutions – the institutions of private property, markets and government. We elaborate this idea in the next section.

3.3 INSTITUTIONAL ORDER

Organisations can efficiently respond to changes in the value of resources and technology by forming, growing, shrinking, merging and dying so long as there are clear rules governing these processes. Informal voluntary organisations rely on informal agreements that govern the coming together of individual resources and rights. Firms and other legal organisational structures rely on laws governing contractual issues such as the allocation of liabilities.

Organisations also exist to create institutions – rules and agreements that re-assign property rights that have been combined. Not all institutions come from organised agreements however. Some rules, such as customs and conventions, can emerge spontaneously without conscious agreement by a group. They are simply rules that spread from individual to individual and group to group because they are successful in reducing certain costs of interaction. In primitive communities taboos about eating certain kinds of meat reduced the costs of either detailed attempts at explaining the dangers of consumption or the more serious costs of individual experimentation by each new generation. In cities, conventions emerge that permit households and firms to interpret the economic and social landscape. The conventions that allow a new business to bid confidently for a location are a form of heuristic rule – locate where similar businesses tend to locate or face failure (or higher costs) elsewhere. Locational rules of thumb are like taboos in this sense. They are shorthand versions of more complex explanations. They are operational rules based on established observations about other people's behaviour. They emerge and persist because they are usually very effective in reducing certain transactions costs – particularly search costs. However, like taboos, they can become anachronisms as their original justification changes.

From the informal rules that structure family life to the conventions that stabilise land markets and the legislative rules of the state, institutions emerge over time to oil the wheels of society, economy and polity. Various typologies of institutions might be constructed. Kasper and Streit (1998) distinguish between *internal* and *external* institutions; the latter being imposed by the state and the former emerging internally within society. This only partially captures the essential distinctions, however, since in most societies, government-imposed rules should be thought of as emerging naturally over time – often as extensions to, or endorsements of, existing customs. The English tradition of Common Law is a case in point. As with customs and conventions, state rules are a response to demands arising from within society – demands for frameworks, for security, for certainty. An internal/external distinction implies a rather static view of the state therefore and is timescale-dependent.

Other authors, particularly those writing from a strong ideological liberal position, have made a fundamental distinction between *voluntary* and *coercive* institutions (for example Foldvary, 1994). This device is also scale-dependent, however – in a spatial sense. Municipal regulations are coercive for those living within a jurisdiction but there are *exit* and *voice* options for those who do not like them. The exit option becomes more costly as the scale increases – a move between jurisdictions in the same city means, in principle, that households may choose between alternative bundles of regulations. There is a large literature on the exit option (see for example, Tiebout, 1956; Heikkila, 1996) and some evidence that where there are many sub-municipal jurisdictions, they compete with each other by reducing regulative burdens (Thorson, 1996). Moving from a large city to avoid certain rules, however, is usually more costly than moving within it; and moving between states and countries all the more so. Similarly, the voice option becomes more costly with increasing spatial scale.

A less scale-dependent view of institutional order is gained by focusing on the nature of the contracts that establish it. In Table 3.1 we identify six categories of institution.

Table 3.1   Typology of institutions

Type of rule		Sanctions
Spontaneous	Conventions	Harmed self-interest
	Internalised rules	Conscience
	Customs	Group disapproval
Organised by private contract	Informal agreements about conduct	Loss of group privileges
	Formalised private codes of conduct	Formal exclusion from group privileges
Organised by state	Public codes of conduct backed by law	Loss of rights, for example by fine or imprisonment

Spontaneous Rules

Many of the rules and norms that contribute to cultural distinctiveness develop over time within a society, within regions, within cities, within neighbourhoods. They include conventions, customs, moral systems and ethics (internalised rules). Their origin often lies in historical practices, values and beliefs; and those that survive have adapted to meet modern requirements and values. They have not come into being by organised agreement, formal or informal contract but persist because individuals find them to be useful devices for reducing the costs of interacting with others. If this were not so, they would have become extinct like the many norms that characterised previous stages of a culture's evolution – superstitions and the closing of a contract with a handshake, for example.

Conventions are rules and practices accepted by others that it would be foolish to ignore. They are sanctioned by harmed self-interest. If a notice was placed at the British end of the cross channel tunnel linking France and England inviting drivers to 'drive on whichever side of the road you wish – you may like to know that most people prefer to drive on the left', most visitors to England would indeed choose to drive on the left. The reason for following well established conventions are usually compelling. American shopkeepers generally advertise prices in US dollars rather than Euros or weight of gold, since to do the latter would be ruinous.

Internalised rules and standards govern behaviour at an even deeper level. We honour an informal agreement because we believe it wrong to renege. In Far Eastern cultures, ethics relating to the bond of the spoken promise, the importance of keeping face and group allegiances are more important than in the modern West. The existence of widely accepted internalised rules governing interpersonal transactions makes for lower overheads in an economy. Conversely, where cultural values permit 'economical use of the truth', outright deception or reneging on verbal agreements, then costs will be raised by broken contracts and by the formal institutions that become necessary to enforce agreements by law.

Customs might be thought of as conventions imbued with specific value – value acquired through the test of time. They are more consciously normative frameworks for action than mere conventions. Customs develop within groups of co-operating individuals and spread between groups, evolving as they do and evolving over time. The traders in Middle-Eastern market towns, New York's financial districts, Milan's fashion industry, Bombay's film industry and London's media quarters all abide by customary practices. Individual traders shunning custom and etiquette would not last long in business. Customs formalise *ad hoc* conventions and provide often-complex rules of engagement, which remove the need for costly repetitive information search. They create inclusion, belonging and membership; they win trust; reduce risk and create sustained relationships. They ease the way for informal agreements and reduce the need for formal contracts. They are analogous to the pooling of individual property rights and the creation of shared rules within a firm; and they have the same rationale and effect – to reduce risk and uncertainty in transactions. In this sense, groupings of firms and households with strong customs – a city's informal spatial clubs – act like an informal and open version of a firm. Indeed, viewed in this way the boundary between firm and a collection of firms that forms an industry, blurs.

Many types of conventions, shared values and customs help to order the life and business of a city. Indeed, it is these institutions that keep markets working. Without making assumptions about the behaviour of consumers (the rules and norms that they follow), entrepreneurs could not supply with confidence. Buyers, too, use rules of thumb to search for seller and to search for co-consumers. Producers adopt customs to help them better identify partners in trade up and down stream. Financial traders develop flamboyant dress codes; patterns of locational preferences emerge as firms and households follow innovators to exploit new opportunities; neighbourhoods of similar households and firms form on the basis of assumptions about and familiarity with the behaviour of others.

Rules Organised by Private Contract

Sometimes spontaneous, non-contractual institutions are not good enough at reducing transaction costs. Stronger rules are sought through the organisation of informal agreements and formal contracts. In most cases these will be an elaboration, extension and codification of more tacitly understood rules.

In the nineteenth century and early twentieth century the informal conventions that governed the acquisition and practice of many fields of specialised knowledge became inadequate in the industrialising economies of Europe and the United States. The speed and complexity of modern capitalist development required greater assurance of standards, greater accountability and greater information about the skills being purchased in a labour contract. The result was the emergence of professional bodies governing engineering, architecture, teaching, surveying, town planning and other modern trades, each with its voluntary codes of conduct. Individuals enter a profession contractually, agreeing to be bound by its formal rules and to accept certain sanctions when these are broken. Most professions are member-organisations which means that changes and additions to codes and sanctions are collective and contractual, rather than spontaneous, or state-imposed decisions.

By the late 1990s, over eight million Americans were living in private neighbourhoods, attracted by market-supplied security, leisure and environmental services and by private regulation and management of the residential environment (Blakely and Snyder, 1997). By 1994 Fred Foldvary estimated that 25–30 million US residents were members of 130 000 community associations – informal private neighbourhood governance organisations (Foldvary, 1994). The number of associations is now nearer a quarter of a million. In the Chinese city of Wuhan, there are two private neighbourhoods, built and managed by entrepreneurial firms that between them are investing in infrastructure to accommodate 500 000 residents. For most members of these residential clubs, one assumes the contractual rules governing shared facilities and neighbourhood behaviour provide greater certainty and lower co-operation costs compared to the equivalent local government rules that allocate public services to open neighbourhoods and regulate various kinds of externalities. They must also be superior to the informal spontaneous institutions that exist in residential areas where government regulations and services management are ineffective or non-existent. Private codes, covenants and restrictions were an effective method of reducing transaction costs in the land and property markets well before the advent of modern municipal government (Beito, 1989). They re-emerged towards the end of the twentieth century as a contractual alternative to both informal spontaneous rules governing the use of shared goods and to government institutions. In Wuhan, approximately 35 per cent of the municipality's five million urban population live in privately managed communities.

As a result of high housing densities on new estates and rising car ownership, many volume housing developers in the UK now contractually allocate on-street parking spaces in public access cul-de-sac developments to individual houses. The informal neighbour agreements that used to keep down the costs of organising parking arrangements are no longer adequate. As the private supply of urban public space and services grows in importance and as public infrastructure gets more congested, contractually organised institutions will become increasingly important in ordering cities.

Rules Organised by the State

Private contractual agreements about rules can therefore sometimes be superior to government-organised agreements. This is one conclusion to be drawn from the inexorable growth of private shopping, industrial, commercial and residential spaces and facilities in cities. More generally, however, it might be supposed that government-organised institutions emerge because of perceived inadequacies of private contractual institutions. This is an unavoidable conclusion to be drawn from the growth of municipal government during the twentieth century.

There are two distinct arguments here, which we shall say more about when we discuss public goods in Chapters 5 and 6. Private rules, regulations, codes and agreements are, from an efficiency point of view, likely to be either under-supplied or not supplied at all. Where they are supplied privately in excludable contexts such as member-only leisure clubs, professional bodies, fee-paying schools, and gated residential, industrial and office complexes, then there is, in theory, no problem of efficient supply. Over time, members will weigh up the benefits of club rules and give voice or exit if the rules are too burdensome. Where the club has a wider social benefit, however, as with professions, schools, health facilities, shopping malls, private beaches, open countryside and so on (all supplying merit goods – private goods with social benefits) non-members will also weigh up the benefits of any private regulations that influence the publicly consumed attributes. Public access residential streets are an interesting case in this respect. The quality of a residential street is partly determined by conventions and values of its residents and property owners – the material expression of which is home investment. Good neighbourhoods are analogous to residential producer–consumer clubs – each property owner individually co-producing a contribution to neighbourhood quality. In the same way, the quality of an entire city is partly a product of the culture of its inhabitants, including spontaneous and organised voluntary institutions.

In all of these cases, where there are spillover benefits from private institutions, be they spontaneous and informal, or formal codes such as covenants and restrictions written into title deeds of properties, they are likely to be under-supplied. This is because third-party beneficiaries free ride on the institutions created and maintained by others. Third party consumers benefit from the order created but do not contribute to the costs of organising the institutions that deliver it. Economically speaking, a benefit implies a demand or a willingness to pay and therefore if the free riders' willingness to pay were captured in some way, order could be delivered at less per capita cost. More of it may also be delivered if that would deliver additional benefits to contributors. In private shopping malls shoppers partially bear the costs of organising institutions that deliver order and lower the costs of transaction by signage, air conditioning, parking, security and so on. Retailers pay for these facilities via rents and, where they can, pass the costs on to customers. Non-spending leisure users of malls free ride, however, making a degree of under-supply inevitable. The under-supply is greater the greater the number of beneficiaries who have no contractual relationship with the organisers of the institution from which they derive benefit.

The non-supply argument is merely an extension of the under-supply argument. All may agree that a rule is a good thing; that a speed limit of 80 km/hour on urban motorways keeps traffic flowing more steadily than a higher limit; that a legally binding agreement by two parties pursuing a house sale avoids the wasteful costs that arise when vendors are allowed to pull out at the last minute if offered a higher price. Acknowledging the benefits of a collective rule is one thing; abiding by the rule is another, however. Faced with no legal constraint, individuals can generally be expected to take the strategy that gives maximum pay-off. While there may be those who voluntarily keep to 80km/hour and resist the temptation to dump a would-be buyer for a higher offer, the performance of housing markets and traffic flows will generally reflect the behaviour of free riders. If everyone free rides, the mutually beneficial restraints that everyone in principle agrees with do not materialise. The larger the individual incentive to free ride, the more pervasive the anarchy. Thus in periods of property market boom, the worse is the behaviour of market participants. The greater the traffic congestion, the worse the behaviour of frustrated drivers.

It was the anarchy of resource allocation in nineteenth century industrial cities that led to the legal foundations of modern municipal government functions. After a century of evolutionary feedback, those rules have changed, adapted, disappeared, been replaced by private contractual rules or been strengthened. Paralleling these changes is the pattern of proprietary order – the fragmentation and combination of private property rights; the enclosure of public domains to form private domains; and the re-ordering of private domains. Proprietary order is created and shaped by institutions. It also shapes institutional evolution. In the next section we explore this co-evolutionary process starting with the primitive emergence of states, territories, boundaries and communal and common property rights systems. Before moving on to this discussion, however, we consider the costs of organising rules via the state and the associated idea of government failure.

Transaction Costs of State-organised Rules and Government Failure

Whereas the critique of government regulation has a long history, going back to the nineteenth century libertarian thinking and the post-war criticism of socialism of Hayek and Friedman, the concept of 'government failure' in direct opposition to the idea of 'market failure' has a recent history. It apparently arose in the 1980s from diverse sources where western democracy is practised. Martin Jänicke advances the concept of *Staatsveragen* (the German expression of *state failure*) (Jänicke, 1990). Citing Gwartney and Stroup (1982) and, Kwong explains four sources of 'public failure' that are specific to a democratic decision-making setting (Kwong, 1990):

(1)   voter ignorance: voters do not tend to obtain costly information except on issues that are important to themselves only;

(2)   the power of special interests: well-informed and articulate interest groups will dominate the political process and receive political favours;

(3)   the short-sightedness of elected officials – election time frames tend to take priority over long term efficiency in decision making;

(4)   lack of incentive for entrepreneurial efficiency – government officials are in a weak position to recoup any personal gain from improved efficiency; and

(5)   imprecision in the reflection of consumer preferences – there is little opportunity for individuals to pick some of one candidate's positions and some of another's. Policy bundles tend to reflect a majority coalition (Gwartney and Stroup, 1982).

Government inefficiency, however, is not limited to the problems of voters' preferences and bureaucratic practices in a democratic setting. The problem of voter's preference is just an example of the problem of using non-price institutions to allocate scarce resources. More generally, the failure of government institutions lead to: (1) the inability of the state to tackle market failures and its ability to exacerbate them; (2) the tendency of the state to create market distortions; (3) the disposition of the state to levy too much tax, in money or in kind, for its services, wanted or unwanted; (4) the tendency in modern democratic society for over-public participation. We comment briefly on each of these in turn.

Failure in addressing market failures. This type of inefficiency can arise where (a) the state intervenes where it should leave matters to the market or even anarchy; (b) the state uses the wrong means to address a market imperfection though there is a social preference for intervention; or (c) the state is not resourceful enough to do anything with the problems (the state does not intervene because of lack of revenue, expertise or political will). Rigid land use zoning is a classic example at the local government level. Zoning is imposed on the grounds that the free land market cannot sort out the problems of externalities. However, many hedonic pricing studies have shown that the imposition of zoning may not lead to the lower incidence of externalities that it is meant to mitigate or pre-empt. Zoning is also widely held responsible for creating sterile – and in one sense uncompetitive – cities (Jacobs, 1962).

Creation of ill-thought out market distortions. As we shall see in Chapter 7, distorting the market in a measured way through taxation is a common method by which states address externality problems. Many interventions cause distortions that are not measured, however, and that are often unanticipated. This happens, for example, when the state, in reaction to political pressures, imposes price controls, output restrictions and excessively high environmental standards. Rent control, for example, reduces the stock of low-cost homes as does over-stringent building standards.

Over-regulation and over-taxation. This can happen when interventions, though perhaps appropriate in terms of direction, are imposed in a draconian manner and are thus wrong in the quantitative dimension, driving out investment, destroying incentive to innovate and develop markets and places and removing pollution but at a high cost in terms of future growth and prosperity. In the land market over-regulation of externalities may occur when a highly costly environmental impact assessment process is imposed on activities that have low pollution potential irrespective of their area. Inefficiencies may also arise when measures are taken to target specifically singled out 'monopolistic' developers or 'obnoxious trades' (say open storage of containers) where the whole land market is not in perfect competition or free from other externalities. In other words the system-wide opportunity costs of regulations can be too high.

Over-participation. To promote public involvement in the government decision making process, the scope and depth of public participation has expanded. The purpose is to facilitate government in obtaining more accurate information and to enhance the legitimacy of government decisions. However, the expansion in public participation, if not properly constrained, raises the costs of transacting with government, creates opportunities for rent seeking which often infringe the rights of the less powerful and can inhibit government responsiveness and spontaneity.

That state-organised rules can fail can be explained by many possibilities: poor judgement; error in judgement; and self-interest. The first is a matter of human wisdom and the last two matters of economics. The high cost of government institutions and the failures of those institutions can be related to two principal underlying problems introduced in Chapter 1: the knowledge problem and rent seeking.

The Knowledge Problem and the 'Fatal Conceit'

When Hong Kong was ceded to Britain, it was agreed that free passage of Chinese subjects into and out of Hong Kong was not to be interrupted. Depending on relative economic performance of Mainland China and Hong Kong, people moved between major cities and areas in the Pearl River Delta Region and Hong Kong. This practice was discontinued after World War II when it was observed that the inflow of population was unlikely to be offset by any meaningful outflow. However, illegal immigrants strong enough to reach urban Hong Kong were given Hong Kong identity. The 'touch-base' policy was discontinued in the early 1980s as there were too many who were physically strong enough to find their way to the urban areas. Yet, an official daily intake quota of 150 persons is still effective. The economy of Hong Kong was able to absorb this scale of immigration until recent years. Indeed, illegal migrants were actually in demand to build housing and offices in Hong Kong during the property boom. More recently a new type of immigration problem has arisen due to a fundamental change in welfare policies: there is no longer a need to stay in Hong Kong for seven years before being entitled to public housing benefits or social security. The drastic change in welfare allocation led to a change in the nature of migrants and their sociological composition. Those who came to Hong Kong in the 1980s or before were young individuals. Now, most are young women (married to elderly Hong Kong men) and their young children. Instead of providing a new supply of energetic workforce, the inflow is mainly a net burden, in the short term at least, on government resources.

Some rules fail because they are inappropriate instruments to achieve desired effects; others because their system-wide impact was not thought through; and others because of unanticipated events. All of these are problems of inadequate information. In the absence of market prices as revealed preferences, the planner and policy maker must find other proxies to measure individual and public interest. Thus, a key cost of using the plan is the cost of trying to ascertain the true preferences of the individuals. This is, however, a formidably costly task.

Government response to problems of information is often inappropriate. Examples of government failure are typically taken as evidence of *occasional mistakes* or *under-capacity* of government bodies due to inadequate financial resources, human capital or legislation. In urban planning, for example, failed plans and policies may be put down to inadequate planning studies or statutory loopholes in the planning system. Solutions offered are better ideas and concepts based on better information and better consultation with better-qualified staff using better techniques and stronger government commitment or sanction. This may be valid in specific instances. However, government failures are often recurrent and persistent in a context where the state has committed full resources and where all the reasons for the intervention were laudable and unobjectionable.

In the absence of complete information about preferences, the government rule-makers inevitably assume a good deal of power in representing the preferences of the whole society. An obvious cost of ordered co-operation arises: the costs of enforcing commands, which may not correspond to the preferences of the recipients of orders. Where individuals are told to do things involuntarily, they have less incentive. Costs must be expended to ensure compliance or to enforce orders.

In urban planning, the concept of the planner as an advocate, notwithstanding good intentions, may dangerously exacerbate these problems. Unlike the counsel in a legal battle, the planner advocate is self-appointed rather than instructed by the relevant party. However, the more serious problem is that the planner-advocate as an employee of the state and educated into a public service culture and ideology is often hostile to economic calculus. Instead of weighing the costs of a particular rule against its merits, decisions are often arrived at a priori from ideological preferences (where the executive government is strong) or in response to powerful lobbies (where democracy is strong).

Rent Seeking

The second root source of failure when a collective entity, like government, allocates resources using plans and associated rules is rent seeking. Rent seeking, like the knowledge problem, may be regarded as a problem of high transaction costs of information when the price mechanism is suppressed. Where the market is not completely displaced by a system of rules that are fully co-ordinated by the plan, rent seeking arises.

The very nature of government and its various arms as a non-price distributor of property rights in cities makes it vulnerable to rent-seeking activity by all kinds of resource owners. This may lead to (a) additional transaction costs in the form of delays and lobbying that benefit interest groups rather than the public at large; and (b) resource use that is less than optimal (as the winner in the non-price competition may not be the highest value user of the resource in question, for example land).

There is an economic tendency for all interest groups to promote their interest at the expense of others if the costs inflicted on others will not harm the groups' economic interest in the foreseeable future – this is but a dimension of human fallibility.

The tendency of regulating professions and government departments to act as interest groups leads them to (a) expand and deepen the law that governs their regulated area; (b) promote more policies for their regulated area; and (c) restrict entry of alternative solutions. The economic effects of over-regulation will however eventually check the ambition of the regulator, but the rest of society may meanwhile have to bear the costs.

In Hong Kong, the high transaction costs confronting developers trying to assemble land under multiple ownership led to the creation of a statutory body with the power to *resume* private property coercively before the contractual expiry dates on land leases. Major developers have become joint-venture partners with government in profit-making urban renewal projects which involve wholesale redevelopment rather than rehabilitation. Forcibly removed residents or shop owners are often not relocated, though they are compensated for their loss. These owners acquired their rights by virtue of their leasehold interests acquired in the open market initially from the Crown in auctions or tenders. The land selected by the statutory body for renewal is often zoned as a 'comprehensive development area (CDA)'. Individual private lots inside a CDA zone cannot be individually redeveloped by the owners themselves. They lose their right of redevelopment even if they all agree to a joint redevelopment scheme that competes with the scheme of the renewal agency, (as revealed in a number of court cases). The joint venture arrangement allows the renewal agency to use its powers to redistribute rent from existing landowners to itself and its private partners. The statutory body is a typical state trading enterprise that was once popular with socialist countries. The renewal authority has systematically favoured larger-scale development projects over smaller ones. Public complaints have led to further increase in the rate of compensation but the more fundamental issue of private property, as a constitutional issue under the Basic Law, or rent seeking, as a matter of just government, has been ignored.

3.4 PROPRIETARY ORDER

Historically, linguistically and legally, 'the common or commons' is common property. Several (many) persons (families) share in the usage of a potentially valued resource. Privatisation involves the partitioning of this resource among separate users with a specific delineation of boundaries (Buchanan, 1993: 1).

The institutional order of a city, we have argued, emerges to lower the costs of market transactions and other forms of co-operation. It only does so, however, to the extent that it successfully delivers efficient order in exclusive property rights. In the example just cited, one state institution rescinds the proprietary order that another state institution created. If a government does this too often – and without a widely appreciated justification – it will come into disrepute.

As the monopoly supplier of violence, the state has a fundamental role in creating a legal environment for market-based exchange and economic growth. At the minimum this includes making rules and sanctions that confer on individuals (a) the secure rights to exclusive use of private property; (b) the rights to derive income from property and (c) the right to trade (alienate) property. Where rights are conferred but are inalienable, inefficiencies arise in the sense of there being unrealised potential gains from trade. The inalienable land rights given to indigenous people groups through reservation policies are a source of frustration to some entrepreneurial members of younger generations wishing to use land to yield more wealth (Frantz, 1999). Similarly, inalienable land-use designations in urban development plans that go against the market, prevent potential gains to contracting parties and to many potential users of a prohibited but beneficial development.

The Emergence of State and Territory

To an urban planner the delineation of boundaries, or zoning, is a well-known tool. But zoning is not only to be associated with government planning, as partitioning of land pertains to all human activities governed by some degree of exclusive property rights. To appreciate the logic behind the emergence of spatial partitioning of land resources, we need to consider how government comes into existence.

Few, if any, single individuals have sufficient knowledge to survive totally alone. Modern day survivalists rely on artefacts made by complex production processes involving thousands of individual processes; each of which is the knowledge domain of other individuals. Primitive survivalists, like most castaway sailors of the great maritime era, did not survive for long on their own. People in primitive society lived together in clans and kinship groups. One of the features distinguishing such groups from groups of non-human animals is the existence of conscious government. Government is an authority backed by force, which constrains the cost of competition by making and upholding rules. Unrestrained competition means anarchy. The logical extreme of anarchy is 'might make rights', where private property, innovation and peace are difficult or impossible to sustain. Government emerges to organise the rules that prevent slippage and meltdown in human co-operation and to build or re-build civil society from various states of anarchy.

Government in a primitive hunter-gatherer society typically comprised a kin chief supported by a group of elders. Inherited rules, mores and customs (spontaneous institutions) interpreted by and adapted and added to by the current generation of leaders, ensured the collective survival of the tribe. Tribal institutions, including family and interpersonal customs, allowed a primitive division of labour – between male and female, ruler and ruled, priest and laity and between different types of hunters and makers. Spontaneous institutions evolved to govern the allocation of food, shelter, material artefacts and activities – between tribe members, over time and between generations. Without rules to create trust, individuals would remain islands of very incomplete knowledge.

With agreed conventions, customs and moral codes governing the allocation of resources, individuals in primitive societies could specialise in knowledge, becoming expert fishermen, priests, trappers and garment-makers. When circumstances changed – social, political and environmental – so the value of a tribe's resources would change and institutions had to adapt. If they did not, a tribe would probably not survive major external threats. Depleted food resources reduce the value of a location and force a move with an upheaval of the institutions adapted for a particular environment. Increasing competition for land from other tribes might eventually force a shift to settled agriculture and permanent settlement. The concept of boundaries of influence then becomes significant, and states with finite territory and restricted entry emerge (Lai, 1996, 1997).

Boundaries and the institutions that support them reduce the costs of protecting lives and property; they reduce the costs of dispute resolution between neighbouring states; and as a result they increase the value of communal, common and private property.

Boundary delineation has long been subject to state supervision. The establishment of a new regime is often followed by land surveys to define or redefine landed properties, as in the cases of the eleventh century Norman conquest of Britain (Doomsday Book of 1086) and various land title censuses in Dynastic China (where the first national survey and standardisation of measures and written characters was in 221 BC). Such surveys may have been driven by fiscal intentions but land boundary delineation makes all forms of social activity and governance more efficient, not just taxation.

The Emergence of Boundaries within States

Within territorial boundaries, the sophistication of property rights systems naturally adapts over time. Many primitive settled communities held property under communal property rights. Alchian and Demsetz characterise this system: 'Under a communal right system, each person has a private right to use of a resource once it is captured, but only a communal right to the same resource before it is taken' (Alchian and Demsetz, 1973: 22).

The deserts occupied by the Hun Khans provide an example with near universal intra-communal rights. The Indians of the Labrador Peninsular who allowed free hunting on land owned by them collectively is documented by Leacock (Demsetz, 1967: 351). Modern variants are found throughout Africa, for example in the Libyan province of Tripolitania (Bottomley, 1963) and rural Namibia, where 27 per cent of arable land is owned by the state and allocated to 60 per cent of the population on a common-hold basis (Noongo, 2001).

A system of communal rights allows individuals to retain the fruits of their labours in capturing resources for themselves. Captured resources are protected from others within the community by a first come, first served understanding and protected from outsiders by force. The two-fold excludability encourages individuals to expend resources in capturing and exploiting resources and adds to individual and communal wealth.

Communal rights become inadequate however when competition becomes more acute. First come, first served is not an adequate institution to protect the fruits of an individual's labour when rights are constantly challenged in the face of resource scarcity. Rising scarcity within the boundary of a state leads to more boundaries forming and the emergence of exclusive property rights. Noongo (2001) reports the fencing off of communal arable land in Namibia in the 1990s as a result of pressure on land. Political battles to reallocate tribal and communal land in urbanising regions are currently being played out in many parts of the African continent.

Traditional systems of property rights evolve and are replaced by private property rights as the value of land, labour and capital change. The doctrine of estates in feudal England and the evolution of the private rights system in feudal China are pre-modern examples. Feudalism consolidated rights to land, labour and capital in the hands of feudal lords who supplied protection, shelter and land and made decentralised production decisions on their patch. The arrangement was costly in terms of serfdom's loss of individual human rights but arguably made life bearable for many. In the absence of effective wider state laws to protect property, transaction costs may well have been higher without feudal order – in terms of risk to property and life from arbitrary opportunism.

Feudalism was established in China in 2698 BC and private rights over wild freshwater fish emerged as early as 2000 BC (Lin, 1940). The latter was achieved by domestication of fish through converting lakes under communal rights into private property; by excavating privately owned land; or simply by combining fish culture and paddy farming on private land. The sophisticated spontaneous zoning pattern of agricultural land in China, which still survives in many parts of Hong Kong's New Territories, bears witness to the evolution of the institution of exclusive property rights over land. Privatisation of marine fishery resources has also become a reality by cage and net culture. This happens in all countries with a maritime boundary and even in a high-density and small area like Hong Kong, marine fish culture has found space to develop into a strong industry. The total world output of cultured fish, once regarded in the economic literature as a classic common or open access property, now exceeds that of cattle in terms of weight (McGinn, 1998).

The fragmentation of land and boundaries within a state requires a complex system of rules and a number of parallel systems have evolved. In England, *land law* has evolved to delineate rights and to adjudicate disputes. Exclusive property rights or 'private property rights' over land are conferred by *fee simple absolute*. The holder of the estate of fee simple has an exclusive right to use and to derive income from land within clearly delineated boundaries. The income derived from a property and the property itself can be freely disposed of (alienated) in whole or in part (subdivided) or in combination with another piece of land (land assembly). Development of land, including the building of structures and changes of use are governed by *planning law*. The rights to decide how private land may be used are severely attenuated by planning law. In addition to land law and planning law, the *tort law of nuisance* allows the courts to deal with conflicts of rights that cannot be resolved by private negotiations. Although planning law is often thought to have the purpose of lowering the social (third party) costs of private exchanges in land and property markets it can also serve to lower the private costs of exchange – by furnishing transacting parties with information that influences their valuation and choice of location.

As land fragments into private estates some land will remain common property, however. Land in states and cities is never fully subdivided. Common-land rights may be found in frontier settlement situations where institutions are in the process of forming, or in anarchic situations where institutions have broken down. They may be found where institutions have yet to emerge because a resource has insufficient value or because the transaction costs of assigning rights exceed the value of enclosure. They may also be found where state, individuals and firms deem that it is desirable to retain common rights of various kinds for various purposes. Municipal governments maintain various levels of common access rights to roads, parks and other facilities that they supply. Owners of shops and malls permit common access to their land because that is how they generate revenue. In Chapters 5 and 6 we develop this discussion of enclosure by looking at the economics of clubs and local public goods.

'Enclosure' of Resources

The emergence of territorial states and of boundaries within states illustrates the wider issue of resource *enclosure* or *subdivision*. Here we widen the discussion from land, to other material resources and their attributes and introduce ideas developed in the remainder of the book. The general principle governing the process of resource enclosure has been stated as the *subdivision* rule in Chapter 1, which may be summarised as: *A change in the value of a resource leads to a demand for institutions that re-allocate property rights over the resource in a more efficient way.*

Greater efficiency in this context means lower costs of transacting with that resource. Institutions enclose resources by assigning various types of rights and create private domains. Resources left fully or partially 'unenclosed' – with unclear property rights – remain in the public domain. Resources may also be purposefully placed in the public domain – a reversal of enclosure. Public domain resources give rise to most of the problems that urban governments seek to address.

Many of the pressing public domain problems arise not from common ownership of land and material property per se, but of common ownership of important attributes of those commodities. Roads may be owned by the state and buildings may be the private property of a firm or an individual. If ownership of the right to use roads is not well defined (by driving licence, regulations or road pricing for example), then that right is common property and may be subject to public domain problems as individuals compete for that right. If the right to pollute others by using a privately owned building for a dirty industrial process is not well defined, then the air in the vicinity of the building is a common good and subject to the public domain problem of unrestrained competition.

The boundaries between public and private realms, common and private property rights shift over time with changes in resource values and institutions. In general, there would seem to be a secular trend towards progressively fine delineation of rights – from common rights to private rights. This is driven by a constantly evolving demand for resources through changes in preference and changes in population and density. In the context of increasing prosperity, population growth and urbanisation the subdivision rule implies increasing fragmentation of all resources.

Where there is little or no competition and congestion, common property rights may be an equilibrium form of institution in the sense of being stable and consistent with the pursuit of individual wealth. Where there is no scarcity, there is no threat to the fruits of an individual's labour and the absence of exclusionary institutions does not inhibit investment, invention, wealth accumulation and social and economic progress. In such circumstances, the costs of creating and sustaining property rights, including the technological costs of enclosure and pricing, exceed the benefits (the *public domain rule* introduced in Chapter 1).

It is rarely the case however that a resource with the potential to raise welfare remains uncontested. In a populous and mobile world most common property resources sooner or later become congested. With the introduction of scarcity and competition, common property rights become unstable. They will not remain for long in a society in which individuals creatively search for new ways of combining knowledge with others in pursuit of greater wealth. In neo-classical terms they are inconsistent with the maximisation postulate.

Anarchy, Congestion and Benefit Dissipation

A scarce resource governed by common property rules leads to allocation by anarchy. Thomas Hobbes' *Leviathan* characterises life in this state as 'solitary, poor, nasty, brutish and short' (Hobbes as quoted in Berki, 1976). Though the term *open access* is used by some in place of *common property*, (from one point of view there is no property in anarchy), the better view is that anarchy results from individuals asserting their *economic right* to a resource by might. Under anarchy, the income derived from a resource (its economic rent) will, in the extreme, completely dissipate through the rising costs of competition (the costs of making transaction in congested and unrestrained conditions).

In a frontier gold rush town, unrestrained competition and the ensuing violence that destroys property and life, might conceivably reduce the net social value of the gold reserve to zero or below (for an analysis of the California Gold Rush, see Umbeck, 1977). Three outcomes might arise in such a situation. A higher state may intervene to impose order for the greater social good; order may emerge internally providing that collective action problems can be surmounted; or the settlement may deteriorate until the rising costs and falling net benefits eventually bring about its demise.

In Figure 1.1 (Chapter 1), point $P5$ defines the point of total benefit (or economic rent) dissipation in a settlement. The gold rush city is an extreme example but the curves may represent any city moving beyond some notional (and unknowable) optimal size. Rent dissipates by the competition costs of commuting along gridlocked roads and overloaded public transport systems; by prohibitively high housing costs caused by restricted land supply and unrestricted speculative investment; by various types of queuing competition for scarce urban services (for a discussion of rationing by waiting, see Barzel, 1974); by urban conflicts (a kind of competition cost) and the violence that emerges to threaten life and property; and by the high costs of policing a lawless society.

Some cities of the former Soviet Union make an interesting illustration of the rent dissipation issue. The mass desertion of some Siberian industrial towns with the removal of central planning infrastructure suggests that when the costs of isolation are added in, locational rent derived from many of these remote places is exceeded by the transaction costs of living, working and producing there. A contrasting Russian example is the relatively well-off settlements built around rich mineral deposits and currently wanting to reintroduce Soviet-style travel restrictions. Under the old system the Soviet government prohibited free migration and visitation from other cities to keep the general public ignorant of the superior benefits offered to workers in these inhospitable locations. Without such controls, migrants from poorer regions attracted by superior urban services and the hope of a good wage are threatening to dissipate the benefits cherished by established citizens. Falling average benefits resulting from rising numbers of free riders could tip the balance and make these single-industry towns unviable. An alternative to immigration controls would be to increase the complexity of welfare institutions in the towns – something that would also cause benefit dissipation by raising organisation costs of government. In 2001 the nickel-mining town of Norilsk re-imposed entry controls it had relinquished at the end of the communist era. The Ural towns of Magnetogorksk and Novy Urengoi and Mirny, the diamond capital of Yakutia are about to close their doors (Jack, 2002).

Problems of congestion, rising competition costs and benefit dissipation are not only found in frontier or underdeveloped settlements. Cities are unavoidably full of public domain resources. Even if land in a state or a city were to be fully fragmented into private holdings, the boundaries between holdings would be sources of shared resources – positive and negative externalities or land use 'spillovers' – a point we pick up in Chapter 7.

3.5   KEY ARGUMENTS OF CHAPTER 3

•   Individuals and firms seek co-operative opportunities with lower rather than higher transaction costs. As they seek exchange partners, five types of order emerge from their cost-minimising behaviour. This chapter discusses organisational, institutional and proprietary order. (The other two types of order, spatial and public domain order, are discussed in Chapters 4 to 7.)

- Organisational order (patterns of planned co-operation) emerges as individuals combine property rights with those of others in order to reduce the costs of co-operating in the market. This order 'supersedes' atomistic market co-operation with exchange that is based on rules governed by consensus, agreement and hierarchical decision making. Central to the market-plan dichotomy is the Coasian notion of the costs of using the price mechanism for co-ordinating division of labour in the land market.
- Institutional order (patterns of rules and sanctions) emerges from agreements made in organisations. Institutions are formed in order to reduce competition costs within markets and within organisations. They do this by assigning exclusive property rights over private goods and attempting to assign rules or rights over contested public domain goods. Three types of rules that are significant for development are spontaneous rules, private contracts and government regulations.
- Imposing order via government rules is a costly business that is prone to failure. Government transaction costs are high because of the information problem and because of the scope for rent seeking.
- Proprietary order (patterns of exclusive property rights) is generated by institutional order. We make a distinction between institutional and proprietary order because it is possible to have the former without the latter – when institutions are poorly designed or otherwise ineffective. Central to this order is boundary delineation and exclusive use of land resources. The transition from common property to private property involves the partitioning and restriction of access to resources.
- As economies develop, property rights have a tendency to fragment – to subdivide with ever increasing sophistication.
- Without property rights, resources are left in the public domain and are subject to dissipation.

4. Spatial order

4.1 NEO-CLASSICAL BID-RENT MODELS – A CATALLACTIC INTERPRETATION

In most Western societies, land is allocated among alternative uses mainly by means of private markets, with more or less public regulations. In such societies, the current spatial structure of a city is thus the outcome of billions of individual actions taken in the past. Hence, one might suspect that the outcome of such unregulated individual actions would be near chaos. However, the history of science suggests to the contrary that the larger the number of individual actors in a system, the stronger are the regularities it will exhibit. Indeed, many studies have revealed that strong regularities exist in the spatial structure of different urban areas (Fujita, 1989: 2).

All physical objects have dimensions and occupy space and hence space is a vital element in human interactions. In this chapter we consider how space is ordered to constrain competition over land and other resources.

Von Thünen's (1826) early nineteenth century model of agricultural producers bidding for proximity to a central market remains an elegant theory of emergent spatial order. Starting with an arbitrary transaction cost map (a single pre-existing central market), Von Thünen demonstrated that concentric rings of similar land uses emerge as competing producers bid away rent and colonise land according to bidding power (profits). The analysis is insightful but comparatively static in the sense that bidding responds to exogenous accessibility-related transaction costs (distance in the original model). Derivative models of urban land use (Alonso, 1964; Miyao, 1981; Fujita, 1989) deepen Von Thünen's analysis, introducing non-uniform accessibility costs via transport nodes, localised positive and negative externalities and so on. These models have the same basic limitation, however, of being unable to complete the loop and render transaction costs a dynamic function of the spatial patterns emerging from bidding.

Recent developments in the economics of geography (Fujita et al., 1999; Krugman, 1995) tackle this long-standing theoretical problem by modelling economies of scale and the growth of agglomerations. Such models capture a more dynamic equilibrium in which producers and consumers bid for locations on the basis of cost advantages but change those advantages by their location decision. Yet, the perfect market clearing mechanisms in all of these models and their underlying assumptions of perfect knowledge render them of intellectual value but lacking as practically useful representations of reality. The bid rent story may therefore be usefully re-told with an emphasis on knowledge imperfection, transaction costs and property rights.

Agglomeration Economies, Transaction Costs and Spatial Clustering

One of the most important decisions made as individuals and organisations seek gains from co-operation is location. This remains so even in the modern *knowledge economy* since face-to-face exchange in production (forging and maintaining contracts) and in consumption (urban living and leisure) seems to remain an essential sinew to modern urban order. Location influences benefits and costs.

More populous locations yield the benefits of greater choice of exchange partners or more strictly, lower search costs and therefore greater choice. The costs and benefits are evaluated differently by different transacting partners, however, and locations specialise. Specifically they become spatial clusters of individuals and organisations that benefit from each other's specialised production or consumption knowledge – either in exchange or in combination. Homogeneous residential neighbourhoods form as households combine publicly consumed attributes of their private property (including their own personal characteristics) with those of others. Commercial and industrial neighbourhoods form as firms locate near similar and complementary firms, effectively combining individual contributions to a location's accessibility and market potential.

Clustering of uses – spatial specialisation – is an ordering process with an analogous dynamic to the grouping of individuals into organisations or 'firms'. To lower the costs of using knowledge in pursuit of wealth, individuals combine private property rights by forming or joining firms. Both the size and existence of a particular firm is determined by the net benefits of so doing (Coase, 1937). Similarly, spatial clusters form, grow, change use-mix and density, decline and disappear as the net benefits to combining shared positive externalities change. The cost-saving rationale for clustering is different for different types of exchange and we can talk of agglomeration economies of production and of consumption.

Agglomeration economies of consumption either lower the costs of searching for products to consume or lower the costs of searching for other consumers with whom to co-consume (and thereby co-produce a desirable neighbourhood). Homogeneous residential neighbourhoods form around locational attributes that are valued by a particular type of household – good schools, specialised schools, scenic lakes, wooded slopes with a view, historic sites. They also tend to generate their own supply of specialised services – shopping streets change to reflect the character of residents. Residential neighbourhoods in this way lower home-movers' costs of locational search and lower transaction costs to residents by reducing the need to travel.

Agglomeration economies of production are of two kinds: those that lower the costs of searching for customers and those that lower the costs of searching for inputs (including labour and supply chain partners). To access higher pedestrian flows, shops locate near to large anchor shops; evolve into spontaneous clusters; and purchase space in malls (organised clusters). Retail firms compare the higher rents of these locations with the costs of alternative strategies of searching for customers. A similar spatial order emerges from an aversion to the costs of input search but the two rationales are distinct. Offices traditionally locate in city centres because that is where urban transport systems converged. The geometry creates a point of peak accessibility to labour, which is the most important factor of production for a commercial business. A weakening of the monocentric geometry through urban motorway construction and other decentralising forces creates polycentric commercial clustering but the clustering is still by and large a strategy that lowers the cost of transaction between employer and employed. Since firms bear the costs of finding a location, location is a part of the labour transaction cost borne by the employer just as the employee usually bears the cost of commuting. We return to this reciprocity in transaction cost sharing in the next chapter since it is fundamental to the understanding of the way order emerges in the consumption of public domain goods.

The spatial specialisation processes we have described are dynamic and evolutionary. They are catallactic. As urban social scientists have observed for a long time, clusters of land-use and knowledge compete against each other for location-derived benefits or cost advantages: they invade and succeed each other; they are dominated and dominate (for a survey of the early urban ecology literature, see Timms, 1971). As new combinations of knowledge are invented and new exchange partners discovered so spatial order changes along with organisational order and the growth and redistribution of wealth. The processes of evolution are simple and understandable at the level of individual behaviour, as we elaborate below, but in combination they are non-linear and path-dependent and systemically hard to understand and predict.

Spontaneous Order by Bidding for Land

At any point in time the city presents to individuals a map of agglomeration (clustering) economies – a map of transaction opportunities and transaction costs. The map will look different to each individual but there will be regularities in subjective evaluations and these will reveal themselves in the bids that households and firms offer to acquire property rights over particular locations. The subjective evaluation of a location (site, plot, building) is a function of the stream of net benefits that may be expected after acquiring rights over it. This may be modelled as the net present value of a stream of revenue (trading income); a stream of recurrent production costs (maintenance, taxation); fixed capital costs (construction, refurbishment, demolition and so on); and transaction costs (legal costs of policing contracts, advertising). For non-trading activities (households) the value may be thought of as the net present value of a stream of residential benefits measured by the opportunity costs of renting similar accommodation; a stream of recurrent costs (maintenance); capital costs (renovation and adaptation); and transaction costs of locational exchange such as search and legal costs.

A distinction may be made between the transaction costs of acquiring rights over a location and the transaction costs (particularly distance-related costs) of other exchanges (which are influenced by location). More remote locations make it more costly to participate in labour, retail, leisure and other markets. In residual land valuation models these distance-related transaction costs are captured implicitly in the discounted benefit stream. Anticipated rental income from a proposed new supermarket, for example, will take account of the spatial distribution of consumers around a site and is inversely related to mean distance. Thus the transaction costs facing consumers becomes an important determinant of the locational value bid by producers. Elaborating a point we have already made, the producer will have a range of bid prices in which the share of exchange costs (or custom/product search costs) is variously apportioned between supplier and consumer. If there are many available sites, a firm may be expected to choose a location that apportions search costs in a way that optimises its trading objective (market share, turnover, profit, costs and so on).

Neo-classical bid rent models assume that these comparative static valuations of individual producers and consumers determine spatial structure through a competitive market clearing process. Different classes of households (low-income, high-income) and firms (commercial, retail, wholesale) make bids for a variable supply of land, which is differentiated in attributes and valued by each class in the way we have described. It is a variable supply because models typically allow agricultural land to be converted into urban uses if urban rent exceeds rural rent. Assuming large numbers of competing bidders, perfect knowledge and no transaction costs other than those relating to travel, producers have the incentive to bid away all profits (rent) in order to acquire the rights to produce at a particular location.

Profits are determined exogenously as a function of price and they decline with distance from points of maximum accessibility (a single central market in the simplest models), reaching zero at a point where profit is equal to transport-related transaction costs. The downward sloping curve mapping economic rent against distance is also the producer's spatial bid rent function and the landowner's spatial revenue function from this type of exchange partner. For a household, the bid-rent curve is downward sloping because, faced with a fixed household budget and a fixed level of utility, the amount it can bid for land falls with distance from the centre as more of its budget is consumed in travel-related transaction costs. Residential bid-rent curves (land value curves) are usually drawn concave to the origin because of intra-marginal utility trade-offs between land and a bundle of other goods.

Whereas competition from similar bidders equates the spatial rent curve with the spatial land value curve, competition between classes of bidders partitions urban space between land uses with the intersections of bid-rent curves forming the boundaries in the segmented land market. The result is a pattern of concentric rings, each defining the space in which a particular class of land consumer acquires the locational property rights by virtue of superior bidding power.

4.2 BIDDING WITH IMPERFECT COMPETITION, IMPERFECT KNOWLEDGE AND TRANSACTION COSTS

Bid-rent theory is compelling because it captures something important about the spontaneous ordering processes that create regularities in cities, which are otherwise diverse in history, culture and economy. However, with the breakdown of monocentric geometry in the post-industrial city it is some of the finer details of the models rather than their partial equilibrium results that are of abiding importance. It is not just the geometry that is unrealistic; the models assume away too much.

First, there are not always large numbers of similar bidders competing with each other for each location. Second, all urban locations are unique, and this alone guarantees that knowledge is far from perfect. Third, there are transaction costs other than the costs of travel – particularly the costs of subdividing property rights, the costs of locational search and the sunk costs of relocation. These three realities have a number of consequences for the spontaneous exchange of locational rights in a city and we address each in turn.

Imperfect Competition

Where there are only a few bidders, rent will be shared between bidder and landowner, not completely bid away in competition. How much is retained by a bidder in the absence of competition is determined by the availability of similar sites; the bidding power relative to other classes of bidders; and legal and statutory attenuation of land rights. A large employer coming to a city in a depressed region is likely to have the choice of several sites and will face little if any competition from similar bidders. It will wield considerable market power and retain rent that would be bid away in a more competitive urban land market. If it receives land free or heavily subsidised by the state by way of regional incentive (not uncommon in lagging regions of Europe, for example) it may not have to cede any property rights over its projected profit from the location. In this uncompetitive situation it is the bid rent of the next most profitable use of the location that determines the cut in the large employer's profits that must be ceded in the exchange for land. Below this level, without subsidy it will be outbid.

Competition from other types of land users therefore provides market discipline even in the absence of competition from similar enterprises. Whether or not the degree of competition between similar land users makes a difference to spatial order depends on the number of locations at which that use outbids other uses – the effective land supply for that use. If supply outstrips demand, bidders are able to offer just above the bid of the nearest competitor use to gain property rights. If demand outstrips supply at this level, bidders start competing by bidding away rent. As they do, their bid-rent curve rises and the quantity of land for which they can offer superior bids expands. If the city is relatively closed in the sense of there being few alternative cities to which individuals and firms can relocate, then spatial order changes throughout the city as all other uses crowd into marginally reduced space. The repositioning of land uses is determined by the intersection of adjusted bid-rent curves – raised as a result of more bidders crowding into smaller areas (for an introduction to the bid-rent analysis of urban structure, see Thrall, 1987). Since it only takes two competitors to start bidding away rent, however, the large numbers assumption of the bid-rent model is probably not too serious a problem. The more general point of interest is perhaps the ways in which rent is shared between exchange partners in the absence of competition.

Imperfect Knowledge

More important is the reality of imperfect knowledge. It will help to make a distinction between random and systematic knowledge variations and then to identify several distinct types of the latter. Random knowledge variations we define as those that arise from individuality. In neo-classical terms they are random perturbations to a household utility function or a firm's profit function.

There clearly exist strong regularities in preferences that characterise different groups of consumers and producers in cities and these regularities must logically be founded on common knowledge. Indeed, in several points of our exposition so far, we have made knowledge the primary analytical device. Individuals and firms cluster to combine and exchange property rights on the basis of knowledge, and spatial order can be understood to be spatial knowledge specialisation. Strong regularities notwithstanding, all individuals and firms are unique and the knowledge of each is subjectively formed from unique histories. Thus while small retailers, heavy industries, media firms, middle-income households, impoverished rural migrants and young professionals tend to locate in predictable patterns, offering similar bids for land rights on the basis of shared knowledge, there are always those that for one reason or another buck the trend.

Many deviations from the norm may be individually rational because of subtle differences in preferences including the desire to innovate in consumption or production. However, it is as likely that many others will be a result of individuals' specific knowledge deficits. The impact of these random acts of non-conformity is subtle but profound. It can easily be shown using micro-simulation methods that when individuals with different preferences for exchange partners openly compete for land rights the result is stable spatial clusters, homogeneous in preferences. When the locational bids of individuals are randomly perturbed, however, simulating either knowledge imperfection or innovation, then the result is spatially unstable clusters (Wu and Webster, 1998; Webster and Wu, 2001). Like oil and water, clusters of co-operating individuals and firms gradually change shape, moving against each other as locations on cluster boundaries randomly change use under 'perverse' bidding.

Non-conforming property right bids resulting from innovative intentions may not, of course, be perverse in the sense of arising from partial or false information. They may turn out to be well judged – by pioneers of gentrified neighbourhoods, new retail clusters, new towns or other new styles of spatial, institutional and organisational order. On the other hand successful innovations sometimes arise as a creative response to an imperfect location decision (spontaneous innovations). This happens when a development project fails in its intended use but succeeds in something else partly because of its unique and possibly unlikely combination of opportunities and constraints. A failed industrial building converts to a leisure centre, for example, using the original office suite as a hotel for innovative weekend leisure breaks. The innovation is copied and the mix of services located in industrial parks takes an evolutionary step.

It is also true that planned innovations can fail through imperfect information – a new business fails, for example, because it undervalued the transaction costs facing targeted customers and consequently overvalued the site's market potential. Individual and unpredictable knowledge imperfections therefore result in unpredictable changes in spatial order. Innovative responses to knowledge deficit can lead to new markets and new regularities in spatial pattern. The long-term effect of random variations in knowledge, however, is likely to be spatial instability in the demand for land rights.

Other kinds of knowledge variation follow more discernible patterns. It will be helpful to discuss these in relation to Figure 4.1, which plots variation in household utility across a city. The figure shows a flattening out of the spatial utility function over time as households relocate in pursuit of utility gains. This is a standard device used in partial equilibrium bid rent. To simplify, assume households and landowners are homogeneous in income and can only raise welfare by relocating to reduce travel-related costs of transacting in the central employment and service district. At some initial point in time utility is higher at the centre where transaction costs are lowest. As households relocate towards the centre, however, densities and, as a result, rents rise and thus utility at the centre falls. With perfect information, property rights over location will be re-allocated and priced in equilibrium such that there is no more incentive for movement and exchange. Households on the urban periphery have lower rents but higher transaction costs; those towards the centre have lower transaction costs but higher rents.

This neatly balanced utopia (invariant long-term spatial equilibrium utility) may fail to emerge, however, through a variety of systematic knowledge problems. Utility peaks may persist where locational benefits are under-valued; and utility troughs may persist where they are over-valued. Both may result from systematic variations in the distribution of households and search costs since households tend to curtail their search of more distant locations and are therefore less knowledgeable about distant opportunities for schooling, jobs, leisure and friends. Stubborn utility peaks and troughs may also result from systematic variations in knowledge distortion – also related to search costs and household distribution. Neighbourhoods that once had a bad reputation, for example, or have otherwise undergone changes may be misrepresented in the various means by which value is tacitly signalled. The result is higher than average utility for residents due to lack of competition.

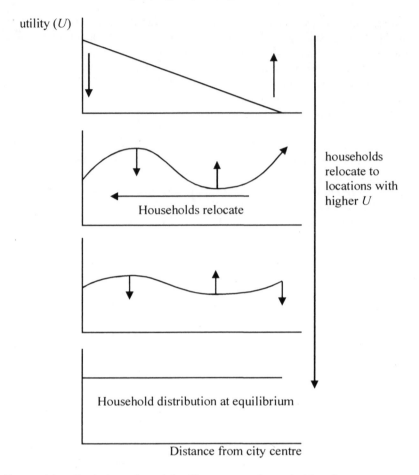

Figure 4.1   Evolution of spatial utility curve as households relocate to avoid travel-related transaction costs

Generally, it is unlikely that households or firms moving within a large city or between cities, possess the information necessary to make a realistic and consistent appraisal of all property rights that would on investigation turn out to meet their exchange requirements. Even though some variations may diminish over time as knowledge disseminates, it is clear from experience that the process is very sluggish. Over 90 per cent of Europeans live within a mile of a church building established in the Middle Ages (Batty, 2001). Over 21 per cent of the UK GDP is generated in London and 13 per cent of this within the 'Square Mile' financial district (Corporation of London, 2001).

Fifty per cent of Thailand's GDP is generated in Bangkok, which handles 90 per cent of the country's international trade (Stubbs and Clarke, 1996). There are reputed to be more Internet hosts in Manhattan Island than in the whole of Africa. Such concentrations of activity are sustained not only by agglomeration economies but also by systematic knowledge imperfection. They are sustained by an aversion to the cost of searching for partners with which to exchange or combine property rights. This includes an aversion to the costs of searching for more complete knowledge about alternative locations within which to search for exchange partners.

An added reason for the long-term stickiness of spatial variations in utility and profit is catallaxis. The neo-classical spatial sorting of households within cities (or sorting of labour and firms within a country) may never happen given the constant innovation in exchange that characterises cities and the constantly changing profit and utility profiles that result. Retailers move into booming shopping quarters as new areas emerge that have improved features. London's leafy western suburbs densify as individuals seek locational rent; but as they do, some of the rent dissipates through congestion and other honey-pot neighbourhoods emerge – suburbs to the east of the city, renovated dockland, gentrified inner city quarters and ex-urban villages and towns. It seems probable that spatial disequilibrium, not equilibrium generally, holds in the long as well as the short term.

So far we have talked principally about imperfect locational knowledge and attributed its existence to the costs of information search and its resilience to the constant emergence of new exchange opportunities. This highlights another important sense in which knowledge imperfection impacts spatial order: and here we broaden a point already made in relation to failed innovations. Competitive markets, we have noted, ensure that new knowledge only survives (as products) if it meets the wants of others. This means that there are inevitably many innovations – new products and the new organisations created to produce them – which fail the test. The spatial consequences of most of these – of many individual production decisions made on the basis of imperfect information about exchange partners – has already been discussed. If they are random imperfections, scattered through industrial sectors and space, then they will have, as we have said, a tendency to randomly re-shape the knowledge and land use clusters that form as a result of more systematic variations in knowledge. If they are relatively minor innovations – a firm experimenting with a small change in product or process – they may, of course, have no appreciable impact on spatial order. An innovating firm may not have cause to re-evaluate its location's attributes and its profits and bidding power may not change substantially. There will be many small innovations that change very little, or at all, the spatial order implicit in the intersection of many bid rent surfaces.

Misinformed innovation that makes its mark on the physical fabric of the city can dramatically affect spatial order, however. This is because investments in built capital are more lasting than in other markets. A bad decision in the stock market can be retrieved immediately – though not perhaps without loss. A bad investment in the labour market might take a little longer – depending on employment contracts. Unprofitable companies can be wound up or merged, and failing product lines adapted or closed. Buildings are less easily removed or changed.

Well before the Far Eastern financial markets crashed in 1997 many people had realised that too many international-sector homes had been built in Asia's booming capitals. The number of vacant new apartments in Bangkok by that year exceeded 330 000 (Yap and Sakchai, 2000). The banks had kept lending on the basis of investment value that could never materialise into use-value. Cities in the region competed with each other for footloose demand and in the end South China, with its plentiful supply of cheap labour and subsidised land won the day. The systematic mis-valuation of property rights in vast numbers of key sites in these cities will influence spatial order for decades to come. Whether it is good or bad for the cities depends on how these property rights are now reallocated. This leads us to our next point: the reality of non-zero transaction costs.

Transaction Costs

Spatial order evolves by subdivision and aggregation of property rights. In the spatially equilibriated neo-classical city in Figure 4.1, households pursue utility gains by moving effortlessly to the city centre or to sources of local public goods. They live at higher densities, implying densification and innovation in the way existing property rights are subdivided and new rights allocated. Asia's failed giant condominiums and shopping malls may lie rusting for a while, but not for long. Given the intensity of demand for space within which to make exchanges, new uses will be dreamt up, new organisations created, property rights reassigned and new bids made.

There will always be benefits to be gained from subdividing and combining property rights over land and buildings. The transaction costs of so doing, however, determine which exchanges are left unrealised. Costs are incurred in searching for partners with whom to combine property rights (merging land, partnering with venture capital companies, creating management organisation); searching for exchange partners (new users, agents, marketing companies); re-shaping a building to make it marketable to a variety of clients; and creating and managing contracts with new users. Where land or a building has become redundant, as in the Asian example, or in the historical industrial spaces of Europe's cities, the onus will be on the current property owners to bear most of the transaction costs. Where subdivision is driven by a natural process of intensifying demand as in Figure 4.1, then transaction costs, especially search costs, may be more easily passed on to those purchasing the re-organised property rights.

4.3   FRAGMENTATION AND SUBDIVISION

A more general principle here concerns the relationship between value, property right subdivision and transaction costs (the *subdivision rule* in Chapter 1). The value of a resource, or of an entitlement, commodity, or attribute of a commodity or resource, changes for many reasons. The value of privately owned resources changes with the numbers of people offering goods in exchange. The value of a good that is subject to unclear property rights changes with the number of individuals competing for it. If the property rights are exclusive, then a change in a resource's value is likely to lead to subdivision of the right as various attributes of the resource are partitioned and exchanged with individuals who value particular parts of the former whole. In this way, urban land and buildings evolve by subdivision. As knowledge about a superior location spreads, the number of bids for land and buildings increases and price rises. At some point it becomes profitable to demolish single homes and subdivide land rights into many smaller plots.

Other privately owned factors are also subject to the process of subdivision. If an individual can increase the value of his labour by subdividing his working time between more than one exchange partner he may be expected to move from a single employer contract to multiple contracts. Capital is valued for its different attributes and if knowledge specialisation is sufficiently developed, different attributes may be sold to exchange partners for whom they can create wealth. Thus the rights to buildings may be divided between freeholder, tenants, mortgage owner, insurance company (who assumes the right to certain liabilities).

Even at the most elemental city scale – the building – the pattern of property rights is complex. Residents have use rights. In the case of squatters the right is only an economic one but most residents of urban land also have a legal right to occupation. The freeholder has the economic and legal right to ground rent and the resident of a leased property may or may not have the right to exchange use rights for rent. In most countries the right to develop or redevelop a building is attenuated by law. In some countries such as the UK and China, the state owns that right in quite a full sense; in others, state and landowner effectively share the right in varying proportions. Where a planning system is weak it may be that the state owns the legal right over development, re-development and changes of use but landowners have the economic right.

Potential for use and potential for redevelopment are both attributes of a building. So too is the building's risk from fire, theft and structural failure. Ownership of these attributes is costly for residents, firms and landowners and is typically sold to third parties (insurance companies). Utility companies may assume property rights over liability arising from failed heating and water systems. Ownership over a building's asset value can be very complex; the more so the larger the building or the more complex the land ownership. As an asset, even a single-room apartment may be co-owned by the occupant and a mortgage company, with the proportion of ownership varying over the mortgage lifetime.

The long-term process of urban development tends therefore to result in fragmentation of property rights over land and buildings, of parts and attributes of land and buildings. Sometimes it will be necessary to combine property rights to better re-allocate them as with big urban development schemes or redevelopment of areas under traditional tenure patterns. But by and large, the trend is to reassign property rights over finer and finer layers of attributes – be they finer spatial boundaries or finer partitioning of commodity attributes within a boundary. Asia's uncontainable urbanisation proceeds by and large by the combination and re-division of property rights. Large redevelopment sites combine many small properties that had arisen spontaneously under former economic conditions. Ownership of the giant edifices that replace the older order combines the property rights of far more individuals, however, via complex modern contracts that assign all manner of rights to commercial firms, employees, residents, estate management companies, shoppers, insurers, financiers and bankers. The subdivision of rights over land and over the resources located on land, proceeds as the transaction costs of rights delimitation fall and as the value of rights rises.

Barzel (1997) proposed that the contracts that govern voluntary exchange tend to evolve in such a way as to apportion property rights in a way that will maximise the total value of the contract (the *subsidiarity rule* in Chapter 1). Applied to the allocation of land rights and the spontaneous spatial ordering of activities, this would mean that rights over land, buildings and attributes constantly change hands and over time form combinations that maximise the total product of those combinations. Cities have a way of spatially ordering themselves in a way that maximises gains to those who have an ownership stake in the resources combined to bid for locational rights.

The spatial order consistent with maximising the value of private contracts is not the same as the order that maximises the value to all stakeholders, however. The reason is the prevalence of third party costs and benefits and it is for this reason that institutions emerge with the purpose of assigning externalities and public goods liability more efficiently. Before coming to that discussion, however (Chapters 5–7), we conclude this chapter by reflecting on the importance of property rights fragmentation to the economic transformation of traditional societies and to the process of urbanisation.

Transaction Costs, Property Rights, Economic Development and Urbanisation

The contracts used to exchange and combine factors of production (or to combine knowledge about their use) are typically informal in developing rural areas. As well as being exchanged through formal wage contracts, labour may be exchanged in a barter system or according to the internal institutions of families and village groupings. Capital is traditionally exchanged on the basis of contracts that rest on trust and sanctions embedded in kinship or inter-group relations. In traditional societies land is shared under communal or common rights as we have seen, or allocated within the family on the basis of traditional rules.

Private property rights are fundamental to the process of knowledge and labour specialisation in developing rural areas. Without formal wage contracts it is difficult for a rural worker to compare the value of one job with another and difficult for employers to compare one worker with another. A wage is a signal of the value placed on a worker's labour and without such a signal the costs of searching for employment and employees becomes excessive. The traditional solution of employing within the family or kin group becomes inadequate. Economic development requires wider co-operation as the knowledge for productive exchanges becomes ever more specialised and dispersed.

If a farmer cannot demonstrate exclusive rights to his fields he cannot use them as collateral for a long-term crop diversification loan. Nor can he easily sell an under-productive field to a neighbour who can better use it to create a pond. Ill-defined land rights may prevent the neighbour from innovating into fish farming and prevent the farmer from raising capital to build a brick house. Institutional capacity building is therefore a vital plank in the modernisation strategies of developing countries and transitional economies. Thailand, for example, is currently in the middle of a 30-year programme to develop an accurate rural land cadastre, replacing one in which boundaries and ownership are frequently inaccurately documented and in which there are unnecessarily complicated categories of tenure and classes of rights. In a developing economy, the high transaction costs of poorly defined property rights create real barriers to progress.

Development brings institutional and property rights reform to rural areas therefore. In urban areas where the process of knowledge specialisation has always focused, exclusive rights developed earliest. Land parcels with well-defined exclusive rights developed first in towns and tended to be smaller and more regular in shape than rural land parcels. Size and shape evolve over time – by aggregation and fragmentation in voluntary exchange or by government design – to reduce the costs of selling land to individuals who have the knowledge to use it more productively. Suburban and intra-urban enclosure and subdivision is a constant process. Several suburban land use patterns in Boston that are often attributed to planning, in fact emerged without planned zoning, taking their shape from pre-existing patterns of land holdings (Warner, 1962). This is visibly the case in many British cities where homogeneous subdivisions of terraced houses created what are now inner suburban neighbourhoods from what were once peripheral agricultural estates under single ownership. Subdivision is even clearer in the endless ribbon developments of Southeast Asia's growing industrial cities. Bangkok's arterial roads stretching far into the countryside, are bordered by a herringbone pattern of long and narrow rectangular industrial and residential plots that intersperse with fields of the same dimension as urban turns to rural. Some are old paddy fields, neglected by the speculators who now own them. Others have been converted to high value market gardens. All take a shape determined by older, more simple systems of land rights. The pattern is the same but the institutions governing land ownership and transactions have had to change.

The conversion of land from one form of agriculture to another and from agriculture to urban uses requires laws that govern all manner of transactions: the transfer of capital from investors to developers; the professional validation of surveyors and architects; the sub-contraction of construction tasks; the exchange of liability for construction material defects; the formal definition of tenant and lessee liabilities; agreements governing the management of common areas; partitioning of liabilities between users and providers of utilities; the resolution of disputes; and a multitude of other co-operative acts.

The history of cities is the history of this kind of *institutional deepening*. Nineteenth century innovations in the laws and practices governing capital markets (the emergence of joint stock companies) allowed expansion of the railway companies and permitted agricultural landowners and urban workers to make mutually beneficial exchanges as suburban and metropolitan regional property markets emerged. The largely unplanned industrial cities of Europe and the United States during the nineteenth century and of Asia during the last half of the twentieth century developed an order of their own, albeit one yielding high environmental and social costs. Those costs notwithstanding, the order generated wealth, and over time, wealth has a habit of fostering new systems of property rights that reduce some of the excesses of earlier stages of development.

The overcrowded and unsanitary cities of nineteenth-century Europe and the United States were unsustainable and eventually gave rise to private and government institutional reforms. The garden city of Ebenezer Howard (1902) that inspired a wave of new forms of settlement and urban governance during the twentieth century started as a spontaneous private entrepreneurial search for alternative institutional, organisational and spatial order (privately owned and managed free-standing industrial towns built on low-value agricultural land).

A hundred years of knowledge specialisation, wealth creation and property rights exchange means that descendants of the workers who once inhabited the terraced cottages packed around Britain's industrial city cores now pay scarcity premiums for the privilege of owning those same cottages. Much of the inter-generational wealth redistribution has occurred through voluntary exchange in land, labour and capital markets; through the creative search for new knowledge and for new ways of combining and exchanging property rights in ways that meet the needs of other individuals and firms. In the same way, Asia's rapidly expanding middle class households, many of them with their roots in impoverished rural areas, are refashioning their cities by their tastes in housing, shopping, leisure and by their demand for new forms of governance, new patterns of public expenditure, new forms of regulations to protect homes, environment and the life chances of their children. In mainland China at the time of writing, there is an unprecedented home decoration boom – following closely on the heels of housing market reform and a widespread new sense of personal wealth. This is a prelude to and a part of housing market differentiation that will transform the social, economic and spatial contours of the country's cities in the years to come (see Wu for a study of Shanghai's re-emerging housing market).

4.4   KEY ARGUMENTS OF CHAPTER 4

* Spatial order (patterns of activities over space) emerges as individual property rights owners and organisations of combined property rights seek to minimise the distance-related costs of co-operating with other individuals and organisations.
* Traditional land use models springing from Von Thünen can be reinterpreted in the light of positive transaction costs of spatial specialisation, imperfect information and property rights. The agglomeration economies of consumption that shape cities are created as individuals seek to lower the costs of searching for products to consume

and other consumers with whom to co-consume. Agglomeration economies of production arise as firms seek to lower the costs of searching for customers and inputs.

* The spatial specialisation processes are dynamic and evolutionary. They are catallactic; a process of evolution that is simple individually but complicated collectively for being non-linear and path-dependent. Being hard to map systematically or predict, this process often frustrates utopian planning.

* Cities grow through the re-combination and subsequent subdivision of rights over land and over the resources located on land.

* The transformation of traditional economies and the social and spatial processes of urbanisation proceed by a process of property rights subdivision over land, labour and capital.

5. Public domain order

5.1 THE INDESTRUCTIBLE PUBLIC DOMAIN

> One household only shovels the snow outside one's door. No one cares about the frost above the roofs of others' homes (Chinese proverb).

But what would happen if the roofs of all houses were continuous? The collapse of one roof may destroy the entire row of housing. The old Chinese saying condemned selfish behaviour at a time when moral norms and self-discipline were the prime forces in ordering a society where the rule of law was not well developed. But even where the state is powerful enough to impose effective laws, there are always lacunas, loopholes, gaps or gulfs in which property rights are not yet defined or are unclear. As the world is always on the move and not static, formal laws often come too late, and in their absence, other rules governing the competition for contested resources under uncertain property rights emerge and evolve.

In this chapter and the next two, we address the question of how urban society creates order over resources characterised by property rights ambiguity. Such ambiguity arises because of positive costs of exclusion, transactions and organisation. In previous chapters we argued that as the division of labour and knowledge causes economic growth and urban development, institutions emerge to reduce the costs of co-operation. They do this by assigning property rights over contested resources. Due to changing preferences, innovation and rising resource scarcity, the proprietary order that arises is never static, however, and the process of allocating property rights is never complete. Even in advanced urban economies, many resources remain in the public domain. Indeed, as more individuals crowd into cities, the patterns and valuation of public domain resources become ever more complex. The more crowded the city the greater the contest for shared road space, sidewalks, waterways, clean air and views. In fact, the problem of shared resources will, by definition, never go away as population and economic growth proceeds and property rights fragment in response to rising resource values. Quite the reverse.

Imagine a square-shaped piece of suburban land divided evenly into four separately owned parcels. If each parcel were subdivided again into four, the length of shared boundaries would rise by a factor of two. For each successive grid-shaped subdivision, the number of plots increases by a factor of m (m=4 if plots are divided into quarters) and the quantity of shared boundary increases by a factor of $m/2$. Land subdividing into ever finer regular intervals therefore tends to increase both the number of private titles and the potential for boundary resource contests by a power function of the subdivision fraction.

More generally, in a population of n individuals any individual faces the possibility of being a third party recipient of the consumption of n–1 other individuals. This leads to n^2–n possible third party interactions and the potential extent or density of the public domain may therefore be said in principle to rise as a power function of population size.

Geometry and numbers are only half the story, however. The degree to which public domain resources are contested will depend on their value, which varies with their quantity, the number of individuals co-consuming them and the spatial distribution of people and resources. In the simple example above, the length of shared boundaries (or roads) doubles while the number of plots (or blocks) quadruples. By the same token, private land consumption per capita falls by a quarter. This suggests that the marginal value of private land is higher after subdivision and the marginal cost of any congestion arising across the reduced length of boundaries, higher. Adjustments in proprietary and spatial order therefore give rise to new property rights ambiguities – something that lies at the heart of the urban governance function.

The Chaotic Balance of Externalities

Airline pilots landing their planes in Hong Kong prior to the opening of its new airport in 1998 will never forget the approach to old Kai Tak Airport. This involved lowering landing-wheels meters above the rooftops of Kowloon City's towers in a breathtaking low-flying approach. The old airport was built just prior to World War II, on a site that became available after the failure of a large speculative housing project. The site, then on the periphery of the urban area, was expanded by the Japanese invaders just in time to surrender it to the Allied forces. As the city boundary pushed outwards in all directions after the war, Hong Kong soon had a busy airport right at the heart of its thriving industrial and housing area. When Sir Patrick Abercrombie wrote his *Preliminary Planning Report* for Hong Kong (Abercrombie, 1948) as the ruins of the war were being tidied up, he saw the need for a new airport. Meanwhile, the runway that projected into Victoria Harbour became longer and longer as aircraft grew in size. Few of Hong Kong's tolerant citizens complained about the noise of the aircraft, the goods and passenger traffic it generated and the existence of low-flying objects over the heads of millions of people (until the Environmental Protection Department emerged to educate people to do so). The British colonial administration honoured the Abercrombie report by starting the construction of the prize winning Chek Lap Kok International Airport, built largely on the levelled island Chek Lap Kok off Hong Kong's largest outlying island. It was finally completed by the Special Administrative Region Government after Hong Kong's return to China.

Kowloon City is now a quiet place and so are its hundreds of street shops that used to be busy restaurants and bars. In the past, taxi drivers earned much income by sending departing air passengers and their friends to Kai Tak, where long queues of arriving passengers waited for their services. Now, long queues of taxis wait for the few passengers who choose not to catch the train into town from the new airport. Noise pollution and the problem of flying objects over Kowloon City have gone but so have the air-forwarding trade and the restaurants that served the huge airport workforce. The residents may have gained, but the owners of buildings as a whole have lost out as the value of their properties has fallen, *ceteris paribus* (property prices in Hong Kong have been falling in recent years). Objectively, the monetary costs to these people of relocating the airport are greater than the benefits of relocation. For Hong Kong as a whole, however, the calculation may be different.

Residents and property owners in the vicinity of the old airport faced third party costs and benefits arising from airport operations. By and large, residents faced environmental costs while property owners faced rental advantages. Some residents who were employed by the airport or in related business will have valued the local employment benefits, including the low costs of commuting, more highly than they valued the environmental disbenefits. However sophisticated a society, the distribution of externalities, by definition, is capricious: third party benefits and costs shift like the sands and introduce an element of anarchy to otherwise orderly interactions.

The Disorderly Consumption of Public Goods

Passengers leaving Hong Kong through the new Chek Lap Kok International Airport can check-in at a downtown Hong Kong shuttle terminal, enjoy a comfortable and scenic train ride, and wait for their flights in an award winning monumental shopping mall-cum hotel building set against dramatic mountain and ocean scenery. Many of the accessibility and consumption benefits that the new airport confers and the travel-related transaction costs it reduces are public goods in the technical sense – jointly consumed and difficult to price. Travellers pay a contribution to the facility via airport tax and shuttle-riders pay for the space they occupy when they purchase a ticket. The benefits of the airport are more far-reaching than the value of these payments, however. The airport's new location raises land values in neighbouring parts of Lantau Island and at locations near to train, road and sea links on the mainland. It is valued by day-trippers who pay no airport tax. It gives Hong Kong firms subtle advantages over competitor firms in the region. Its prestige attributes confer benefits to the Hong Kong government, people and economy and it is valued by some for the potential use that might one day be made of it. It is valued by others for the improvement it makes to Hong Kong's environment and for the benefit this brings to future as well as present generations.

But because the technical, organisational and legal costs of measuring and organising payments for these dispersed benefits are prohibitive, there is no knowing how well the new airport matches up to demand in its fullest sense. It may be that an airport provided by an entrepreneur without public subsidy would have been under-supplied in terms of these wider benefits – less accessible, less prestigious, smaller, of poorer design and less environmentally friendly. Because of the size of the project and the risks, it may not have been provided at all by the market. On the other hand, it may be that government subsidy went beyond the demand of the public. Whereas externalities tend to be oversupplied by the market, there are strong arguments to suppose that public goods are oversupplied by government (for a lucid portrayal of this popular theme from the public choice literature, see Foldvary, 1994). One thing we can be sure about is that when it comes to shared consumption goods, we can rarely tell with any great accuracy how much should be supplied to satisfy demand.

5.2   MARKET FAILURE AS A PROBLEM OF PUBLIC DOMAIN ORDER

Externality and public good problems are endemic in society but particularly in cities where many different types of people and firms locate in close proximity. Conventionally, externalities and public goods are viewed as a problem of *market failure*; a view attributed to Arthur Pigou's seminal analysis of externalities (Pigou, 1920, 1946) – hence the ascription 'Pigovian'. The existence of market failure provides the rationale for most of the functions and programmes of modern urban governments throughout the world. The market oversupplies goods that yield third party costs and undersupplies or fails to supply goods that yield third party benefits. Municipal governments therefore seek to regulate production and exchanges that yield social costs – land development, traffic movement, air and water quality, noise, street-trading, waste disposal – and supply goods and services that might not otherwise be in sufficient supply – social housing, open space, security, transportation infrastructure.

Externality and public goods problems may also be understood to be problems of undeveloped markets or more generally underdeveloped institutions. They arise when resources have a value, but are ill-defined in terms of property rights and as a result of proprietary ambiguity, remain unpriced and inefficiently allocated. Inefficiency in this sense simply means that gains from trade are not exhausted.

Several important distinctions can be made between the property rights view and the traditional market failure view. We introduce three distinctions here and elaborate the discussion in the remainder of this chapter and in Chapters 6 and 7.

First, the idea of market failure implies the existence of a perfect market – a utopian benchmark that only exists in theory and not in reality. This is not so with the idea of ill-defined public domain rights, which directs attention towards the comparative analysis of alternative systems of institutions and property rights that yield different resource allocations. Pigovian market failure analysis is therefore institutionally specific and specific to a particularly unrealistic institution at that – the perfect market.

Second, a market failure analysis requires discrete categorisation of goods and services on the basis of consumption characteristics. Public goods and externalities are defined as such by virtue of being jointly consumed and non-excludable – in contrast to private goods and internally costed factors of production. The property rights view is a less static one in which any resource or attribute thereof may move into or out of the public domain, depending on its value and the transaction costs of marketing it. It is also more able to cope with the reality that any particular physical good or resource has multiple attributes, which are consumed in a number of different ways by different individuals.

Third, the property rights approach offers a more dynamic analysis of urban markets and of the scope and requirement for intervention. If property rights are understood to be a function of resource value and the transaction costs of excluding others, then the boundaries of the public domain will be understood to be constantly shifting. The market will spontaneously re-order property rights to cope with some kinds of public domain problems, for example when a factory owner transfers the ownership of certain liabilities to a private security firm. Under the constraints of the courts, other externality problems may be resolved by internalisation, as happens when a polluter compensates a pollution victim by a buyout – say an oil refinery buying up neighbouring residential properties (Webster, 1998a). In either case, market-based exchange and the legal institutions that support the former can turn external costs into internal costs and render previously unmarketable goods marketable by introducing exclusion mechanisms.

As soon as the public domain boundaries are redrawn, however, a new set of externality and public goods problems emerges as we have already illustrated. The tolling of a highway or river crossing or the introduction of electronic congestion pricing helps reduce congestion of a public domain resource but moves congestion to other parts of the transportation system. Condominiums with security guards, sports facilities and underground parking shift the balance between negative and positive locational externalities sufficiently to induce professional classes back into city centres (Webster, 2001a). In sufficient numbers their presence may confer third party benefits that raise the residential value of other sites on the fringe of the centre. The higher travel-related transaction costs faced by relocated low-income residents become a third party cost, however, as the neighbourhood gentrifies. The contested public domain resource in this instance is the positive externalities generated by production and exchange opportunities clustered in the city centre. The change in net social wealth arising from the shift in the public domain pattern might be positive if rental gains resulting from gentrification exceed the net costs faced by displaced activities (higher travel costs minus lower rents and so on). It involves the redistribution of a public domain attribute (city centre accessibility) from the poor to the rich, however, and society might take a view about whether any net social gains infringe shared values of fairness or are outweighed by long-term social fragmentation costs.

The pattern of a city's public domain resources is therefore constantly changing through evolutionary and iterative processes that are dominated by local learning and feedback. In such a system, an urban management agenda defined narrowly by a set of deviations from some agreed ideal is bound to cause as many new externalities as it alleviates. It is also bound to supply many public goods that the market might itself have supplied, often in greater quantities than is strictly efficient (Foldvary, 1994). This is so whether the ideal that governs intervention is the perfectly competitive market model of a public-sector economist or the goals of a plan created by politicians, professionals and perhaps the public.

In the remainder of the chapter we elaborate the discussion of market failure and critique the conventional externality and public goods arguments by dropping the assumptions of zero transaction costs and perfect information. In the next two chapters we elaborate the discussion by presenting a typology of urban management interventions that emphasises alternative approaches to allocating property rights over public domain resources.

5.3   THE EFFICIENT SUPPLY OF PUBLIC DOMAIN RESOURCES

Externalities

The first theorem of welfare economics, also known as the *invisible hand theorem*, states that under conditions of perfect competition, market-based exchange leads to an equilibrium state in which all gains from trade are exhausted.

Markets, in other words, can be shown under certain restrictive conditions, to be socially efficient in the sense that they allow individuals and society as a whole to concurrently maximise gains from trading property rights over resources. What is in the interest of individuals is also in the interest of society. Adam Smith stated this prosaically:

> As every individual ... endeavours as much as he can ... to maximise his own economic wellbeing, every individual necessarily labours to render the annual revenue of the society as great as he can. He generally, indeed, neither intends to promote the public interest, nor knows by how much he is promoting it ... by directing ... industry in such a manner as its produce may be of the greatest value, he intends only his own gain, and he is in this, as in many other cases, led as if by an invisible hand to promote an end which was no part of his intention (Adam Smith, 1776).

Perfect competition is not, however, a reality in many, if any, markets. Several key assumptions need to hold in order to obtain the first theorem of welfare economics. First, consumers view the products sold by different firms in an industry as perfect substitutes so that firms have to compete with each other for customers. Second, consumers and firms are all price-takers, none being individually powerful enough to influence prices. Third, entry and exit of firms into an industry is unrestricted in the long run by start-up costs, regulation or other constraints. Fourth, information is perfect and symmetrically distributed to sellers and buyers such that all parties to an exchange can weigh up all alternative uses of a resource. Fifth, transaction costs are zero, meaning that there is no friction of cost inhibiting the movement of resources to their highest value uses. Sixth, property rights are completely assigned, meaning that there are no resources valued negatively or positively by society that are not priced.

The fourth and the fifth assumptions are essentially the same since transaction costs arise principally as a result of imperfect information. If consumers and producers can see into the future and have all knowledge necessary for perfectly efficient decisions, then there are no transaction costs.

Arthur Pigou's critique of the invisible hand in *The Economics of Welfare* (1932) amounts to a challenge of the full assignment of property rights assumption. Pigou argued that production and exchange invariably impose costs – and benefits – on individuals and firms not party to production or exchange decisions. In the presence of externalities, private costs and social costs diverge and an equilibrium allocation of resources arising from private contractual market decisions may not, therefore, exhaust gains from trade. Compared to the perfectly competitive neo-classical economy, the ubiquitous presence of externalities means that the market fails to produce a Pareto optimal allocation of society's resources. Pigou saw the market as failing, therefore, and proposed corrective mechanism in the form of marginal taxes equal to the marginal value of externalities. This, he proposed, would induce those responsible for generating externalities to cut back production or consumption to a socially optimal quantity.

The idea of a market-correcting tax implicitly recognises the property rights issue at the heart of the externality problem. A Pigovian pollution tax has the effect of pricing the unpriced. Clean air, rivers and road space are congested by unpriced use in a production process or in the course of consumption because those resources typically lie in the public domain. A Pigou tax imposes a price and, in effect, assigns a liability to a would-be user of a public domain resource. With the tax, use of the public domain resource has an opportunity cost and individuals react with restraint.

Pigou's analysis was not based on the economic analysis of property rights, however, and as a result it was one-sided. This is the thrust of the argument in Ronald Coase's 1960 paper, 'The problem of social costs' (Coase, 1960). Coase argues that Pigou's view is flawed because it fails to appreciate the reciprocal nature of externality problems and because it fails to understand the implication of full information and zero transaction costs. He pointed out that if transaction costs are zero, as assumed by Pigou, the generators and recipients of externalities would come to agreements that balanced their respective interests. With perfect information about the value of pollution to the polluted and about the value of polluting production to a producer, bargaining would lead externalities to stabilise at levels from which no further gains from trade are possible.

Furthermore, the Pareto equilibrium would result whether producers have the right to pollute or whether the polluted have a right to be free from pollution. Where producers have unfettered rights to use public domain resources, third parties bearing the costs of externalities have an incentive to compensate producers to cut back production. This remains true so long as the marginal cost of pollution to third parties is greater than the marginal private benefit of production to the producer.

Alternatively, where a producer's right to use a common resource is constrained by some form of institution such as convention or regulation, the producer will have an incentive to compensate third parties so long as his marginal gains exceed the marginal externality costs imposed on the third parties. Coase demonstrated that the equilibrium resource allocation arising from bargaining is identical, whichever way the property rights fall. Pigou was wrong, therefore: with perfect information, the market does not fail.

It is an absurdity, however, to propose that information is anywhere near perfect in any but the very simplest of externality situations. The principal illustration in Coase's 1960 paper has neighbouring cattle and wheat farmers considering alternative courses of action including paying and receiving compensation for trampled grain, erecting fences and shifting production to something else or somewhere else. Even in this simple agricultural tale, the assumption that each party has perfect information about its own and the other party's valuation of costs and benefits is unrealistic, particularly when the opportunity costs of alternative production processes and relocation are thrown into the calculation. In cities, externalities are everywhere and dense, and the possibilities for efficient voluntarily negotiated solutions to externality problems that involve complicated specificities, are limited. Most attempts will be confounded by the inhibiting transaction costs of bringing together multiple third parties and multiple polluters.

Coase did more, however, than suggest that efficient resolutions to public domain problems can be achieved by voluntary exchange. In fact, the Coasian literature on externalities makes three distinct contributions to the analysis of markets and public domain order in cities.

First, is the proposition that *where information is complete, or at least sufficiently good, the market, or more generally voluntary exchange, need not fail*. This is tantamount to saying that in such circumstances so-called externalities are not, in fact, externalities. Where private negotiations, through the courts or less formally, can establish a compensatory contract over a contended common resource, a price and a distribution of liability is established and the externality is internalised. Reciprocal bilateral restraint by neighbours who depend on each other's goodwill, for example, undoubtedly contributes towards neighbourhood stability (Webster, 2001b). Where the contested resource is sufficiently well defined and the affected parties sufficiently organised, the transaction costs of multi-lateral negotiations may be worth it. Residents of an urban neighbourhood might, for example, organise themselves to lobby against a unwanted change of land use, or to compensate the existing landowner by outbidding the would-be polluter (Webster, 1998a). By and large, voluntary solutions to third party spillover problems will be more tractable in rural areas where population densities are lower and land use and land users less heterogeneous.

Second, is the so-called Coasian invariance theorem: the proposition that *with perfect information, negotiations will reach the same Pareto-efficient allocation of output and externality regardless of whether polluter or polluted hold the property rights.* Some have sought to use this strand of Coasian analysis to show the futility of urban land use regulation (Mark et al., 1981; Maser et al., 1977). The same kind of land-use order, it is suggested, will tend to emerge with or without zoning or other land-use controls. Since it is generally unreasonable to assume that much compensation flows from community to polluting land developer or user, such studies have really only succeeded in investigating the convergence of land market performance under varying degrees of regulation and the willingness of municipalities to reach negotiated land use outcomes regardless of what a land-use plan might specify. These applications pay scant regard to the invariance theorem's perfect information assumption and are, in any event, mostly inconclusive because of the explanatory limitations of cross-sectional statistical studies (for a critique, see Lai, 1994).

A third and more significant contribution is implicit in the first two. If information is incomplete or is not perfectly distributed and transaction costs are not therefore zero, then *the outcome for any externality problem will depend on the distribution of property rights* (Lai and Yu, 2002). In this situation, the state has a role to play. Since this is the case for nearly all third party problems in cities, an understanding of property rights is crucial to the analysis of externalities. Furthermore, it will be more useful to compare the efficiency of externality situations under alternative property rights distributions than to compare any particular externality problem with an ideal model of the perfectly competitive market. The solution to an externality problem is to assign property rights, and the efficiency of any particular solution depends on the externality costs saved less the cost of creating institutions that create the property rights. Solutions may not be Pigovian since the common law or other institutions that deliver them may be compromises that fail to exhaust gains from trade.

Following Coase's critique of Pigou, a vast literature developed debating the scope, technical definition and properties of externalities. Arrow (1970) conceptualised externalities as additional commodities for which markets are missing. This facilitates analysis using neo-classical tools, although it leads to the abstract practice of analysing equilibrium quantities of 'commodities' that are theoretically separable (one attribute of a resource is consumed as a private good, another as a public good) but not separable in reality (for an example, see Webster, 1998b). Like Pigou, Arrow defines externalities with reference to a specific kind of institution (competitive markets).

Meade (1973) represents a contrasting approach in the debate, defining externalities much more broadly and independently of particular institutions:

merely as discrepancies in the way different individuals value marginal changes in the quantity of commodities. They are in other words, third party effects. Discrepancies may arise whatever the institutions that govern transactions. Government allocation, altruistic giving, primitive bartering and well developed competitive markets all make resource allocations that confer a wide range of costs or benefits on individuals directly or indirectly affected by the allocation.

At the heart of all discussion about externalities, however, lies the issue of ill-defined property rights, joint consumption of public domain resources, information and transaction costs. The reasons for Arrow's missing markets include the absence or poor definition of property rights; the high costs of creating a market, entering a market and transacting within it; and the costs of obtaining information.

Generalising this to institutions other than competitive markets, third party costs and benefits arise due to the inability of government, an altruist, bartering parties, members of a household or a club, to contract with all parties with whom mutually beneficial transactions may be made. The inability is due to the absence of clear property rights over resources that are valued differently by the affected parties; to imperfect information; and to high transaction costs of assigning property rights and negotiating deals.

Public Goods

The problem of joint consumption (or third party effects) was formally recognised long before Pigou discussed externalities. Adam Smith (1776) identified certain types of good that the invisible hand of market-based exchange would not provide adequately. These included national security and schools. Before him, David Hume (1739) had succinctly portrayed the underlying behaviour that accounts for the public goods problem, the latter being one of the most thorough modern expositions of the problems of collectively consumed goods:

> Two neighbours may agree to drain a meadow, which they possess in common; because it is easy for them to know each other's mind; and each must perceive, that the immediate consequences of his failing in his part, is, the abandoning of the whole project. But 'tis very difficult, and indeed impossible, that a thousand persons should agree in any such action; it being difficult for them to concert so complicated a design, and still more difficult for them to execute it; while each seeks a pretext to free himself of the trouble and expense. And would lay the whole burden on others. Political society remedies both these inconveniences (Hume, 1739: 538).

Paul Samuelson's analysis of the conditions required for the efficient provision of this type of good produced a public goods literature that parallels and overlaps the externalities debate started by Pigou. Samuelson (1954, 1955) characterised a pure public good as being non-excludable and as being in infinite supply such that consumption is non-rivalrous or non-exclusive. With such a good, the collective amount consumed by a group of individuals equals the amount consumed by each, and the efficient quantity to supply is given by equating the summation of each individual's price (marginal willingness to pay) with the marginal cost of the good's provision. This contrasts with a pure private good, where quantity is summed to get collective demand and efficient supply requires each individual's marginal benefit to be equated to price and to the marginal cost of producing the good.

James Buchanan (1965) generalised Paul Samuelson's analysis by showing that pure public and pure private goods are special cases of a more general class of good that he called 'club goods'. Buchanan's great contribution was to bring the number of consumers into the efficiency analysis such that an individual's utility depended not only on quantity consumed but the numbers of co-consumers too. This produced a theory of co-operative membership in which a pure private good lies at one extreme ($n=1$) and a pure public good lies at the other ($n=$infinity). In between, ($1<n<$infinity), lie most public goods of practical interest – those which are consumed by a finite set of individuals and can in principle be priced, so long as appropriate exclusion mechanism can be designed.

Mancur Olson published his own *theory of groups* in the same year as Buchanan's paper (Olson, 1965) which was more extensive in scope but less general in its analysis of the efficiency conditions for optimal group formation and group size. These two contributions resulted in a literature on impure public goods – public goods which are both congestible and excludable under certain conditions but remain uncongested and/or non-excludable under other conditions.

Ten years before Buchanan published his theory of clubs, Tiebout (1956) had suggested that local public goods might be supplied efficiently if a sufficient number of competing cities supplied different bundles of community goods from which mobile individuals can choose. Local public goods are public goods for which consumption benefits fall off with distance – hence they are also known as spatially impure public goods. With perfect information and mobility, individuals might be expected to select the bundle that best suites them. Tiebout proposed that they are attracted to cities in which community goods are not yet congested (cost per resident has not yet reached a minimum) and avoid congested cities in which the cost per resident has risen beyond the minimum. There are similarities between Tiebout's spatial clubs and Buchanan's entrepreneurial clubs. Both explore institutional arrangements for efficient supply of collective goods other than Samuelson's two extremes: private goods efficiently supplied by a perfectly competitive market and public goods supplied by state-organised collective action. Tiebout's idea is that local governments can supply local public goods efficiently if there is sufficient choice between jurisdictions. Buchanan's idea was that entrepreneurial clubs can supply excludable public goods efficiently.

When the institutional context for Samuelson's, Buchanan's, Tiebout's and derivative analysis is generalised beyond the perfectly competitive market, the public good problem is essentially the same as the externality problem: ill-defined property rights, imperfect information and high transaction costs. A thorough synthesis by Cornes and Sandler (1996) views pure public goods, local public goods, club goods and common resources as special cases of the more general externality problem. Externalities to Cornes and Sandler are, from the point of view of an individual consumer, goods that are consumed by others but which raise or lower an individual's utility. They are third party effects that remain non-excludable, unpriced and in the public domain. Anyone can choose to benefit (or disbenefit) from the set of goods consumed by others by exerting an economic right, for example by moving into a city or locality. Pure public goods are a class of externalities in which everyone's individual quantities of goods demanded combine together into a single collective good which all co-consume. Local public goods and club goods are externalities where the influence of other people's consumption is moderated by the number of co-consumers and in the case of the former, by distance from the source of the public good.

All are problems of public domain order and the differences between them are differences in the way costs and benefits are apportioned, and ultimately, differences in the way information and transaction costs are distributed. These different information and cost structures determine the shape of the institutions best suited to creating order in any particular public domain problem. We shall elaborate these points in the next two chapters.

In those chapters, our analysis of institutional choice and public domains retains the conventional distinction between public goods and externalities as an organising device. It should be understood, however, that there are three kinds of symmetry in the analysis of the two categories. First, any institution created to reduce externalities is itself a public good that by nature, is likely to be under-supplied by the free market. Second, negative externalities can be thought of as public bads and analysed using public goods ideas with negative valued demand schedules. Third, public goods can be thought of as positive externalities and analysed using externality concepts with negative valued externality cost schedules.

The unifying and more important idea underlying the next two chapters is that a wide choice of institutions may emerge to assign property rights in the face of public domain problems in cities. They may emerge voluntarily or by government imposition and the efficiency of any institution will depend on the costs of creating and maintaining it and the benefits of reducing property rights ambiguity.

5.4   KEY ARGUMENTS OF CHAPTER 5

- Public domain order (patterns of rights governing common resources) emerges as organisations create arrangements to govern the consumption of resources with incompletely assigned property rights. A distinction is made between public domain and proprietary order because the property rights that attempt to govern the consumption of shared resources are more contestable, less easily protected by law and consequently more fluid. In fact they can never be solved.
- Externalities and public goods give rise to public domain problems and can be thought of as problems of undeveloped markets or, more generally, underdeveloped institutions. Such problems arise when resources have a value, but are ill-defined in terms of property rights and as a result of proprietary ambiguity, remain un-priced and inefficiently allocated. Inefficiency in this sense simply means that gains from trade are not exhausted.
- The Pigovian concept of market failure regarding externalities and public goods is problematic because it unrealistically implies the existence of a perfect market – a benchmark that only exists in theory and not in reality. It implies discrete categorisation of goods and services on the basis of consumption characteristics and is thus incapable of coping with the reality that any particular physical good or resource has multiple attributes. It also disregards dynamic aspects of property rights, taking for granted their existence.
- The Coase Theorem helps us understand the inadequacy of the Pigovian thesis in three senses. First, where information is complete, or at least sufficiently good, the market, or more generally voluntary exchange, need not fail. Second, with perfect information, negotiations will reach the same Pareto-efficient allocation of output and externality regardless of whether polluter or polluted hold the property rights or bear liabilities. Third, as a corollary of the above, if information is not complete or is imperfectly distributed (and transaction costs are not therefore zero), then the outcome for any externality problem will depend on the distribution of property rights. The way in which property rights are organised becomes a relevant consideration.

• The property rights approach offers a more dynamic analysis of urban markets and of the scope and requirement for intervention. If property rights are understood to be a function of resource value and the transaction costs of excluding others, then the boundaries of the public domain will constantly shift. Markets will spontaneously re-order property rights to cope with some kinds of public domain problems, rendering previously unmarketable goods marketable by introducing exclusion mechanisms. The pattern of a city's public domain resources is therefore constantly changing through evolutionary and iterative processes that are dominated by local learning and feedback.

• Property rights ambiguity is therefore not a sufficient ground for state intervention as individuals invent means to remove ambiguity.

• Knowledge specialisation and the division of labour means that everything is connected to everything else. All actions are unwittingly vicarious. When property rights are assigned in a solution to one set of public domain problems, a new set immediately arises. Property rights ambiguity is unavoidable since the specification of all dimensions of rights over resources is impossible.

6. Public domain order – public goods

6.1 SHARED CONSUMPTION, INFORMATION AND TRANSACTION COSTS

The Chinese proverb quoted at the start of Chapter 5 implies that when adjoining roofs collapse under a weight of frost, everyone suffers loss. A more efficient organisation of the shared roof structure – or shared liability – would assign each neighbour a degree of responsibility for the entire roof. This would stop an individual householder waiting for others to address what in reality is his problem too. The legally enforceable concepts of the Deed of Mutual Covenant, strata corporation, owner corporation and other notions in modern estate management practice are means of assigning such responsibility or liability. So too is the leasehold land system at a higher level of urban management (Lai, 1998; George, 2000). They are indispensable institutional arrangements in an age where reliance on convention, custom and shared values (such as the respect for 'fung shui' by villagers in old China) is too uncertain.

The London Underground provides another scaled-up modern example of problems that arise with common goods. The Underground is a massively complex transport system, carrying to work 35 per cent of those who work in central London. It has 275 stations, 4000 carriages, 16 000 staff and 12 lines; covers 253 route miles, 42 per cent of which are underground; carries 3 million trips per weekday; over 1 billion passengers each year; and generates over $US1.6 billion of revenue income annually. In 1998, the British Government announced a major new Private Public Partnership (PPP) initiative to tackle a backlog of maintenance and capital improvements with an estimated value of $1.8 billion. Management of the Underground during the years of neglect was in the hands of various public sector bodies. It had initially been developed by separate private companies starting as early as 1863 but gradually came under public control during the twentieth century. Mergers and a form of public control occurred as early as 1933 and full nationalisation in 1948. In 1970 control passed to the Greater London Council – London's municipal government – and in 1984 it was taken back by Central Government. The PPP was finally given the go-ahead in January 2002. It is a $24 billion scheme; secures $6 billion of private money; is $3.5

billion cheaper than the public sector comparator plan used by government to assess value for money; and requires about $1 billion of taxpayer subsidy each year.

An interesting question posed by the London Underground PPP is why subsidy is paid to a crowded transport system heavily in demand by one of the world's richest urban economies and a leading international financial centre. The UK Government estimates that for the eight years following the start of the partnership, 45 per cent of the cost of running, maintaining and renewing the Underground under the PPP package, will fall to the taxpayer, 30 per cent from fares and 25 per cent from private finance. The main reason, of course, for the funding gap is the age of the physical assets and the prolonged neglect. The New York and Paris Metros also require subsidy. Why should government willingly bail out the Underground, however, rather than leaving it to raise fares and introduce other efficiencies? The answer, of course, lies partly in the political fallout in a democratic polity from taking the latter course of action. But, if the subsidy were only a matter of keeping fares down, it would soon be recognised for what it was – a redistribution of wealth from the general taxpayer to London commuters. The ease with which subsidy flows and the language used to justify it tells another story – that politicians value the Underground beyond the immediate commuting benefits conferred to its paying riders. In fact, the value of the subsidy might be taken as an approximate measure of the wider benefits conferred by the Underground on the capital and to the British economy more generally. Just as these are revealed in the subsidies the UK Government is willing to make, they are also revealed in the contributions developers are willing to make to improvements and extensions to the Underground. The principal developer of London's flagship Canary Wharf dockland redevelopment contributed almost $US 1 billion to extend the Underground to the site. The private expenditure was easily justified by the huge predicted impact on property prices.

From the point of view of the general public, employers, governments, property developers and landowners, the Underground has multiple benefits that are not captured in the fares paid by daily commuters. To the extent that wider beneficiaries rely on commuters to fund the system through fare box revenues, they free ride on others. If such benefits are not paid for, the Underground will be under-provided (as has become the case during the years of government funding). Like the Chinese householders, ambiguous rights and liabilities over a communal resource leads to inefficiency and to shared loss.

By contrast, Hong Kong's 23-year-old Mass Transit Railway (MTR) system built by the executive-led colonial administration and run by a public corporation (and recently floated as a gesture of privatisation), has been earning huge profits through station property development and charging at marginal cost. Property development projects associated with stations are a means of recouping improvement of land adjacent to stations. They involve contractual agreements between the MTR, landowners, developers and land users, which allocate the benefits derived from improved accessibility. We shall look into the London Underground PPP in greater detail in the last chapter.

Two practical questions lie at the heart of these illustrations and at the heart of theoretical and practical debates about public goods: (a) how much of a shared good is required (bearing in mind that many different people want to consume it)? And (b) what institutions will best ensure its efficient supply. Answers to both questions are fundamentally dependent on the distribution of information and transaction costs.

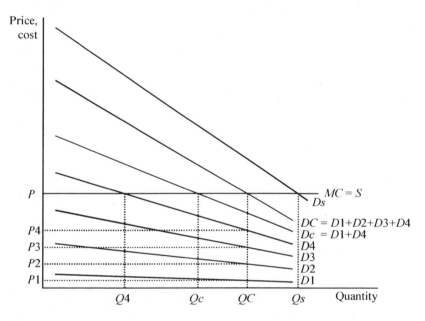

Figure 6.1   Efficiency of alternative institutions for supplying a shared good

Consider Figure 6.1, a graphical representation of Samuelson's conditions for the efficient provision of public goods. To recap, these state that a shared good is efficiently supplied when the cost of supplying an additional unit equals the benefit of that additional unit to the consumer group, the latter derived by summing individual benefits (or marginal willingness to pay). Four neighbouring households living in an informal settlement on the edge of a poor city are each willing to make a contribution to pave a muddy path fronting their homes and leading to a nearby road. Their demand schedules, $D1$ to $D4$ reflect the price each is willing to pay for additional cubic metres of paving material. More material will make the path wider, longer and more robust and the marginal benefit of additional material falls with quantity, reflecting diminishing returns. An entrepreneur is willing to supply the path at a fixed unit price represented by the marginal cost curve MC.

Note first the public domain problem arising. Once the pavement is built it is available equally to all four households. Without the possibility of exclusion, property rights are ambiguous and none of the households have an incentive to reveal their true preference when discussing how much paving they should buy.

In the remainder of the chapter we consider the outcomes and alternative institutions that might arise to create and deliver order within the public domain under four headings. (a) The utopian community – market supply with perfect information and zero transaction costs; (b) the imperfect community: market supply with imperfect information and positive transaction costs; (c) the entrepreneurial club: market supply with contractual collective action: (d) government supply. With the exception of (a), which is a fiction in all but exceptional circumstances, these institutions compete in the real world over time. Municipal governance systems evolve as the institutional mix changes in response to resource scarcity, technology and transaction costs.

6.2 THE UTOPIAN COMMUNITY – MARKET SUPPLY WITH PERFECT INFORMATION AND ZERO TRANSACTION COSTS

If each household is able, without cost, to assess its own willingness to pay and to ascertain how much its neighbours value paving and if there are no costs of collaboration, then the quantity they will jointly purchase is QC. All four households combine their valuations of an extra unit of pavement and are able, as a consequence, to purchase more than any one household on its own. DC, the collective demand schedule, is the summation of $D1$ to $D4$ and intersects the entrepreneur's supply schedule further to the right than any of the household schedules. The outcome involves households 1 to 4 paying contributions $P1$ to $P4$ respectively and is efficient in the Pareto sense because all gains from collaboration are exhausted. To the left of QC the collective valuation of an additional unit exceeds its marginal cost and the community of four will gain by purchasing more. To the right of QC the cost of additional pavement exceeds any additional benefits yielded.

The institutional requirement for this utopian (perfect market) outcome is a community of households, preferably headed by or advised (costlessly) by an economist, and sharing conventions that value honesty and community. In reality, even a community of four neighbourly households might find it difficult to arrive at efficient contributions *P*1 to *P*4.

With perfect information and costless collaboration there is no ambiguity about liability for provision. The perfect knowledge of the mutual gains from collaboration gives each household an incentive to reveal its true preference. Using Cornes and Sandler's (1996) model, the *externality* problem can be described as follows. Each household has a preference for expenditure on a good that also benefits others. *P*1 to *P*4 are the utility maximising prices paid and these are pooled to provide *QC*. Household 1 consumes *QC* of paving, paying *P*1, and as a result, households 2 to 4 receive third party benefits. This is a rather more convoluted interpretation of Figure 6.1 than the one we have already given, but it has the elegance of identifying the third party (public domain) effects in the public good problem and calling them externalities.

Having said this, the perfect information assumption in the utopian or perfect market scenario really means that there is, in fact, no public domain problem. The informal utopian institutions that render transaction costs zero also mean that property rights over the shared good are completely allocated – at least in terms of liability for ensuring its supply. With only four households, the path is unlikely to become congested so that there is no need to assign property rights over *utilisation* – only over financial liability (contributions). There is no missing market here – the social institutions that comprise the perfectly functioning community are all that are needed to induce correct demand revelation.

Buchanan (1968) showed that with small numbers, efficient contributions (the tax prices *P*1 to *P*4 in Figure 6.1) can be arrived at by bargaining and that the negotiated equilibrium exhausts gains from trade. His analysis does not require assumptions about perfect information and zero transaction costs: only about an agreement to negotiate with a view to resource pooling. In reality, however, the model Buchanan poses is probably only applicable to bilateral bargaining. Even three or four individuals trying to negotiate a mutually agreeable set of contributions *P*1 to *P*4 would seem to pose problems and require something of the utopian community already described. The two-party problem is an interesting one, however, and we adapt a graphical version given by Cullis and Jones (1992).

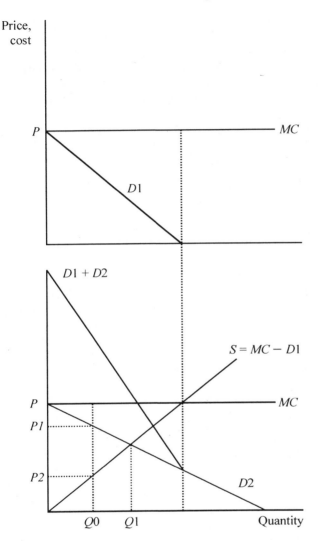

Source: Adapted from Cullis and Jones (1992: 72)

Figure 6.2 Bilateral negotiation exhausting gains to trade

$D1$ in the top part of Figure 6.2 and $D2$ in the lower part respectively show two households' demand for a public good. The households negotiate because both realise that neither on its own can afford any of the good (like households 1–3 in Figure 6.1). S is the minimum contribution household 1 requires to pool with its own contribution to see the good supplied and is the difference between *MC*, the supply curve and household 1's demand curve. In the lower part of the figure we see that household 1 would be willing to accept *P2* to have *Q0* of the good while household 2 is willing to contribute *P1*. There are therefore advantages to both parties in bargaining. This remains so until *S* and *D2* intersect each other. *Q1* is an optimal quantity of the good judged against the criteria that both parties have to consent to the outcome. It also happens to be the point at which the summed demand curves intersect the supplier's marginal cost curve. This is Samuelson's condition for the efficient supply of a public good but it has been derived from assumptions about bargaining rather than perfect information.

6.3   THE IMPERFECT COMMUNITY: MARKET SUPPLY WITH IMPERFECT INFORMATION AND POSITIVE TRANSACTION COSTS

In the presence of positive transaction and other co-operation costs, the outcome is unlikely to exhaust gains from trade. Transaction costs might be incurred in the example as individuals seek to value the pavement for themselves. They may spend time and money finding out about alternative products and trading off quality, quantity and the opportunity cost of making a contribution. Other costs arise as members of each household discuss the problem and as members of the community sound each other out about the idea, discuss different products and negotiate on contributions.

Imperfect information leads to various second-best outcomes (compared to the utopian outcome) including non-provision; under-provision and over-provision. We deal with these possibilities in turn.

Non-provision

In the absence of community values and conventions it could be that each household has a demand for pavement but none is willing to make a unilateral contribution either to the cost of the good or to the transaction costs of organising collective action. Buchanan (1968) represented the free-riding problem as a pay-off matrix. In the face of uncertainty about the behaviour of neighbours, the maximum pay-off to self-centred households is to free ride.

Imagine that *QC* in Figure 6.1 is an arbitrarily chosen quantity of pavement considered by a household as a reasonable amount given the length of the path and what it knows about price and quality. It may or may not coincide with the largely fictitious utopian amount defined under perfect information assumptions. *P4* is the amount household 4 is willing to pay for units of material at this quantity and *P4×QC* is the total contribution it is willing to make and is a measure of the benefit enjoyed. Imagine that *P4×QC*=$100 and that the sunk transaction costs of exploring collaboration with others and searching for a supplier is $40. Table 6.1 represents the prisoner's dilemma facing the household in the face of uncertainty about others' behaviour. The lowest payback arises if the household takes the initiative to organise collective action but no one agrees to the scheme (–$40). The sunk transaction costs are lost. If others agree to the scheme, each agreeing to contribute a quarter of the transaction costs, the household gains $100 benefit once the pavement is built less $10, its portion of the costs of collective action. If the household free rides, waiting for someone else to take the initiative and absorb the transaction costs, its net gain is $100 (lower left). If everyone waits for someone else to underwrite the co-ordination costs, no liabilities or losses are incurred but neither is anything gained (lower right).

Table 6.1   Pay-off matrix with co-ordination costs

	Others contribute (good is provided)	Others free ride (good is not provided)
Household contributes	90 (100–10)	–40 (0–40)
Household free rides	100 (100–0)	0 (0–0)

In the absence of institutions that increase a household's information about the likely behaviour of others, there is a risk that all households will choose the maximum pay-off strategy (lower left) and the good will not be provided.

The outcome becomes more likely as the number of households (*n*) rises, of course. There are actually three contributing factors at work here. First, the costs of acquiring information about costs and benefits tend to rise with *n*. Second, the costs of organising collaboration rise with *n*. Third, any household's contribution as a proportion of total cost falls as *n* rises, making individual household contributions appear increasingly insignificant and encouraging free riding.

Under- and Over-provision

Non-provision is by no means inevitable, however. A certain quantity of the collective good may be supplied by single individuals or by groups of individuals able to overcome the collective action problem. Prohibitive transaction costs and information problems notwithstanding, $Q4$ amount of paving material will be supplied in Figure 6.1 by the purchasing power of household 4 alone. None of the other individuals can unilaterally afford to purchase the good, however, and in the absence of collaborative institutions, are likely to free ride on the $Q4$ amount purchased by household 4. The good is supplied, but undersupplied in the sense that households 1–3 have a positive demand that they have not chosen to reveal, due to problems of co-ordinating.

A friendship struck between households 1 and 4 might be sufficient for each to reveal its true preferences, yielding mutual gains from co-operation irrespective of the other two free-rider households. Two households may also bargain with each other with a view to producing the good bilaterally, as in Figure 6.2. The outcome may exhaust gains from trade between the two of them but will undersupply the good to the community if other households free ride.

Under-provision as well as over-provision can arise in another way – through voting and through more informal non-price decision making. Imagine that being aware of the problems of honest and accurate preference revelation, the community of four decided that it should organise the pavement on the basis of equal contributions and a collective decision about quantity and quality. A first meeting might distribute the tasks of researching products and suppliers. A second meeting agrees the project and a total cost to be shared. The only institution required for this arrangement is an agreement to co-operate. With small numbers and a freedom to drop out, the outcome is unlikely to be far off that which is acceptable to any one household. However, the institutional framework guarantees (a) a degree of collective under-provision and (b) over-provision from the point of view of those with the lowest demand. The agreed level of contributions might end up corresponding to the preferences of household 1 (the lowest bidder) or perhaps at a point representing average willingness to pay (somewhere between the preferences of 2 and 3). Even with small numbers there is clearly scope for re-distribution between individuals. If household 4 is powerful as well as being a higher bidder it may abuse the community spirit, forcing household 1 to contribute an amount higher than $D1$. If households 3 and 4 push through a project that delivers QC for a common contribution equal to $P4$ then households 1 and 2 will have effectively been taxed for their collaboration.

Collective action can rarely avoid such redistribution and it becomes a significant problem when n is large; when parties to collaboration have unequal power; and when they have unequal access to information. We elaborate these points further in the following sections and in the next two chapters.

It is important to note that our use of the terms *under-* and *over*-provision is with reference to the outcome predicted under utopian institutions. Given that the utopian context is in most cases a fiction, it should not be assumed that under- or oversupply in this sense implies inefficiency – the mistake of the traditional welfare economic approach. If there are real costs to collaborating with neighbours, then there is a sense in which the deficit $QC-Qc$, created when households 1 and 4 co-operate but 2 and 3 free ride, may be in equilibrium. It may be an efficient allocation of public domain resources given the reality of transaction costs.

6.4 THE ENTREPRENEURIAL CLUB: MARKET SUPPLY WITH CONTRACTUAL COLLECTIVE ACTION

Where informal institutions are incapable of surmounting collective action problems, a public good will only be supplied if there is some kind of third party intervention. The arrangements we have looked at already might be viewed in this way: single consumers or small groups of consumers taking it upon themselves to purchase a good that supplies others with positive externalities.

An increasing number of urban public goods are provided on the basis of *formal* contractual arrangements, however. Inefficient and poorly ordered public domains make rich pickings for entrepreneurs. They represent potential markets and the entrepreneurial challenge is to find methods of pricing the public domain resource.

Buchanan's notion of the club is a useful one for thinking about all kinds of organised approaches to the voluntary supply of public goods. We have already noted that the club idea can usefully be extended to understand local and national governments and urban neighbourhoods. Here we use the term in the more conventional sense to mean firms (including voluntary and non-profit organisations) that contractually supply a public good to a group on the basis of membership contributions or fees.

A community organisation such as a village council, church, mosque, temple, neighbourhood association, labour organisation, ethnic community association or local political party may discern a need and organise the supply of a community service or infrastructure investment. Settlements throughout the world are supplied with all kinds of services and infrastructure by a rich tapestry of voluntary organisations. Initially perhaps, an organisation may use its existing institutions as the contractual basis for organising the public domain. Very often, however, what starts locally and informally can grow and diversify.

In nineteenth century Britain, impoverished urban workers fearing the prospect of dying without funds to pay funeral expenses clubbed together into local mutual savings societies. Many *mutuals* have survived into the twenty-first century as national and international member-owned companies, the largest having multi-billion dollar portfolios and offering a wide range of financial products.

Since the 1970s, in a wave of incipient economic co-operation reminiscent of the nineteenth century self-help institutions, agricultural co-operatives and rural credit circles in many parts of the developing world have been transforming themselves into diversified commercial enterprises.

In many cities of the developing world, the most prestigious schools and hospitals started life as informal programmes organised by foreign religious missions. Education and health systems in developed countries similarly had their origin in locally oriented philanthropy. Globalisation of labour mobility in the last quarter of the twentieth century gave rise to many examples of voluntarism among expatriate communities, with informal educational co-operatives and cultural clubs for example, developing into international schools and commercial enterprises.

The distinction between voluntary (non-profit) association and commercial firm is a grey one therefore in this respect. Both represent the emergence of organisational order – a pooling of property rights – as a voluntary solution to a public domain problem (or missing market problem).

What makes a difference to the provision or non-provision of public goods, or to their undersupply or adequate supply, is not so much the manner in which any operational profits are distributed (for-profit versus not-for-profit organisations) but the existence of an organisation that overcomes the collective action and ambiguous property rights problem. This crucially involves four things: a source of investment and working capital; a management capability; a constitution; and a membership.

Consumption-sharing clubs emerge, therefore, through the evolution of more primitive organisations and institutions; through the actions of community entrepreneurs (visionaries) and through the actions of financial entrepreneurs (often in partnership with community leaders or visionaries).

Clubs will form where institutional, technological and demand conditions foster them, and these conditions are constantly changing. Until quite recently there were few private sports and leisure clubs in British cities, and municipal authorities by and large saw it as their responsibility to supply sports centres. This they did with a flourish between the late 1960s and early 1980s, carefully locating facilities to maximise accessibility, particularly to disadvantaged groups. By the turn of the millennium, however, the private health and leisure market had become firmly established as tastes changed and real incomes rose. Public and private leisure facilities now regularly invest in new programmes and equipment in order to keep up with changing tastes and both are now used by individuals across a wide income range.

Technological change is as important to the development of club-markets as changes in tastes and fashions. Club–community innovations such as gated suburbs, city centre condominiums, gated social housing estates, tolled express ways, shopping malls and industrial parks would not have spread as rapidly had it not been for rather simple security and access to technological developments. The development of competitive markets in urban utilities, notably telecommunications, water, gas, electricity and postal services have been made possible by advances in supply and pricing technology and a liberalisation in government regulations. Deregulation may have been spearheaded by ideologically driven governments but was only possible because the transaction costs of switching suppliers and of measuring and charging had fallen due to technological advances.

Technology also has the effect of weakening or removing natural monopolies and thus making market-based club provision more acceptable. State monopolies of urban utilities tend to be justified on the basis of national security and the problems of natural monopoly. No longer can it be said, however, that all urban utility provision is naturally uncompetitive due to high entry costs and captive markets. A British home owner at the time of writing might buy a mix of telephone, internet and TV services from AT&T, a local cable company and one or more discount international phone services and is likely to have switched gas and electricity suppliers at least once in the past five years. Technological and institutional innovation has transformed urban utility markets from publicly organised collective consumption clubs into competitive goods and services markets. Certain attributes of the services retain public goods qualities but others have been transformed into private goods or into more efficient clubs. Internet services over a telephone line are excludable and accessed for a monthly fee but lines are shared and can become congested.

The market responds to the congestion of shared infrastructure by product and price differentiation. High bandwidth is offered to customers for whom congestion is more costly and who are willing to pay a higher fee, thus creating new communities of co-consumers. This is an example of a newly emerged public domain problem (congestion on communication cables) submitting to market-based order as property rights are more clearly defined and assigned. It is also an example of the fragmentation of rights as value, transaction costs and technology change.

The process of refining co-consumption communities – redrawing club boundaries – is an important part of the evolution from public to club to private domain and an important process in ordering cities. It is seen particularly clearly in public transport markets. Informal transport solutions emerge to mop up gaps in the market. Squads of motorcycles wait at the junctions of Bangkok's arterial roads to distribute commuters to their homes in the Sois (lanes). The number of motorcycles rises and falls as major transport infrastructure projects cause changes in the level of congestion and producer clubs form to regulate the behaviour of motorcycle owners. Travellers quickly adjust to new travel opportunities and constraints and adjust habits and loyalties. When air-conditioned bus services and executive coaches were introduced on certain routes in Bangkok in the 1980s, those willing to pay a premium for the advantages offered switched mode. Others chose between non-air-conditioned buses, trucks with seats, pick-ups with seats, taxis and three-wheeled tuk-tuks. Many private car drivers formed car-sharing arrangements as congestion rose. When Bangkok's sky train and elevated expressways appeared in the 1990s some travellers switched from buses, cars and taxis. Travel club boundaries were redefined again.

In all these examples, the space that travellers individually occupy on a journey (seats) are private goods, but travellers join a club in which they share certain facilities – air conditioning, video, drinks, air, cigarette smoke, fumes, noise, quiet, furniture and décor, queuing arrangements, travel times and frequencies, and the attributes of fellow passengers.

These are illustrations of the sophisticated and often spontaneous way in which public domains are re-ordered as the competition costs of using them rise with congestion. Roads get congested, causing their value to change. A constantly logjammed section of road is nearly valueless as a means of commuting. An unreliable bus service is less valuable than a reliable one. Congestion-induced changes in accessibility and transport service are valued differently by different individuals according to preference and wealth. Entrepreneurs (including entrepreneurial governments) spot opportunities to use transportation land and infrastructure more efficiently from the perspectives of particular types of traveller. Innovations that succeed reduce the costs of competing for congested transportation space (and reduce the transaction costs of participating in urban labour market). As the urban transportation market diversifies and matures, new public domains are created, with travellers paying for a travel package that suits their preferences and means. The evolution of public domain order typically involves the fragmentation of the public domain into smaller public domains or the proliferation of clubs.

Entrepreneurial clubs introduce exclusion and lower transaction costs including the costs of competition for and congestion of shared resources. Buchanan, in his 1965 paper, developed a theory of efficient club size by considering how the quantity of a shared good and the number of co-consumers co-vary. The precise details of his model and the mathematically dense (and overly abstract) literature that developed from it are not of great interest to our discussion. Its general principle is, however, since it elegantly portrays the conditions under which a club can efficiently organise collective action to avoid the public domain problems of congestion, over-use, competition costs and benefit dissipation.

We reproduce Buchanan's three key diagrams and comment on the institutions and information required for the emergence of efficient club domains.

Many antagonists in the discussion of privatisation and the demise of public realm resources in cities base their objections on social exclusion and community fragmentation arguments. Their conclusions may in the end be correct, but their arguments are typically incomplete because of a failure to consider the potential gains from a shift from *public* to *club domain*. Buchanan's theory of clubs may be viewed either as a *theory of optimal inclusion* or a *theory of optimal exclusion*. The idea of optimal exclusion is a fact of life for a market economy. Only a political philosophy that denies the legitimacy of *any* private property can ignore the issue of optimal exclusion. If we accept the market as an allocating institution then we accept exclusion since, as we have noted, markets cannot function without exclusive property rights.

Consider a household living in a predominantly owner-occupier single family dwelling neighbourhood adjoining a lively inner city residential quarter where the houses are mixed tenure and mainly in multiple occupation. The household shares pavements, roads, views, schools, parks, playgrounds, bus services, cleaning, planning and environmental regulations and many other civic services with a hundred other similar households in the same street and hundreds of others in its own and in the adjacent neighbourhood. The joint-consumption services are paid for from local taxation, and elected politicians and their professional officers decide on the type and quantity of the services. Applied in this context, the question posed by Buchanan's club theory is how do the costs and benefits of consumption sharing arrangements vary with the numbers of joint consumers? What sort of consumption-sharing arrangements (spatial and aspatial) would emerge if households were able to purchase their own choice of shared services, bearing in mind that larger groups mean more people with whom to share costs but that after a certain point congestion sets in? What spatial and sectoral groupings would emerge to share streets, community halls, schools, parks, street-planting, security services, waste disposal, potable water supply and other environmental services?

Figure 6.3a (after Buchanan 1965) shows the total costs and benefits per person of some good or service of fixed quantity, against the number of people jointly consuming and paying for it. Imagine that the service in question is a neighbourhood park which adds to household utility by the view that it creates, the recreational space it provides, the added house values it creates and so on. Benefits might be expected to rise initially as more join the club until such time as congestion sets in and they start to fall. Hence the benefit curves *B* are drawn convex. Average costs start off high with small numbers (spread over just one household in the extreme left) and fall off as additional members join, forming the concave curves *C*. At the point where distance between the benefit and costs curves is greatest, maximum net benefit is derived for club members and this defines the optimal membership given the fixed quantity of good. There will be a different set of curves for each quantity of the good. *B*1 and *C*1 might represent benefit and cost curves for a park of a certain size and *B*2 and *C*2 the curves for a larger park. The benefits from the larger park are greater as are the costs, but its capacity is greater and congestion (the apex in the curve) is further to the right as is the optimal size of consumption-sharing group (*N*2 compared to *N*1).

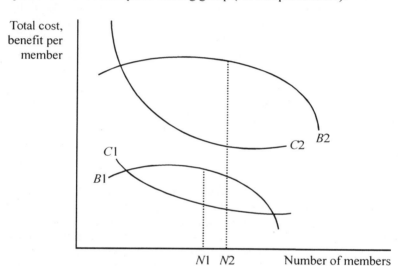

Source: Figures 6.3a–c are adapted from diagrams in Buchanan (1965: 7–10)

Figure 6.3a   Optimal club size for two differently sized facilities

There is another way of looking at the problem of optimal size however: what if we start with a fixed number of members and vary the quantity? Figure 6.3b shows total costs and benefits per person against quantity of service (park size). Benefit curves increase at a decreasing rate reflecting diminishing returns, either flattening out or down-turning if the surplus actually reduces a household's utility (the park gets too big to feel safe within). Cost curves rise with the size of the park. There is a set of curves for any given number of joint-consumers. $B1$ and $C1$ are for a small group and $B2$ and $C2$ for a larger group (with lower average benefits because of the greater numbers, but lower average costs because of the greater cost-sharing). For each club size there is as optimal quantity given by the maximum distance between cost and benefit curves. Now consider Figure 6.3c, which shows the size of facility against the number of people sharing it and plots both optimal community size N_{opt} as it changes with facility size, and optimal facility size Q_{opt} as it changes with community size.

For an entrepreneur supplying a club good, the optimal membership is given by N^* and the optimal quantity of the good Q^*. These are the design parameters of public domains organised by entrepreneurial clubs.

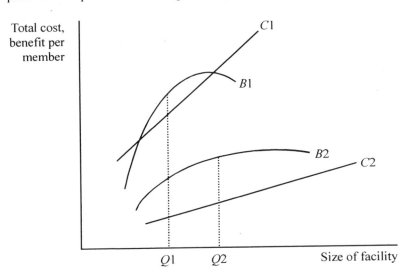

Source: Figures 6.3a–c are adapted from diagrams in Buchanan (1965: 7–10)

Figure 6.3b *Optimal facility size for two clubs with different numbers of members*

Returning to Figure 6.1 and the illustration used at the start of this chapter, imagine that there were many more than four households using the muddy path in the informal peripheral settlement and that each would be willing to pay a small contribution towards a linked network of paths that joined each of their homes to a nearby bus route. The (unmeasurable) collective demand may be Qs in Figure 6.1. Buchanan's pay-off matrix (Table 6.1) suggests that the pavement would not materialise, however, as everyone would be likely to free ride. Figures 6.1 and 6.2 show why some parts of the network might be produced by small numbers collaborating, but by and large, the collective action problems caused by ill-defined property rights might be assumed to be too powerful to see the neighbourhood upgraded by voluntary action and market forces.

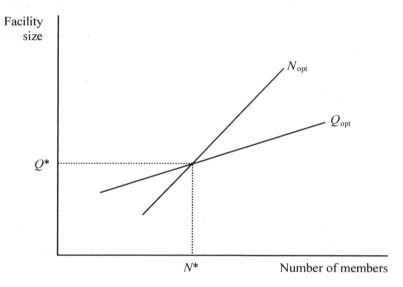

Source: Figures 6.3a–c are adapted from diagrams in Buchanan (1965: 7–10)

Figure 6.3c   Optimal club domain: optimal facility size against number of members and optimal number of members against facility size

Buchanan's club analysis, on the other hand, demonstrates the possibility of efficiently supplying the pavement and other neighbourhood goods. What are the institutional and informational requirements for the efficient provision of club goods?

First are the institutional preconditions for creating an organisation. Owners of resources must have the right to combine their property rights with others to form an organisation mandated to supply the public good to members, be it a commercial company, co-operative, home owner association, mutual society, condominium or non-profit organisation. This right does not always exist. At the time of writing, some London Boroughs are drafting planning policy that would require restricted-access residential developments of ten homes or more to include a minimum quota of low-income homes. Whether the policy is aimed at protecting the capital's diminishing stock of key-worker homes; averting social fragmentation; or is motivated by a sense of fairness, the law will mean that land owners do not have the right to form residential clubs exclusively for those with middle and high income.

In most countries, residents do not have the legal right to barricade streets with the intention of improving neighbourhood security and traffic problems. This does not stop neighbourhoods exercising their economic right to do so in some cities and thereby challenging the laws that deny local resident rights over local streets (Jones and Lowrey, 1995).

In many congested cities with water-supply problems, laws have been enacted that forbid the sinking of private boreholes. Many older residential and industrial compounds in Asian cities have private wells. Costs are recovered via ground rent or connection fees, demonstrating the economic feasibility of water supply clubs.

Private policing is forbidden in many countries, although laws are rapidly liberalising in this area. In the US, there are more private security personnel than state police (Blakely and Snyder, 1997) offering security as a club good to groups of commercial, industrial and residential interests. The British government is currently revisiting the laws that govern private policing.

Where countries and states have not liberalised urban utility sectors, there is no institutional base to support the emergence of competition and the fragmentation of public domains into new markets and into potentially more efficient club domains. India is currently reforming its state monopolies over many municipally supplied public goods. France is resisting EU calls to liberalise its energy markets, particularly its state-run monopoly electricity distributor.

Until recently in Britain, there was no legal provision for the creation of common-hold land tenure; for the enforcement of positive conditions exchanged with landed property; or for the private management of neighbourhood assets. Neither was there legal provision for low-income households in state subsidised homes to manage their own housing estates. These institutional constraints to club reformation are changing under market and political pressure.

The second requirement for the efficient provision of club goods is the technological and institutional preconditions for exclusion. Generally speaking, technology for measuring, pricing and controlling access needs to be available before an entrepreneur can supply a club good. Where geography and social–cultural institutions create natural clubs with existing conventions of mutuality and personal and community responsibility, club goods are likely to be forthcoming. In such instances, traditional methods of raising and collecting funds and traditional methods of social disapproval form the pricing and exclusion technologies. Many English villages have acquired their pristine picture-postcard quaintness by voluntary community effort and unwritten standards of home maintenance and investment. They function like clubs and in many cases it is geographical distance that prevents benefits leaking away through non-member congestion. Where there is a problem of congestion, from through-traffic for example or weekend visitors, villagers are likely to lobby government for additional exclusion measures, such as a by-pass road, speed restrictions and parking restrictions.

Club rules are sometimes strengthened by the creation of law. On Victoria Peak in Hong Kong before World War II, Europeans were permitted by law to create a protectionist enclave above the 788-feet contour that excluded the Chinese (rich or poor; educated or otherwise) from residing (Lai and Yu, 2001a). A Residents' Association was set up for holding social functions as well as for vetting details of European living on *the Peak*. Even European governesses had to be vetted by this exclusive club before they were allowed to accept employment (Morris, 1997).

In cities, where the possibility of free-riding is much greater than in rural areas, modern developments in metering and security technology have permitted all manner of club innovations in recent years and will continue to do so. Singapore charges road users to enter the central business district using electronic pricing technology. At the time of writing, there are discussions about restricting access to central London's residential quarters using electronic pricing or barriers. The allocation of water is made more efficient by metering technology.

The third condition for the efficient club supply of public domain goods is effective organisation and decision making apparatus. A set of institutions is required for making decisions about the *quantity* of club good and the *size* of the club. Clubs arise both spontaneously and as a result of conscious planning. They are started by community entrepreneurs who have an interest in consuming and/or supplying the club good and by third parties that supply capital and management know-how to incipient community organisations. At some stage, however, most clubs require a formal constitution that governs decision making, in particular, questions of membership criteria, membership numbers and quantity and quality of club goods supplied. Crucially, the decision making apparatus will need to be able to address the problem of congestion within the club and the possibility of congestion of club goods by free-riding non-members.

Figures 6.3a–c illustrates the idea of an optimal club configuration (membership size and quantity of good) for a given technology and set of preferences. In theory, the constitution and management of a single-good club should be capable of guiding the club towards this ideal point. Buchanan's model is static in terms of technology and transaction costs, however, and in the real world, N^* and Q^* in Figure 6.3c will change as the club invests in new facilities, equipment and practices.

It is worth considering how transaction costs and information problems constrain the attainment of the perfect club. Buchanan's perfectly efficient club requires perfect information and it is, of course, very unlikely that a club's management could accurately gauge the benefit and cost curves in Figure 6.3a and b. The information problem here is fundamentally different to that in Samuelson's perfectly efficient public good supply problem however. The problem of preference revelation is overcome by membership fee: if individuals do not value the public domain resource at the price offered they will not seek membership. The information problem in a club is the same as that in any market and it reduces with competition and market maturity. Clubs operating in a well established market are able more accurately to judge the demand for new services; the response to a price change; and the impact on benefits and costs arising from changes to membership size and changes in the goods supplied. Clubs operating by informal co-operation, clubs in newly emerging markets, and clubs with natural monopoly memberships or otherwise protected from competition will find it more difficult to make decisions leading to club configurations that exhaust gains from trade.

The issue of competition between clubs is important in understanding the emergence of public domain order because of the effect competition has on information and transaction costs. In a competitive club-good market, poor management decisions are quickly detected by market feedback; clubs have to expend resources to discover ways of improving benefits for members and winning new members; a natural discipline exists to keep management costs down; and clubs will assume a greater amount of search and other transaction costs by advertising, offering discounts, locating near to customers and so on.

Commuters travelling the London Tube are currently bombarded by the adverts of dozens of firms competing for custom in the cheap international telephone market; the newly established but thriving cheap European airline market; the travel insurance market; and the city centre apartment market. These are all sophisticated club goods markets in the sense that their products have strong collective consumption attributes. The adverts testify to the impact of competition on the distribution of information search costs: commuters can make their choice about which of these clubs to join while travelling to work. When they arrive home at the end of the day, they are likely to find that another set of membership invitations has arrived by post – invitation to switch electricity company, to sign up with a new Internet Service Provider, to switch car insurer, to join a new health club, to transfer their home loan to a different building society.

Retirement communities are becoming popular throughout North America, Europe and Australasia. Townsend (2002) illustrates the tensions that arise as consumers and producers interact to create new forms of residential clubs in Canada. Consumers do not always seem to get a good deal. This is either because they are the relatively powerless partner (when the product is new and collective knowledge about it not well developed) or because the innovation was poorly designed in the first place. Retirement developments seem to be a popular idea in principle, however, so one assumes that there is a process going on by which the concept is refined as the niche housing market becomes more competitive, and consumers, developers and government regulators become better informed.

6.5　GOVERNMENT SUPPLY

Just as a club that started as a voluntary association bound by informal conventions may evolve into a large commercial enterprise bound by commercial laws and operating in a sophisticated competitive market, so too may a local club evolve into a fully constituted government. Leisure World Laguna Hills in Orange County, just to the south of Los Angeles is a club-community of over 22 000 residents. Founded in 1964 as a private residential development it gained city status in 2000 (Frantz, 2000).

The contemporary US debate about communities ceding from mother cities is an exceptional case however. Elsewhere, change in jurisdictional geography is a more fundamental constitutional issue. The emergence of new municipal jurisdictions is more usually a result of planned local government reform; planned new town development; regularisation of unplanned squatter settlements; and planned or spontaneous frontier settlement development.

Whatever their origins, cities and the jurisdictions within them, as we noted when discussing Tiebout, perform in many respects like clubs. Indeed, the market failure thesis interprets Figure 6.1 as demonstrating that only a government with the legal power to coerce tax payments can supply public goods efficiently.

Municipal governments (bureaucracies, elected or appointed political leaders and sometimes a separate elected or appointed executive) are often thought of as the natural and even rightful supplier of public goods and services. There are strong arguments for government-organised supply in the case of particular goods. These include merit goods (security, education and health – private goods, the consumption of which yields wider benefits to the economy) and regulations (those aimed for example at mitigating social costs that arise from externalities, monopoly behaviour and uneven distributions of wealth and market power – see below and Chapter 7). It is worth considering, however, how municipal governments differ from other organisations that supply club goods in cities.

Local Government Suppliers of Public Goods Face an Inherent Information Disadvantage in Measuring Demand

The information problem facing government was introduced in Chapter 1 when contrasting centralised planned order with decentralised spontaneous order. The problem is captured graphically in Figure 6.1. If a local government sets itself the task of delivering an efficient quantity of a good (pavement in our example) it faces the costly task of trying to measure demand – to discover the utopian planning parameter Qs. Ironically, the greater the number of individuals there are with positive demand for the good, the stronger the argument for government intervention but the more costly it is to discover demand information.

The idea that government can rectify the market failure implicit in Figures 6.1 and 6.2 is implausible for two important reasons that relate to information and transaction costs.

First, if a community of four households finds it difficult to reveal true preferences to each other ($P1$ to $P4$ in Figure 6.1) then it is unlikely that a government agency will discover any method to induce hundreds or tens of thousands of households to reveal their true preferences. Economists have devised clever mechanisms that aim to elicit true preferences but these largely remain theoretical and laboratory ideas. An example is the Clarke Tax, which converts a large number problem into a small group situation in an attempt to induce honest preference revelation – see Clarke (1971) and Tideman and Tullock (1976). In the absence of prices, government resorts to more costly methods of discovering information about demand and need such as market and political research, election campaigns and surveys. The information these yield is less accurate than market price; is likely to reflect average benefits rather than marginal benefits; is more open to manipulation; and is more costly to produce. When the transaction costs of creating centralised information are taken into account, the optimal points of public good supply may be very different to the theoretical zero-transaction cost optima in Figure 6.1 (or the optima in Figures 6.3a–c if local government jurisdictions are thought of as Buchanan style clubs).

Second, even if a set of true preferences were to be measured, a political decision is required to aggregate them. Each individual in a community might be thought to have a preference ranking of alternative public goods allocations. The tax prices $P1$ to $P4$ in Figure 6.1 are the households' preferences for just one public good. Kenneth Arrow famously demonstrated the impossibility of designing a constitution that yields a complete and consistent social ranking of individual preferences (Arrow, 1951). There is no set of rules that will produce a unique social ranking of alternative resource allocations consistent with the rankings of individual members of society. Government's use of information is unavoidably re-distributive therefore and the way the redistribution falls depends on voting and other decision making mechanisms.

Local Governments have Particular Supply-side Constraints

The bulk of locally-generated municipal revenue usually comes from property tax – a kind of compulsory membership fee. Local taxes in many parts of the world are notoriously difficult to collect, requiring an institutional and technical infrastructure base that is often not there. In developed economies where the institutions of government are more stable, the revenue basis of 'municipal clubs' is more reliable but still subject to fluctuations with economic fortune. Financial uncertainty may be compounded where a significant proportion of local authority budget comes from central government's tax base.

As well as being dependent on central government transfers, local governments also face constraints on capital borrowing. This is for good reason: an insolvent local authority has to be bailed out. It is also a handicap. An educational reform act in the late 1980s gave parents in Britain the legal right to choose their children's high school. The right to choose was accompanied by a regulation requiring schools to publish performance information – considerably reducing parents' search costs. What the act didn't do was to deregulate the supply side to match the unleashed demand. Apart from a one-off disbursement of central government funds that allowed selected 'popular schools' to undertake a limited number of building projects, successful schools could not freely borrow in order to expand. The result by and large was to increase congestion in the popular schools; to frustrate parents whose legal right to choose was overridden by local capacity problems; and in the end to revert to a spatial rationing system. The combination of better information about school performance and rigid catchment areas has exacerbated severe house price differentials as better-informed parents pay house price premiums to buy into 'good school' neighbourhood 'clubs'.

Property Rights are Generally Less Clearly Assigned by Government than by Entrepreneurial Organisations

Entrepreneurial organisations assign rights to shared goods by legal contract. Informal voluntary organisations may assign property rights on the basis of the trust and a strong sense of social contract in a community. Governments assign rights by policy, regulation and bylaws. While such devices are contracts of a kind – formalised social contracts over resource entitlements specified by government – they are inherently less stable and binding than the contracts that bind market-based transactions or the conventions that bind transactions within community groups.

Government educational planners, for example, draw up school catchment boundaries, assigning educational services to households. Where school standards sharply vary across a jurisdiction, planners find themselves allocating significant wealth-enhancing benefits. School boundaries change, however, with demographic change, political ideology and educational strategy and as they do, important property rights reassignment takes place.

Statutory land-use plans attenuate the development rights of some landowners and enhance or protect the rights of others. The pattern of rights may change, however, through re-zoning, periodic policy review or by successful legal challenges that render the plans powerless. Where powers to enforce regulations are weak, the legal rights assigned by municipal planning and policy instruments may not confer or attenuate rights in practice. The uncertain status of regulations may lead to greater property rights ambiguity than may have existed in the absence of regulations.

The political nature of decision making in local government means that the order that can be imposed upon a public domain problem is often short lived and frequently leaves ambiguities in the assignment of property rights. One consequence of this is that high transaction costs are incurred through lobbying, legal challenge, appeals and the other activities that become necessary to resolve those ambiguities.

Local Governments have Explicit and Implicit Redistributive Goals in Supplying Public Goods

Local authorities are multi-product clubs, collecting anonymous (pooled) tax revenue and using it to supply a great variety of goods and services to a great variety of groups. This renders their task inherently redistributive as we have noted. Indeed, many elected decision makers and local authority administrators view redistribution as a principal rationale for their existence.

Because of this, public goods allocation becomes politicised when administered by government. This is not so in the same way when administered by entrepreneurial clubs. Private firms delivering club goods have their own internal politics in boardrooms and management committees, but access to their goods is on the basis of price. The price mechanism in this sense is a less costly rationing device and less open to abuse by lobbyists and by managers and decision makers seeking property rights assignments that benefit particular individuals or groups.

The possibility of decisions being influenced by self-interest would seem to be greater in government than in entrepreneurial clubs, especially where the latter operate in competitive markets. Politicians go to the electorate on the basis of big issues and many smaller issues are decided without true electoral endorsement. Large mistakes or abuses of power are limited by the competitive discipline of periodic elections but local politicians have, in practice, a great deal of discretion in spending 'club fees'. As a general rule, politicians can be expected to seek to redistribute tax revenue towards groups and areas that they represent or are otherwise associated with. Professional officers who administer town hall functions on behalf of elected governments have their own margins for discretion which allow them to pursue self-interested goals at the same time as fulfilling the terms of their employment contracts. The oversized bureaucracy has been the preoccupation of public choice writers for a long time (see for example Racheter and Wagner, 1999).

The cause of the problem is the complexity of the information requirement in multi-product, multi-user clubs like local government and the unequal distribution of information and power that naturally develops. Professional officers become monopoly suppliers of services to politicians and have generally far better information about demand for (need of) and supply of the public goods that politicians commit themselves to provide. In such circumstances it is understandable that bureau chiefs will tend to argue for allocations that promote the interests of their staff; that increase their sectional budgets; and that appeal to their professional, personal and ideological values.

The ability of local politicians and public officers to redistribute tax revenues to groups they represent or are members of is enhanced by geography. This is true in two senses.

First, municipalities tend to have a spatial monopoly over their members. Members can move out of a jurisdiction but usually incur considerable transaction cost in doing so. Occasionally a local government's monopoly position has been broken by a higher power as was the case when the British government dissolved the Greater London Council in the 1980s or when an administration is forcibly removed. In the 1990s, several inner city educational authorities in Britain were forced by the central government to bring in external management of failing schools. Failing health authorities, police authorities and even failing London Borough administrations now face the same threat.

Second, local governments are typically well protected from the effects of competition. The vast majority of towns and cities are managed by a single local authority. Only in very large cities is there any real prospect of competition emerging between authorities. London has 33 boroughs, for example, and Metro-Phoenix, Arizona has 23 towns and cities. Calcutta Metropolitan Area has 35 municipalities and 20 elected rural bodies (Panchayat samities) and Jakarta, covering 650 square kilometres, comprises five city jurisdictions, 43 districts (Kecamatan) and 265 subdistricts (Kelurahan). The transaction costs of relocating are always high but in large cities such as these there is the real possibility of residents and industry choosing between jurisdictions on the basis of the bundles of club goods on offer. It is reasonable to suppose that footloose taxpayers may encourage local governments to operate as more efficient and more innovative clubs.

6.6 A TYPOLOGY OF PUBLIC GOODS AND PUBLIC DOMAIN PROBLEMS

We generalise the discussion now by offering a typology of public goods, which is also a typology of public domain problems, and we consider the institutional requirements for efficiently assigning property rights in each category. The taxonomy of public domain goods given in Figure 6.4 is a common one in the literature and a good starting point for understanding the appropriate organisations and institutions for delivery. Without the arrows, it is a static typology, however. It is improved by understanding that any particular good can move between categories with changes in value; changes in exclusion costs; and changes in institutions. We introduce arrows to indicate the dynamic process in which goods can transform between categories, as changes in their value lead to the reallocation of property rights.

The letters in the table represent categories of goods, or more precisely, categories of attributes possessed by goods. If a good has both public and private good attributes it will be located in different parts of the table. This suggests that different institutions may emerge to supply different attributes separately. Whether this happens or not depends on the technical feasibility of subdividing rights and the transaction costs of doing so.

Category A goods are pure private goods and D represents pure public goods. There is no public domain problem with goods of type A. Since consumption is rivalrous, an entrepreneur will seek to assign property rights to each consumption unit. This will be possible if the value of the commodity is sufficient in relation to the cost of the technology and the costs of the institutions required to achieve exclusion. With an exclusion mechanism in place, goods are completely divisible among individual consumer units and entrepreneurs can be assured of revenue since unambiguous property rights can be traded for the market price.

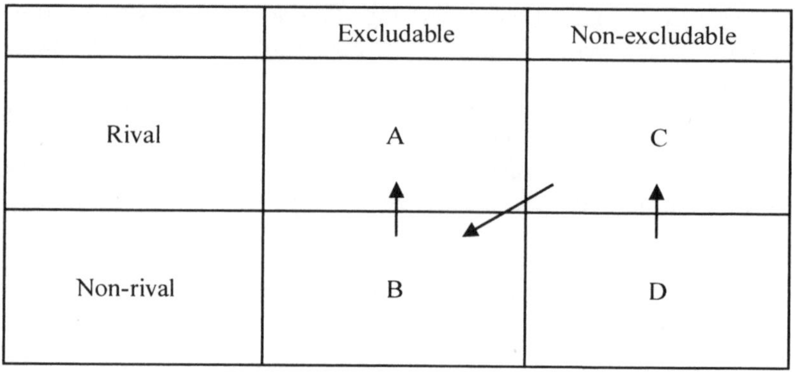

	Excludable	Non-excludable
Rival	A	C
Non-rival	B	D

Figure 6.4   Dynamic typology of public goods

Goods of type B are excludable but non-rival, exemplified by a swimming pool, toll road, shopping mall or school operating below congestion levels. Entrepreneurs have an incentive to supply these goods but will not need to incur the cost of assigning property rights to each unit consumed. It would be inefficient to do so because the consumption of one user does not reduce the amount consumed by another. Instead, entrepreneurs assign rights to a good that is consumed collectively within an excludable public domain (club domain). These are clubs in the sense that we have been using and in the sense of Figure 6.3. Entrepreneurs will provide a club good so long as the value of the good covers the cost of providing it, including the cost of making it excludable; and so long as there are institutions that permit it to be made excludable.

If a type B good becomes congested, however, its suppliers will seek ways of reallocating property rights to reduce the competition costs incurred by club members. Mild or periodic congestion may be handled by informal institutions that emerge within the club – for example, members of a health club readjusting visiting patterns to find quieter periods. Serious congestion requires formal reallocation of rights or the club may be depopulated. This may involve raising fees to expand facilities; rationing facilities; fee-banding; or charging for certain services. One result of reallocating property rights is to transform some attributes of a type B good into type A attributes. A health club in which membership fees cover all facilities except racket sports, charged per court per hour, treats court-use as a private good, (ignoring the public domain created when four players share a court). More strictly, a badminton court hired for an hour by four players becomes a club domain for four for a fixed period. Introducing user-charges for fitness machines, sun beds and saunas reduces congestion and forces members to be more efficient in their use of facilities. If there is no congestion, a club may charge user fees for specific services if the technology permits but may lose out to competitors who do not charge for these services.

The allocation of property rights within public domains in this sense may equilibriate in the short run under the influence of competition. Property rights are reassigned within a club because congestion creates new markets for what were once un-marketed public domain resources. When the costs of competing for space on highly congested urban roads becomes sufficiently high, some will be prepared to pay an expressway toll.

Type C goods are rival but non-excludable. Few goods can be said to be inherently non-excludable and so this category really suggests that there may be goods which cannot presently be rendered excludable for technical and institutional (including cultural and political) reasons. This leads to a focus on the reasons for non-excludability.

The use of over-crowded city spaces on publicly-owned land cannot usually be made more efficient by exclusion because urban governments are committed to open access and underlying distributional goals. The wider adoption of private health care in Britain has been thwarted by the British population's deeply held commitment to the ideal of the National Health Service. Cultural values act as an institutional constraint on the growth of the health-care 'club' market. The National Health Service is grossly congested and one might assume that if NHS managers and government financiers cannot resolve the problems, then the cultural constraints might continue to erode and more might opt for private health schemes.

Category C is a transitional category therefore. There may be an equilibrium that renders the institutional–technological value mix stable (or even oscillating) for a while, but each of these three variables is subject to change from a variety of influences, including each other. If the value of a non-excludable resource continues to fall as a result of over-use, there is bound to come a time when property rights will change. Type C goods are goods that are ready to be transformed from public goods to club goods; from club good to more exclusive club good; or from club good toward private good. They are goods subject to institutional stress and the resulting institutional evolution. They are goods for which there is scope for entrepreneurial and technological innovation.

The roads in London's central area are rivalrously consumed but currently non-excludable. This is about to change with the onset of congestion pricing – championed by the city's first executive mayor. The transformation of urban infrastructure and services from category C to category B goods is a natural evolutionary process. Governments as well as firms will act to introduce exclusion. The London case is particularly interesting in this regard in that the Mayor leading the charge on the creation of this new market is a famously left-wing municipal politician. Ideology co-evolves with resource scarcity, technology and institutions.

Goods of type D are completely indivisible, either for technological or institutional reasons. They are consumed jointly without disbenefit to anyone and are not excludable. This makes for a *de facto* theoretical case for government supply. For the good to be provided by an entrepreneur, there would need to be a mechanism for organising group payment. This happens, it may be noted, when private firms provide public goods on behalf of local governments via contracting-out. Such cases should be understood to be examples of government supply, however, since it is government that organises the supply – via private firms who may be viewed as *providers* rather than *suppliers*.

Public–private partnerships (PPPs) are an interesting innovation in this respect. They are joint supply ventures in which the different parties to an agreement take responsibility for organising various inputs into the public good production process. Analytically this may involve government assuming responsibility for supplying attributes of the service that are less indivisible – such as safety, reliability and capital security – while private partners organise the supply of excludable attributes. A PPP creates, in effect, a new organisation or firm in which property rights are combined for mutual benefits. Barzel's theory of the firm (1997), which places an emphasis on capitalisation as a reason for property rights combination, offers particularly helpful insight into this modern method of supplying urban public goods.

Pure public goods of type D are notoriously difficult to find and most writers of textbooks resort to the obvious candidates of national defence; clean air; open countryside; and lighthouses. All of these are capable of transforming into category B and category C goods, however. Ronald Coase's famous investigation of the lighthouses stationed around the British coast (1974) found that rather than being provided by government, most were supplied as club goods on the basis of harbour fees. The introduction of strategic alliances, tactical and smart weaponry and defence technology means that regional-level national defence is also now a club good. It is not true that the services of NATO are freely available to all in the European region. There are, of course, spillover benefits, but non-members are excluded from the alliance's services. Why else would former Soviet states be queuing up to join the club?

Clean air and water, once taken for granted as free and uncongested resources of type D, are clearly consumed rivalrously. In many of the world's urbanised regions, open countryside, developable land and wilderness areas are becoming truly scarce and therefore subject to rivalrous consumption. Governments, typically believed to be the rightful curators of natural resources, find themselves under pressure to introduce exclusionary institutions and technology.

6.7   REORDERING WEALTH: 'REDISTRIBUTION' AS A PUBLIC GOOD

The last point introduces an important idea in relation to the kind of pure public goods that governments find themselves supplying. A government may legislate to introduce protected area status in order to conserve ecologically vulnerable or recreationally important areas. By so doing it aims to transform land from a congested or potentially congestible good without exclusion, to a non-rivalrous good with exclusion. It turns a public good subject to congestion into a club good by restricting access (for example by charging entry fees or forbidding land development). It restricts access, often benefiting particular groups, in order to yield benefits that, ostensibly at least, are enjoyed by all. Two interpretations of public exclusionary policies may be made with respect to our discussion of public domain order.

First, restrictions placed on public goods domains by government and which result in degrees of exclusion, invariably result from the lobbying activities of those who stand to gain (psychically if not materially but usually both). This is the rent-seeking thesis. Public domain order, from this point of view, is shaped by the interests that dominate decision making in the public arena, and these are not always the interests of the public at large or of deserving groups within it. Much redistribution, from this point of view, is inefficient, as are the government institutions that deliver it.

Second, ethical standards and expectations broadly shared by society may give rise to collective demand for redistributional interventions. Redistribution, or the resource distributions that they hope to achieve, are public goods. The idea of a redistributional policy as pure public good that only government can provide is an important one since it crucially underpins many functions of modern government.

Imagine that most individuals have a preference for contributing a certain proportion of income to the destitute and to a social security safety net fund. Large numbers and the public good nature of both examples ensure that there will be problems of preference revelation and free riding. Prisoner's dilemma is likely to mean that these goods will be under- or un-provided. Voluntary sector provision of services to the poor may be very successful but remain inefficient if some individuals free ride on the contributions of others, failing to reveal their own willingness to contribute. More could be collected and redistributed if contributions were organised through the tax system.

The same may be said of all kinds of redistribution. Most residents of London, New York and Tokyo, for example, may lament the shortage of affordable homes and understand the problems this creates for the efficient working of the urban economy. Wealthy suburbanites might form this view as bus services are repeatedly cancelled because of driver shortages; as train services suffer due to maintenance staff shortages; and as shortages of builders and school teachers affect quality of life in other ways. If pressed, businesses may in principle be willing to contribute to a fund that ensures an adequate stock of social housing. Firms aware of the importance to the national economy of a well-educated workforce may be willing to pay a certain amount to a fund that sustains a national educational system.

It matters not, therefore, whether the motivation for giving is self-interest, pure altruism or enlightened self-interest. Redistribution and the outcomes it attempts to achieve are pure, non-excludable, public goods and free riding and undersupply arguments for government supply are strong.

The case for government supply should be moderated, however, by two considerations: the costs of organising supply of the public good (organisational or agency costs); and the inevitable tendency of decision makers, administrators and lobby groups to capture benefits for themselves or for those they represent as they redistribute resources 'on behalf of' society. These two sources of inefficiency are in essence one and the same since it is rent seeking by individuals within an organisation that gives rise to alleged excessive agency costs of government.

6.8   KEY ARGUMENTS OF CHAPTER 6

* The problem of public goods may be discussed in terms of four scenarios: a utopian community with a market supply under perfect information and zero transaction costs; an imperfect community under market supply with imperfect information and positive transaction costs; an entrepreneurial club or market supply with contractual collective action; and government provision.
* To achieve the efficient voluntary supply of a collectively consumed good, all individuals in a community have to be able to perfectly and costlessly discover each other's willingness to pay for the good; requiring largely unrealistic institutions of perfect honesty and trust.
* Without perfect information, the costs of discovering other individuals' willingness to pay and of organising collective action ensure that the good is either undersupplied or not supplied at all. For some individuals,

a collective agreement may mean oversupply even though the total amount is undersupplied in respect of the community's aggregate demand.

- Entrepreneurial clubs overcome the collective action problem by enclosing a public good and charging a membership fee. They tackle the public domain problem by fragmenting the *public* into smaller (and generally more homogeneous) *publics*; by subdividing public domains.
- Municipal or local governments differ from other organisations that supply club goods in cities in a number of ways. Local government suppliers of public goods face an inherent information disadvantage in metering demand and face binding supply-side constraints, notably unpredictable local taxes and central government transfers, and in many cases an inability to raise finance from capital markets. They are also less capable of clearly delineating property rights and have explicit and implicit redistributional goals in supplying public goods.
- Imperfect voluntary institutions, entrepreneurial clubs and governments jostle to supply public goods. To the extent that governments, club owners and participants of voluntary institutions have information and are responsive to market and political market signals, competition might be expected to result in the survival of the more efficient institutions.
- As institutions compete and adapt, so the nature of public domains in cities changes. Property rights theory suggests that there is a dynamic relationship between goods classified using the conventional cross tabulation of excludability and rival/non-rival consumption. Through the processes of rising demand, institutional evolution and property rights reassignment, pure public goods tend to become congested; congested but non-excludable goods tend to become club goods; and with in-club congestion, club goods tend to subdivide towards private goods ($D \rightarrow C \rightarrow B \rightarrow A$) in Figure 6.4.

7. Public domain order – externalities

It takes a decade to grow a tree but a century a person.

It is much more difficult, according to the Chinese saying, to shape a person or a society of people than to shape nature. However, the way we shape nature is bound up with the way in which we shape society, in particular with the way in which property rights are organised. You can plant a tree in the open with the purpose of providing shade for your family, future income or a forest for future generations but others may fell it for cash. You can grow a cherry tree in your backyard but not in the space in front of your home; not because the ecology is different but because you have no right to do so. You can raise fish in your own ponds but if your right to drive out herons is curtailed by the bird watcher's lobbying in parliament, your fish pond will become a killing ground for species with wings.

Natural resources and other public goods change in value with demographic pressure, technological innovation and shifts in taste. As societies become more urbanised and cities get more dense, the spillover costs and benefits between private activities change, becoming more numerous and more problematic. Greater competition for shared resources like roads, open space, rivers, water, air and views mean that physical externalities spun off from production or consumption processes – airborne particles, noise, traffic, waste material – cause greater nuisance.

This is so in two senses. The more people affected by pollution, the higher the aggregate level of nuisance (the summed value of individual nuisance costs). Also, the more a public domain resource is congested with spillovers from private activities, the greater the sense of loss as additional units of the river, countryside, view and so on are lost. Increasing scarcity means increased value – increased positive value of the diminishing shared resource and increased negative value of externalities that further diminish it.

Another Chinese proverb says:

The previous generation grew trees and the future will enjoy their shade.

This may be both a word of thanks to the past and a declaration of trust for the future with regard to private investment in the public domain. The social contract and continuity that it implies, no longer holds however. The shade will be contested by too many people wanting to share it; the quality and health of trees and shade will be contested by pollution from traffic and industry; and the land on which forefathers planted trees will be contested by uses that will yield greater present benefit to society.

Institutions evolve to cope with these externality problems. Without institutions and the property rights they attempt to assign, contested public domains are apt to deteriorate chronically to the point at which any benefits they might provide are eroded by the costs of congestion and competition. Large tracts of North Africa's arid wastelands were once a breadbasket for the Roman Empire. Their demise followed a switch from private property rights to a common property system of grazing rights (Bottomley, 1963).

7.1 PROPERTY RIGHTS AND EXTERNALITY ABATEMENT

Economists like to use examples from nature to illustrate theories of resource allocation. The choice between oranges and apples illustrates models of consumption behaviour in many elementary economic texts. In the literature on externalities, the examples are equally pastoral: Ronald Coase's parable of cattle and wheat in explaining the problem of negative externalities (Coase, 1960); Steven Cheung's 'fable of the bees' where pollinating bees and apple farmers in the State of Washington contract with each other to keep reciprocal positive externalities flowing (Cheung, 1973). Agricultural fables make good illustrations but the theatres of most intense daily conflict over externalities are the world's cities or regions, with cities as the core. This covers not only observable pollution and congestion in the three-dimensional space but also the invisible space of frequency bands.

In Chapter 5 we introduced several perspectives on the externality problem. Externalities are resources for which markets, or more generally allocative institutions, are undeveloped, missing or artificially restrained (the latter possibility being a case of 'public failure'). Depending on one's position, they are resources with positive or negative value but ill-defined property rights. From the wheat farmer's point of view, invading cattle are negative externalities and from the apple farmer's point of view, the visiting bees are positive externalities. Fish-eating birds and illegal loggers generate negative externalities in the aquaculture and arboriculture industries while fish farmers and tree growers generate positive externalities for tourism and leisure industries. Users of radio frequencies encounter problems of mutual jamming – an externality problem in which it is hard to point one's finger at any specific wrongdoer (discussed by Coase in a 1959 paper).

From the neo-classical perspective, externalities are by-products of private consumption or production decisions that are consumed by third parties. They often form important inputs to production processes and are therefore also unpriced factors of production. More generally, they are third party effects that remain unpriced due to the high transaction cost of exclusion. Most sublimely, externalities are differences in individual valuations of a resource.

At the heart of each perspective lies the issue of ill-defined property rights, incomplete information and the problem of a poorly-ordered public domain, vulnerable to wasteful competitive behaviour. If rights and liabilities over externalities could be clearly established and accurate information obtained about their incidence and value, then markets might develop and they would cease to be externalities. Governments, firms, individual consumers, bartering parties, members of households and clubs, would contract with all parties with whom mutually beneficial transactions may be made. That they do not is largely due to the high costs of assigning property rights; obtaining information; and negotiating deals.

Hence the importance of the corollary to the Coase theorem: *If information is not perfectly distributed and transaction costs are not zero, then the outcome for any externality problem depends on the distribution of property rights.*

The solution to any externality problem may therefore be said to lie in the clarification of property rights. Whether or not a clearer assignment of property rights is possible depends on the costs of making and policing the assignment. The efficiency of any solution obtained, depends on the gains realised less the cost of creating, upholding and transacting property rights over the contested resource. It also depends on the way in which responsibility, ownership, rights or liabilities are apportioned between affected parties (Barzel, 1997 and the *subsidiarity rule* from Chapter 1).

In the next section, we use this set of propositions as a basis for considering alternative approaches to moderating externality problems and pursuing order in urban public domains. Before doing this, however, it will be useful to be more specific about the reason why externality problems are, in fact, problematic. This allows us to elaborate the criteria by which alternative classes of externality solution might be evaluated and to emphasise the point that all externality solutions involve redistribution of resources. Externalities are problematic in four important senses.

Externalities Mean Unexploited Gains from Trade

First, because they are unpriced, it is likely that there are unexploited gains to be made from trading in them – gains that might be realised if certain transaction costs can be lowered. This might be achieved, for example, by better judicial clarification of legal rules; a breakthrough in the technology of exclusion (which facilitates metering demand and hence direct pricing); or by relaxing certain obstructive regulations. The initial pattern of benefit and cost 'endowment' created by an externality is capricious – a matter of chance; of who located where at some point in history. If rights can somehow be more clearly assigned, then co-operative acts of negotiation and exchange can potentially raise the welfare of some without lowering it for anyone else. In other words, there are potential Pareto improvements to be made in any externality situation where initially high transaction costs can be lowered. The state's intervention in the freedom of contract (via regulation) is one possibility, but not the only or even most likely option.

Until the transaction costs of property rights assignment are actually reduced, externalities remain public domain phenomena that coexist with the market. Care needs to be taken in the precision with which any intervention to tackle an externality is administered. It is all too easy to design overkill solutions that not only leave gains from trade in externalities unexploited but also weaken or destroy the market activity responsible for them.

Following privatisation and a decade of growth in private residential care for the elderly in the UK, the British government (probably rightly) took action to address problems of poor standards of accommodation and care. Its choice of action was, however, almost certainly wrong. An overly fussy list of regulations meant that the many care homes operating in relatively cheap and accessible converted large inner-urban houses had to close. The result was that large numbers of the vulnerable elderly were housed in temporary 'bed and breakfast' (B&B) accommodation that fell below the standard of the homes that were thought to be in need of regulation. Politicians and experts judged that the standard of care and accommodation resulting from contractual agreements between elderly people and care-home owners was unacceptable to society. The offence thus caused was a third party effect or an externality arising from the care-home industry. The regulative solution had the perverse effect of sending old people into poorer living conditions, destroying a young market and ignoring gains from trade. Society, home owners and residents might all have gained if society – the injured party – had offered subsidies to home owners to improve conditions.

Externalities Lead to Wasteful Competition Costs

A second reason why externalities are problematic is that as they are resources that are unpriced but nevertheless valued, other resources will be employed by individuals in trying to capture that value. This includes efforts to avoid negative externalities and to capture the benefits of positive externalities. Both kinds of behaviour give rise to competition costs, since to avoid certain externalities (typically by avoiding certain locations) is also to compete for others (other locations). Given that many of the costs incurred in seeking to capture or avoid externalities are sunk costs, such activity inevitably involves wasteful dissipation of time and other resources. There is also no guarantee that the sunk costs will yield commensurate gains, since the latter can usually only be fully appreciated *ex post facto*.

The process of searching for a location for home or business is largely concerned with navigating through 'externality space'. Not all externality effects are captured in property markets and building prices. Indeed, it might be said that much of the 'hunting' that goes on in the search process is about looking for advantages that are not reflected in the price – looking for the 'good deal' – which might be different for different types of buyer. Estate agents reduce search costs but do not remove them – and indeed their commission is part of the search costs. Neither is their packaging and labelling always accurate in terms of the valuation particular buyers have of particular externalities. The externalities in land and property markets are generally well understood in mature cities with stable growth. In such conditions many, but not all, tend to be reflected in property prices. In fast-growing cities and markets where there is less collective and individual experience and the signs are less easy to read, this is less likely. Choosing location here is more of a lottery. In these conditions it may be rational to spend a good deal of resources searching for and competing for a suitable location.

Roads are more dynamic systems than land and property markets and the spatial pattern of externalities has predictable and unpredictable elements that interact in complex ways. Navigating through an urban road network at rush hour by trial and error involves wasteful search costs. The probability of finding an optimal route (for example, one that minimises journey time) is related to but not determined by the quality of the driver's knowledge and the efficiency with which he translates this into an active search strategy. It is also related to events outside the driver's control such as unusual local congestion, accidents and road works. Like an estate agent, a traffic information service reduces competition costs, but not completely. Information may be wrong, out of date, incomplete or imperfectly used. Real-time in-cab information systems may commit a driver to switch to a route that immediately becomes sub-optimal as the initial congestion disappears.

Externality Solutions Impose their Own Transaction and Third Party Costs

A third reason for externalities being problematic is that the institutions that inevitably emerge to deal with the unpredictable costs of externalities (congestion, avoidance and capture) impose their own costs. The transaction costs of governance are discussed more broadly in the next chapter. Where the political context is open, accountable and responsive, checks and balances may prevent institutional costs rising disproportionately to the externalities they seek to tackle. In all too many cases, however, policy interventions take on a life and rationale that is semi-detached from the problem they were invented for, and costs escalate. In this sense externalities are problematic because they often trigger political interventions that impose more costs than they save. This is all the more likely when single-issue pressure groups successfully lobby the public and governments to regulate externalities. Well-organised lobbies can effectively collude with the self-sustaining dynamic of government bureaucracies, to sustain inefficient regulatory regimes. These organised interest groups can affect the rise and decline of nations by affecting the transaction costs and property rights structure of society (Olson, 1982; North and Thomas, 1973).

As well as imposing administrative costs on society (often hidden from clear view), government policy can often lead to new externality problems. We have already cited the case of the British government's intervention into home care for the elderly. In Hong Kong, a form of low-income accommodation emerged that involved low-income single person households occupying narrow bed units with low headroom not dissimilar to the cabins in public mortuaries. These were housed in so-called 'cage' or 'plank' rooms in private pre-war tenement buildings. The externalities of fire and health hazards were abundant – and this happened partly due to rent control imposed on these buildings. The intention to cater for low-income earners via rent control resulted in intensive use of the rent-capped resource.

Moral Arguments

A fourth reason why externalities are problematic is the moral case against certain activities and commodities. The censorship by various governments of liberal reading material, pornography, drugs, firearms, prostitution, alcohol, black market currency trading and export of ancient artefacts is enacted to reduce third party effects such as financial or moral destabilisation, loss of national heritage and the health and policing costs of violent crime. The sophisticated UK development control system effectively censors 'bad environmental design' (as judged by a particular group of experts). Bad design is an externality of the property market, which in the absence of planning regulation, would allegedly be oversupplied to the detriment of citizens at large.

There is a particular morality and ideology underlying all forms of externality abatement argument and these vary in the degree to which they insist on their position. Some are negotiable while others are not.

Dominant among moral arguments about public domain problems at the present time is the sustainability argument. This too comes in negotiable and non-negotiable versions (weak and strong sustainability). The problem of third party costs borne by future generations is the universally recognised problem at the heart of the sustainability debate and ideology. Without intervention, the present generation will take insufficient account of the state of the world's future generations when it makes present consumption and investment decisions. The externalities that present and near-off generations may be expected to accumulate are believed to be so great that the world will be a much worse place to live in for far-off generations. As the future generation is not directly represented in the present generation, no Coasian contractarian solution is possible. Neither can future generations directly negotiate a political deal over present restraint. Three solutions remain. First, the preferences of future generations may be represented by experts – lobbyists, academics and others who espouse particular strands of the sustainability cause. Second, future generations are placed at the mercy of the altruistic preferences of the present public, as expressed through collective decision processes. Third, future interests are safeguarded by private property – by individuals practising restraint in resource use for a mixture of self-interested and altruistic motives.

All three have their place in ordering public domain problems in cities and their hinterlands and all three have their limitations. Experts who profess to represent the preferences of future generations may be expected to derive much of their motivation from their own preferences. The latter are often non-negotiable and related one way or another to a green ideology that is not generally fully accepted by those whose actions they would seek to control. Sustainability policy emerging from public debate and enacted through democratic processes may be expected to reflect less of an absolutist view of the requirements of future generations. Even members of the public who are sensitive to sustainability issues are likely to vote for some degree of habitat destruction for the sake of economic growth. Private conservation action, on the other hand, can be very effective but limited in scope and extent.

The danger of relying on experts is the risk that they commandeer the political process through organised lobbying, and society finds itself subject to a coercive regime of environmental regulation that is then difficult to keep in check. The danger of relying on the public to safeguard the interests of future generations through democratic processes is that too little action emerges because of various collective action problems. The danger of relying on private conservation is that too little conservation will be supplied due to lack of altruism and the problem of free riding.

Sustainability has become a grand and very effective rallying call. Throughout the globe, it has given a new focus for collective action in urban communities and a new rationale for the actions of politicians and professional urban managers and planners. Sustainability is a rather high-level label, however, and most discussion in urban communities focuses on specific externalities – traffic congestion, refuse disposal, water quality, historic sites, green areas, cultivable land and so on. Some sustainability experts may take a moral or ideological position on sustainability as a general idea. For most of those faced with real decisions about reducing externalities, the moral imperative for action is as much to do with costs borne by the present generation as costs borne by future generations. Sustainability rhetoric, it should be understood, is frequently used in political processes to achieve redistribution between current interests – from car drivers to non-car drivers, from manufacturers to consumers, from rural dwellers to urban dwellers, from inner city dwellers to suburbanites, from poor to rich.

This underlies the Coasian idea that all solutions to externality problems are redistributive. To tax gasoline is to shift a cost to car owners that was previously borne by the general air-breathing public (many of whom are also car owners). One result of the now well-embedded sustainability agenda has been to make it easier for such redistributions to occur. This can be for good or bad.

7.2   CRITERIA FOR EVALUATING ALTERNATIVE PROPERTY RIGHTS ASSIGNMENTS

Any approach taken to address externalities therefore involves value judgement. To ignore an externality is to confer rights to the agent that generates it. To seek to reduce it by the intervention of a governing power is to reallocate rights from that agent to some other. All action is redistributive. Economic analysis can treat efficiency as a criterion distinct from moral value judgements only by first agreeing on a definition of *efficiency* – such as the Pareto criterion. This is itself a value judgement or moral position.

Broadly speaking, two kinds of position are taken in assessing alternative solutions to externality problems. First, are those that look at the net gains to economy and society irrespective of the distribution of costs and benefits. A solution is efficient if the costs of administering it are less than the net gains achieved. Moral arguments about the rightful ownership of property rights are subsumed by the moral imperative of improving net welfare in society. Second, are those positions that are not indifferent to alternative resource distributions. Privatising a forest or a river's fishing rights to prevent natural resource depletion may yield net welfare gains to society. Judged against an absolutist view of the right of public access, the solution may be unacceptable, notwithstanding the fact that the resource may eventually become totally depleted. On the other hand it may be the *existence* of a natural resource that is non-negotiable when assessing alternative courses of action – as with the inviolable green belt or heritage area.

Relative as well as absolutist values feature in debates about externality solutions. Buchanan, for example, suggested that *existing* property rights over a contested public domain resource should have pre-eminence. In this, he was addressing the moral conundrum posed by Coase's invariance theorem. Should a polluting firm have to compensate the residents of a new housing development when the latter have consented to locate next to its factory? The same socially efficient solution is possible if residents compensate the factory owners for reduced pollution. If an absolute (negative) value is placed on the pollution then the question of who located first is immaterial. If air pollution is negotiable (its costs can be traded against gains to society from the goods and jobs that give rise to it and against compensation payments), then the question of who located first becomes a potentially relevant issue in judging between alternative solutions.

Buchanan's rule is an ethical equivalent to Barzel's efficiency rule, which we introduced as the *subsidiarity rule* in the first chapter of this book:

> The total value of a contract or of any collective action is maximised when agents with an ability to influence the value of the contract or the outcome of collective action bear the full effects of their actions. This will be achieved when agents are residual claimants over the resources they influence – such that they have an incentive to deploy their resources efficiently in the attainment of the contract of collective action goal.

Applied to contracts (social and public, informal and formal) that are designed to resolve externality problems by apportioning rights and ownership, the rule suggests that liability should be assigned in a way that gives all parties an incentive to seek the desired result (lower externalities). In the case of land being developed for housing next to an established factory, a contract that makes the developer liable for the costs of installing soundproofing equipment in the factory would give it the incentive to deploy its resources to reduce the externality problem. It might do this by planting landscape buffers; adjusting the layout; and installing heavier duty soundproofing in the houses. Faced with the costs of mitigating the sound pollution that its action has created, the developer is a residual claimant in the sense that efficiencies in site and house design will save costs in soundproofing the factory equipment. The arrangement would be less than optimal, however, if the factory owner did not bear some of the liability for noise, subsequent to installing the new equipment. The factory owner has control of the noise source and must be given the incentive (via noise limits, penalties and incentives to reduce noise, for example) to act with restraint. The factory owner then also becomes a residual claimant in the sense that keeping noise below agreed limits saves penalty costs. The efficient allocation of property rights in a solution to an externality – or more generally a public domain – problem, will invariably involve a division of ownership and liabilty between polluter and polluted. Put another way, the *subsidiarity rule* implies that the externality should be internalised by all major parties to the problem, in proportion to their ability to influence the outcome.

To illustrate the points we have made so far about values, criteria and the choice of externality solution, consider Figure 7.1, which plots private benefits and social costs in relation to a polluting factory.

In a free market regime in which a factory owner has the right to pollute, output will be $Q2$ and externality costs equal the area $B+D+C$. This is inefficient in a Pareto sense since at this level of output, the pollution-related cost of an additional unit of output is greater than the benefit of that unit to the factory owner. This remains true for the region $Q2$ to $Q1$ and there are potential gains from negotiating reduced output (equal to the triangle C).

An absolutist view of the right of individuals to exploit private resources for private benefit might accept the externality problem as the price of individual liberty. At the other extreme, an absolutist view of the right to be free from pollution is consistent with banning the polluting activity completely ($Q0$). In terms of the figure, the externality valuation curve for someone with this view is vertical at the origin – any amount of output is too much because it pollutes. If a single-issue lobby group succeeds in achieving a ban, then other members of society will pay a price. Compared with the free market outcome, the price of removing the factory owner's right to operate is equal to total benefit to society ($A+B+D$) less total externality costs ($B+C+D$). This is negative if $C>A$, in which case a ban yields net gains to wider society and the lobbyists have done everyone a favour. It is positive if $C<A$, in which case a ban yields net losses and the lobbyists have effected a

redistribution of wealth equal to the difference (*A–C*) from the community at large to themselves.

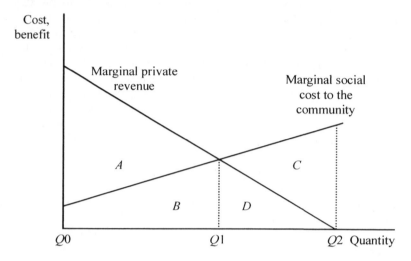

Figure 7.1   Efficiency of regulation, exaction, censorship and de-regulation

If the factory is permitted to operate but on condition that it compensates the community for externality costs imposed, it might be expected to cut back production to a level at which the value of its liability for an additional unit of output equals the marginal profit yielded (*Q*1). This is an efficient outcome, with property rights over the contested public domain resource (say air), assigned to residents in the form of compensation valued at *B*. If the community has the power, it might seek to assign to itself rights to a share of the factory's wealth in excess of the value of the externality, that is a portion of *A* as well as *B*. If it attempts to redistribute all of the factory's profits (*A+B*) then it removes the firm's incentive to operate and the outcome has a similar effect to a complete ban. This happened for a short period in the UK development industry immediately after World War II when government attempted to impose a 100 per cent improvement levy on land development, and entrepreneurial activity slowed to a halt as a result.

If the factory is permitted to operate but only at output levels somehow judged to be socially acceptable, say *Q*1, and without having to pay compensation, then the factory owner gains *A+B* and residents face externalities valued at *B*. In this case, rights over clean air (valued by residents at *B*) are assigned to the factory up to the permitted output level *Q*1. The factory has the right to pollute up to a certain density of pollution and beyond this density (represented by the height of the externality curve at $Q1$), residents have the air rights.

In terms of the *subsidiarity rule*, the object of an agreement ('contract') might be to maximise the value $(A+B+D)-(B+D+C)$. This requires incentives that induce the factory to move from $Q2$ towards $Q1$ and, if appropriate, incentives that induce the polluted party to reduce the size of the externality $(B+D+C)$ by taking evasive action.

With the foregoing discussion of distributional issues in mind, we now turn to a systematic consideration of property rights realignment in the face of externality problems.

7.3   APPROACHES TO TACKLING EXTERNALITIES

In Chapter 5 we caricatured the urban externality problems as one in which a city's n inhabitants produce n^2-n possible inter-personal consumption spill-overs. Imposing order on n^2-n unpriced resource flows may be attempted in a number of ways. Missing markets may spontaneously turn into markets as contested resource values rise. Governments may promote new markets in sectors of the economy or in city neighbourhoods blighted by poor image, high risk and other public domain problems arising as third party effects. Small numbers of individuals or firms may negotiate compensation or bribes to solve local externality problems. Communities may negotiate with polluters. Governments may regulate or tax. Entrepreneurial residential, commercial, industrial and leisure clubs may supply shared facilities that yield positive externalities to members. Residents and firms may sort themselves into homogeneous neighbourhoods, cities, regions and countries in pursuit of positive externalities and to avoid harmful third party effects.

A wide choice of institutions may therefore emerge to assign property rights in the face of externalities. They may emerge voluntarily or by government imposition and the efficiency of any institution will depend on the costs of creating and maintaining it and the benefits of reducing property rights ambiguity. First we discuss the *do nothing* option. Private individuals, firms and governments may all choose to do nothing about an externality after weighing up the costs and benefits. If the costs and benefits demand it, voluntary solutions of various kinds can emerge and we discuss these briefly. We then discuss a range of collective action solutions normally associated with government. It should be understood, however, that any form of governance, including the private governance within firms may resort to the strategies of information and persuasion, direct investment, taxation, subsidy and regulation.

In our discussion we take the negotiable view of social welfare (or wealth) in which a solution is superior if it raises total wealth in society (the economy, the city, the club and so on). However, we point out the distributional consequences of each class of solution and use the notion of net social gain/loss to make explicit the opportunity costs of different property right assignments.

Do Nothing

Individuals and even organised groups of individuals can choose to ignore third party costs. It is not difficult to think of examples in which individuals weigh up the costs of a fight and decide against it. Home owners tolerate bad neighbours up to a point. The owners of a water-using factory may accept a degree of upstream pollution. Commuters submit to traffic queues. Inhabitants of cities like Athens, Santiago and Bogota learn to live with dangerously low air quality.

Non-response is always measured and conditional, however. There must always be a point at which noise, water quality, commute times or air quality trigger action (the *subdivision rule*). Individual action includes complaining to and negotiating with the originator of a point-source externality; seeking a settlement via the courts; asserting economic might by force; lobbying government; organising or participating in collective action; and changing behaviour to avoid the externality. Conversely, no actions are costless. *Voice* options (see Chapter 4) require an investment of time and other resources in searching for the right person to talk to; researching the issue; litigation; and forming or joining an organisation. *Exit* options give rise to costs of relocation, switching transport mode, switching products and so on.

The *do nothing* option is an equilibrium response only so far as the costs of action and the degree of the externality problem remain within bounds. If either the transaction costs of exiting or giving voice change, or the nature or degree of the problem changes, then action might become a rationale response. When the State of California enacted its *Whistleblower Protection Act*, supported by a confidential whistleblower hotline, the personal cost of making a complaint about misconduct, incompetence, or inefficiency by a state employee was reduced. As a result, more people will have taken action to report opportunist behaviour that imposes third party costs on customers, colleagues and the tax-paying public.

Where the anticipated payback from action is low compared to the cost of action, externality problems can drift on. Societies appear willing to accept spectacular secular declines in welfare if externalities proceed by stealth. Traffic congestion and air quality in many major cities of the world had reached crisis point by the end of the twentieth century with little sign of net out-migration to secondary cities or abandoning roads for public transport. It often takes a crisis or political intervention to trigger action where the transaction cost threshold for action–non action has settled at a high level. It took the 1984 methyl isocyanate gas leak in Bohpul, India to galvanise action against firms like Union Carbide. The tragic death toll and large numbers of chronically ill survivors made it politically more feasible to give voice in other cases of industrial pollution, raised the anticipated gains of action and generally lowered the costs of joining organised action.

Returning to Figure 7.1, the economy-wide cost of doing nothing compared to an outright ban depends on the relative size of the private gain and social costs. If $C<A$ then leaving a polluting activity alone is a better option than banning it from the point of view of total social product. If $C>A$, then a ban is better. This is a static analysis, however, and an increase in the value of social costs or falling cost of action might give rise to solutions in the course of time. This is true of individual and collective action and the different kinds of response discussed below will be triggered at different points as these values change.

Voluntary Solutions – Negotiation, Mediation, Litigation and Unitisation

Some externality problems yield to privately negotiated solutions. Organised mediation can reduce the costs of voluntary solutions (see below) and formal resolution in the courts provides solutions for those who deem the costs worth it. Unitisation is a different kind of voluntary solution and closely relates to our discussion of clubs in the previous chapter. Being un-marketed goods, externalities as we have noted provide opportunities for entrepreneurs. An economic principle that might guide an entrepreneur in this respect is to look for opportunities to combine property rights into new forms of organisation that supply goods and services with lower externalities than close substitutes. Hotels, malls, multi-product hypermarkets, department stores, condominiums, gated suburbs, university campuses, airport and hospital concourses and science parks all provide pleasant environments for trading, with on the whole fewer externalities than substitute locations. The advantages are due to the superior way property rights are combined and managed. Shop units and perhaps customers too, pay rental and price premiums for cleaner, safer, air-conditioned and more attractive environments and have a say in management decisions. The nexus of contracts within a science park gives individual businesses something of a co-ownership stake and they are likely to act more responsibly in their consumption of shared goods. Indeed, their contracts may oblige them to, so making property rights over contestable goods clear.

The collective behaviour of individual shops in the Stanley bargain market at Stanley Bay and the Lan Kwai Fong precinct off D'Aguilar Street in Hong Kong (the latter known to expatriates as 'Soho') testifies to the possibilities of privatising positive externalities and internalising negative externalities by voluntary organisation. The Stanley market was originally a run-down residential area with a few shops along a narrow lane (Stanley New Street) that sold clothes and daily necessities to the British garrison stationed at Stanley Fort. A more entrepreneurial shopkeeper stocked some export garments with tourists in mind. In due course, the entire lane became a shopping area for tourists. There being no centralised property management, each individual shop has air-conditioning units. The cool air of each shop escaped into the lane as a kind of positive externality – cool air mass in front of each shop is an asset for shops in sub-tropical Hong Kong. Given the narrowness of the lane as well as the frontage of each shop, it pays for each shopkeeper to construct a transparent canopy over the stretch of lane in front of his or her shop to retain as much cool air as possible. It was not long before a contiguous canopy appeared along the entire shopping area, serving as a facility not only for air-conditioning but also acting as a rain shelter.

Lan Kwai Fong was initially a backyard area in the foothill area of Central District (in which the traditional CBD of Victoria City lies) with a supermarket and a few Chinese restaurants. The opening up of an English pub soon became an anchor for the proliferation of places for drinking, dancing and other western entertainment. Eventually, a trade association was organised which holds festivals and lobbied government for improvement to the locality (planting, street paving and pedestrianisation). The business success of this 'Soho' district has also led to gentrification and re-development of its hilly hinterland areas: all without any high-handed state intervention (from, for example, the Land Development Corporation or Urban Renewal Authority). Indeed, the incremental and piecemeal but stylish redevelopment triggered off by the English pubs would not have been possible if the government renewal agencies had become involved. They tend to develop in large blocks and the choice of shop tenants would be the top-down decision of a property manager rather than the spontaneous choice of individual entrepreneurs.

Individuals and firms can also take bilateral action to combine the property rights of producers and consumers of externalities. A smart hotel that buys out the scrap metal yard on neighbouring land can remove the externality and rent the land for a use complementary to its own business and yielding positive externalities. A factory owner can buy the rights to use river water. A waterfront property owner can buy rights to reclaimed land in front of its properties to optimise sea views, layout, rents, welfare and profit on the combined site.

Information and Persuasion

In the absence of voluntary solutions, or perhaps in response to their high costs, collective action may give rise to strategies that rely on the provision of information or more active persuasion.

Urban plans provide information that helps private and public investors in property and infrastructure to make good decisions – decisions that reduce the social costs of their decisions on others and reduce their own exposure to third party costs. Urban renewal plans and campaigns aim to persuade private investors, by vision and public sector investments, to act collectively to eliminate the externalities that plague blighted areas. Hearts and minds campaigns by governments and other groups aim to change tastes, preferences, values and fashions. Campaigns to drive more safely, wear seat-belts, give up smoking, eat more healthily, avoid jay walking, burn green fuel and to stop spitting in public all attempt to reduce consumption externalities that have high social costs.

Direct Investment

Externality problems may alternatively be addressed by increasing capacity of the contested resources. Governments build more roads and widen existing ones to reduce congestion and related third party effects of driving. Manufacturing firms buy more land to avoid spillover costs between different production processes. Master planned communities buy out adjacent land to remove an eyesore. Buying your way out of an externality problem is both a limited and often a shortsighted solution, however. The British government cut its road investment plan in the 1990s, including a planned widening of London's peripheral motorway when research told them what they already knew: building roads only increases traffic. Most externality problems require more sophisticated management.

Subsidise Transaction Costs

Our analysis of non-action suggests that one approach to resolving externality problems is to lower the transaction costs that inhibit collective action and negotiated settlement. This may be interpreted in the widest sense to include action that supports lobbying organisations; legislation that oils the wheels of legal resolution; and subsidy of advocacy, mediation and brokerage services.

At one level, national governments subsidise dispute resolution by making laws of Tort. Laws covering environment, planning, transport, health and safety and so on, subsidise other kinds of transaction cost by clarifying rights, liabilities and procedures. Zoning ordinances and other statutory controls over urban land development reduce information costs and uncertainty in the land market. By designating preferred patterns and densities of land uses they make the avoidance of externalities less costly and can speed a resolution in the case of a dispute. The UK government has been exploring the idea of an environmental court similar to those in operation in New Zealand and Australia (Grant, 2000). This would create a specialised judiciary body (for example an environmental division of the High Court or a separate court similar to the UK Employment Appeals tribunal), which in principle would handle environmental disputes more efficiently.

Mediation services exist to facilitate dispute resolution without resort to the courts. Many municipal governments offer mediation services for disputes arising from local externality problems, especially neighbour problems. State and national governments subsidise mediation services to lower the costs of resolving conflicts that arise from their own programmes, for example the Florida-based agricultural mediation service run for the United States Department of Agriculture. Brokerage and advocacy services such as citizens' advice bureaux reduce information costs faced by those exploring various kinds of action in response to third party costs.

It is not only governments that invest resource in order to lower the costs of dispute resolution. Firms and voluntary organisations may do so for their own reasons. Well established professions have their own institutions for handling internal disputes. Voluntary agencies provide services for their target groups and firms may subscribe to commercial mediation services that will save them costs in disputes with customers and suppliers.

The efficiency of these services as an alternative to – or supplement to – the more usual governmental tools of tax and regulations, is an interesting and under researched issue. To the extent that mediation allocates contested property rights by negotiation and consent suggests that at a microanalysis, these services are more efficient than blunter instruments that assign property rights by regulation or fiscal measures. They also have the effects of keeping a proportion of cases out of the courts. Against this should be set the costs of running the services.

7.4   FISCAL APPROACHES TO TACKLING EXTERNALITIES

Compared to the measures already discussed, taxes and subsidies are more general incentive structures that attempt to order contested public domains by assigning (and pricing) liabilities.

Tax the Polluter

An obvious way of tackling wasteful competition over unpriced resources is
to price the resources. Pigou's tax solution (1920, 1934) is one approach. A
tax equal to marginal social damage levied on a polluting producer has the
effect of internalising the externality. The tax liability is a surrogate liability
for the externality, and if it is tied to the externality effectively, it gives the
polluter the incentive to operate at a socially efficient level of output – where
the marginal value of externality equals the marginal benefit to the producer.
The Pigovian logic is illustrated in Figure 7.2.

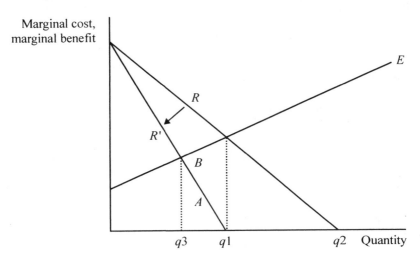

Figure 7.2   Tax the polluter

The figure shows marginal private benefit R (net revenue) against
marginal third party cost E (externality value) for different quantities of
output. E can also be thought of as marginal abatement cost – the amount a
polluted individual or community of individuals is willing to pay to reduce
output by one unit. The non-zero intercept of E indicates that the mere
presence of the producer imposes a degree of social cost even when there is
no production. The upward slope of E means that the intensity of pollution
rises with output.

It is of interest to consider the problem purely in efficiency terms by
assuming that the polluter is a public company owned by the polluted
community, all members of which are shareholders. The community has the
incentive to find ways of keeping the firm's output at $q1$ since beyond that
point, marginal pollution costs exceed the marginal gains from production. It

might achieve this by taxing output with a tax calibrated such that production is optimised at $q1$. In the figure, R' (marginal revenue net of tax) becomes negative after $q1$. Assuming that the tax revenue is used to benefit all members of the community, the tax is not redistributional in this hypothetical case; it is just a device to correct the misallocation of production resources arising from the unpriced externalities.

Reality differs in at least five important respects.

First, pollution tax normally means redistribution from polluters to the polluted. Pigovian pollution tax assigns property rights over contested resources in favour of the polluted. As we have seen, this is a moral position and public policy that redistributes via tax, needs to be legitimised through public discussion. There may be certain circumstances where it is morally more acceptable to subsidise the polluter or tax the polluted to achieve the same result in terms of reduced pollution (as suggested by Buchanan and as illustrated in our story of the factory and house developer).

Second, information is not perfect in the real world. It is neither possible to measure marginal abatement accurately nor to aggregate individual valuations (the former due to problems of preference revelation discussed in the previous chapter and the latter demonstrated by Arrow's impossibility theorem). The curve E in Figure 7.2 is therefore a useful qualitative analytical device at best. If E cannot be estimated accurately then neither can $q1$ and the calibration of any tax designed to align private and social costs must rely on past experience, guesswork and assumptions about what the market can bear. The tax calibration problem is compounded where externalities exist in markets that are monopolistic or oligopolistic and where there are many other forms of state intervention. The practical reality of pollution taxes is often far removed from Pigou's notion of a levy equal to marginal abatement cost. It should be noted, however, that digital monitoring and pricing technology improves the chances of getting it right. More accurate information about the behaviour of externalities can lead to more informed public debate and better aligned tax regimes (congestion pricing on roads, for example).

Third, and more technically, critics of Pigou have pointed out that where the technology and economics of production do not conform to the neat assumptions of micro-economics, for example because of increasing returns to scale, then there may be many local output optima. In such circumstances, equilibrium prices adjusted by a Pigovian tax do not necessarily lead to the optimum (Baumol, 1972; Shibata and Winrich, 1983).

Fourth, transaction costs are not zero. Taxation is not a costless exercise. A minimum requirement for an efficient Pigovian tax, is that the unit cost of administering the tax should be less than the externality costs saved. Beyond this, however, the benefits should outweigh the benefits of alternative deployments of public resources. Consider again the choice between a total ban on a polluting activity and some other form of intervention – say a Pigovian tax. If the transaction costs of implementing a tax are sufficiently high – for example, the costs of educating the public, softening those to be taxed and designing and creating the legal and bureaucratic system – then it might be a rational option either to ban the activity altogether or to leave it alone. This is especially so if there are large sunk transaction costs involved (for example political campaigns) with unpredictable outcomes. We have already explored the efficiency of these options in Figure 7.1.

Fifth, tax interferes with the price incentive mechanism and can have unforeseen and sometimes perverse effects. Buchanan and Stubblebine (1962) noted that the classic Pigovian tax solution illustrated in Figure 7.2 could induce producers to reduce output not to the socially optimal level $q2$, but to something less than that – $q3$. This is because between $q2$ and $q3$ the polluted parties face third party costs equal to the two triangles $A+B$ while the value of output to the polluter is equal to only A. If the two sides can negotiate, the polluter will accept anything above A to reduce output. Depending on the power of the two sides, B will get distributed between polluted and polluter, with negotiation stopping at $q2$ at which point the polluted parties can no longer offer enough to compensate for further losses. It might seem improbable that bargaining would ensue subsequent to the imposition of a tax regime (Mishan, 1988), but the conditions are in place for this to happen whenever there are multiple layers of regulatory and fiscal interventions influencing market transactions, particularly where discretion is involved, leading to the negotiation of the public 'take'.

Where pollution taxes are used directly to mitigate the problems of pollution (hypothecation), perverse incentives might unwittingly be created that lead to sub-optimal outcomes. Olson and Zeckhauser (1970) note that if victims are compensated for the full loss caused by an externality they have no incentive to protect themselves from it. If a polluted community negotiating with a polluting firm receives compensation equal to area B in Figure 7.1, equilibrium will prevail with the firm, taking into account the social costs of its activities. The equilibrium is only a local and partial one, however, and ignores other resource deployments such as the residents or polluting firm relocating. Olson and Zeckhauser's point is that it may be cheaper for victims to take evasive action than for a polluter to compensate.

This is similar to a point made by Coase in his 1930 paper on social costs. Local equilibria achieved through bargaining may be inferior to alternative system-wide solutions (general equilibria) in which the resources that cause the externality problem (be they the resources owned by the polluted or the polluter) are redeployed in some other activity. Webster and Wu (2001) explore this idea in an urban land market simulation. They show that where property rights over land development (including the right to tax polluting land users for externality costs imposed) are assigned to residential communities, polluting land users have the incentive to locate away from residential neighbourhoods. If on the other hand, communities compensated polluters to reduce output (which in principle would lead to the same locally efficient levels of output and externalities), polluters would have no incentive to avoid those that their activities harm, and total quantity of externalities in the city would be higher. Indeed, some firms may seek to locate near to residential neighbourhoods in order to maximise compensation revenue. Bowyer (1992) considers a similar perverse effect of Pigovian taxation (taxation in the form of 'planning gain'), demonstrating that municipal authorities invested with property rights over externalities may seek to maximise compensation revenue rather than to optimise externality abatement.

All these examples demonstrate that the distribution of property rights (over land, development rights and local externalities) has a bearing on the total welfare in a city or an economy. This seems to contradict Coase's invariance theorem. It is, however, a special case of Coase's own argument that locally acceptable solutions to externality problems (which in principle can be achieved whoever has the property rights) should be evaluated against alternative system-wide deployments. Alternative *spatial order* in a city is a special case of this general equilibrium or opportunity cost argument.

Subsidise the Polluter

The reciprocal nature of externality problems means that in some circumstances it might be expected that solutions evolve in which payments are made to the polluter. We have already given an illustration. Such payments are sometimes referred to as bribes in the literature, but this often seems to reflect a lack of understanding of reciprocity. Subsidies paid by governments to polluting firms to invest in pollution-reducing equipment or practices involve redistribution from the polluted (or potentially polluted) parties to the polluter. This happens routinely through tax credits for clean investments, conversion of energy supplies, home insulation and so on. In such circumstances polluters are given a right to a certain amount of the polluted community's wealth on the condition that the transfer is invested in a way that will lessen externality costs. The polluting firm or household voluntarily cedes economic rights over the contested resource (air, water, road space and so on) by entering into a contract with the subsidising authority. If the polluter is required to make a matching contribution from its own wealth, then liability is shared and the polluter cedes rights over some of its own resources as well as rights to pollute.

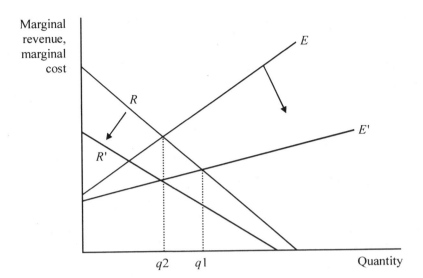

Figure 7.3   Subsidising the polluter

The case is illustrated in Figure 7.3. If the subsidy covers 100 per cent of costs of externality-reducing investments (emission filters, landscape buffering and so on) the effect is to reduce third party costs (*E* moves to *E'* in Figure 7.3) without changing private revenue. Socially optimal output rises from *q*1 to *q*2 and there is a net gain to society so long as the cost of the investment (not shown in the figure) is less than the gains to the economy from increased production. Where some of the costs fall to the firm then its marginal revenue will fall (*R* moves to *R'*). In the special case shown in Figure 7.3 output doesn't change despite the subsidy since the lower revenue and lower externality costs intersect at the output level prior to subsidy. Social gains have been achieved, however, since there are fewer externalities in the system.

Subsidise the Polluted Party

As we have already noted, government may choose to compensate victims directly with taxation raised from polluters. In the UK, landfill tax is hypothecated by being placed in a fund that can be called upon for local projects that have remedial effect on the local environment. A form of indirect hypothecation (in kind) occurs when convicted criminals are required to undertake activities that remedy their crimes or otherwise compensate their victims. In all such cases, property rights over a portion of the externality producer's wealth are redistributed to the third party.

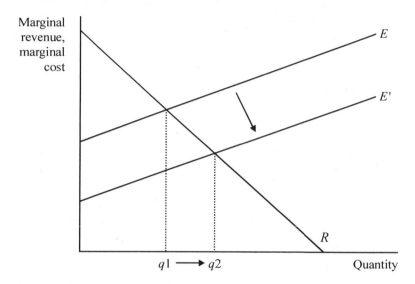

Figure 7.4   Subsidising the polluted

Public subsidy to third party victims of private transactions (as opposed to public sector action) may otherwise be justified on grounds of maintaining stability in a vulnerable market or economic sector or on grounds of vicarious suffering (society *cares* about innocent third parties).

Diagrammatically, subsidising victims of externalities to take evasive action has the effect of reducing the level of E, as in Figure 7.3. Figure 7.4 is drawn with E' parallel to E, however, making the point that evasive action can lower 'existence' externalities as well as output-related externalities. Subsidising the relocation of a village from the shadow of a heavy industry plant or from a location down stream to a new dam reduces E at all levels of output.

Some externality solutions involve a redistribution of property rights between individuals in the community. This happens when a government compensates a group affected by a local externality using general taxation revenue, for example, by subsidising the cost of relocation away from a new road or soundproofing homes near an airport. The rationale for (and justice of) such action is stronger when the externality arises from a public infrastructure project, in which case general taxpayers, being beneficiaries of the infrastructure, may reasonably be expected to assume liability for third party costs.

Tax the Polluted Party

A less intuitive fiscal solution to externalities, but nevertheless one that as we have already suggested, may yield efficiencies, is to tax third parties. Taxing victims seems unjust – unless the victims consciously bring the problem upon themselves. Making oneself a victim of third party costs and then seeking to penalise the perpetrator is by most reasonable criteria, unjust. Taxing third party communities to subsidise or compensate polluters may also be the only option where the latter have the greater power.

Buchanan and Stubblebine (1962) contend that both the polluted and the polluter should be taxed in order to overcome the problem of negotiating output reductions subsequent to taxation (Figure 7.2 above) – their reasons corresponding to Barzel's (1997) analysis of efficient ownership division and what we have called the subsidiarity rule. Taxing a polluted community is also the flip-side of subsidising the polluter since the latter has to be funded somehow. The population of a town whose water supply is polluted by effluent from a major industrial employer may have the incentive to subsidise the fitting of clean technology via their taxes. The firm's importance to local employment may give it a strong enough position to resist coercive attempts to make it clean up its act. The town's inhabitants broadly accept the pollution as a cost of jobs but individually would be willing to pay something to see the factory made cleaner. Cleaning up the factory becomes a public good that is unlikely to be delivered efficiently because of free riding and preference revelation problems and the government therefore assumes the liability on behalf of citizens. This scenario assumes that the factory owners have the *de facto* (economic) property rights to pollute, due either to the absence of regulative or fiscal powers or to the ineffectiveness of such powers in practice. The latter is very common in developing and transitional economies. In terms of Figure 7.1, the community has the incentive to pay the factory anything up to *D+C* and the factory has the incentive to accept anything over *D*, but collective action problems inhibit such a solution. Government taxation of a polluted community is a way of organising the transfer of *D* plus a portion of *C* from the community to the polluting firm.

7.5 REGULATIONS

Regulations provide an alternative means of correcting public domain resource allocations in the absence of market prices. Regulations confer *legal* property rights by the assertion of statutes and rules. They confer *economic* property rights only by effective policing of those rules, however. They may seek to control an externality directly, as with emission controls on car engines or indirectly via the regulation of inputs to a production process or the regulation of output.

Regulation of Product Output

Figure 7.5 plots demand and supply curves (*D* and *S*) for a production process that generates externalities *E*. A tax equal to the marginal abatement cost *E* would move the private cost curve *S* to *S* ' and reduce output to a level (*m*') that takes account of the share of production costs borne by third parties (point *q*1 in Figure 7.2). Imposing a production quota of *m*' achieves the same effect. This is what happens, in effect, when a government sets production quotas for a polluting industry; limits development densities in certain zones; restricts the number of gambling premises in a city; limits the opening hours of gasoline stations and food and drink outlets in residential neighbourhoods; and restricts entry of tourists or recreationalists to sensitive natural or historic sites. In practice, it is unlikely that social or private cost schedules will be understood with any accuracy, however, and the theoretical optimum *m*' is to all intents and purposes unknowable. Regulators therefore have to rely on the judgement of experts, the public and public administrators when setting output regulations. This gives a double imprecision – on the one hand, output is being used as a surrogate for the externality and on the other, crude judgements are made about the efficiency of different outputs.

Regulation of Inputs

Instead of regulating production, a government may restrict the overall level of externalities by regulating factors of production. It is rather more usual for regulations to impose limits on land for polluting activities than to impose output quotas on those activities. The allocation and control functions of land use planning and zoning may be viewed in this way. Traffic externalities are now commonly addressed in European cities by limiting land allocated to public car parks and restricting the parking spaces permitted in private commercial – and even housing – developments. Housing development in land-scarce countries and regions is controlled by land quotas. Quotas, it may be noted, serve different purposes for different actors. The British government imposes *minimum* housing quotas on UK local authorities for the purpose of ensuring a sufficient national and local housing supply. Local governments in congested areas contest the quotas on the basis of their own *maximum* quotas of housing land derived from capacity studies.

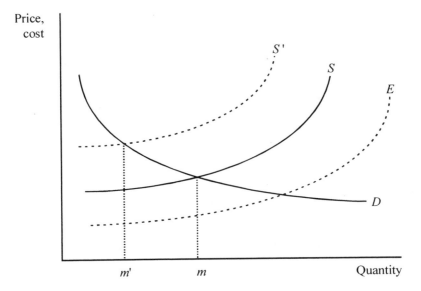

Figure 7.5   Regulating production output

Zoning and development control regulations regulate not only the quantity of land in different uses but land use *patterns*. This may be viewed as a co-ordinated regulation of the land input across all sectors of the urban economy. One of the strengths of land use planning is that it is a multi-sector or system-wide device that considers trade-offs in the allocation of land between sectors. In fact land use regulations typically attempt to control the quantity of production output via planning conditions and density controls; the quantity and spatial allocation of land inputs; and the quantity of certain externalities such as traffic, noise and visual pollution, directly via development permit conditions.

Regulation of Externalities Directly

Legislating against the physical source of externalities generally requires more information than does the regulation of outputs or inputs. Indeed, one of the reasons for the presence of land use controls in all countries of the world and its resilience over time must be the low cost of obtaining information about land. Unlike other resources, land cannot easily be hidden or creatively accounted for. Effective emission regulation requires investment in sophisticated technology and must be policed by experts. Policing health and safety, noise, water quality and design regulations is a very costly activity by virtue of the uniqueness of each externality problem and its local nature. Generally, externalities arising from single-source activities and with ubiquitous effects are easier to control directly. Externalities that build up from multiple small and individually insignificant sources (such as those that blight 'bad' neighbourhoods) and those which impose very localised costs are more costly to regulate directly.

In terms of Figure 7.5, since direct regulation of externalities will usually impose additional costs on a producer, they will have the effect of both lowering E and moving S to the right. As in Figure 7.3 (where the same effect is shown by a move of net revenue R to the left and a fall in E), this can mean that output remains the same, but with lower private benefits and lower social costs; that output is increased (due to the fall in E counteracting the effect of a rise in production costs); or decreased (due to the opposite effect).

7.6   CONTESTED INSTITUTIONAL ORDER

Regulations and taxation are used to 'correct' market inefficiencies due to property rights ambiguities, and they do this by assigning rights and liabilities over various resources that have a bearing on externality problems. They make their 'market corrections' by reassigning rights over wealth in the form of compensation, tax and subsidy; by reassigning rights over land and other factors of production; and by attempting to assign property rights over public domain goods such as clean air and water.

The redistributional nature of all interventions means that certain approaches will inevitably favour certain groups. Even an approach that subsidises transaction costs is bound, in practice, to favour some groups over others. While the specific equity outcomes will be different for each externality problem, there are certain general principles that can be established in respect of the preferences that different groups in society have for different forms of intervention. Competition between groups for methods of ordering public domain resources has an important influence on the path through which cities evolve. In the following, we caricature the nature of this competition by way of a set of propositions relating to the preferences of different groups for different types of intervention. The wealth transfer implications help shape the form of rent-seeking behaviour.

Producers

As a general rule, producers may be expected to prefer regulations to taxes because regulations tend to confer upon them the right to obtain greater profits from market transactions. Where regulations restrict both the quantity of output (directly or via restricting inputs such as land) and the entry of new firms into the industry or the local market, then existing producers will find themselves able to charge premium prices. They may also be able to lower investment, marketing, labour and other costs. In the extreme, a small group of producers may be able, in the absence of competition, to act as a cartel with the costs of protecting their favoured status borne by government. Consider Figure 7.6, which shows supply and demand curves for the house building industry in a congested region such as South-East England or Northern Italy. The effect of local governments limiting the quantity of land for housing development is to provide producers with the opportunity of charging premium prices (*Pr*). To the extent that competition prevails in the market, producers will have the incentive to pass the premium (*Pr–P*) on to house buyers. In a mature congested housing market it is likely that economies of scale and other forces will have led to the dominance of a small number of large firms, however, and it can be expected that some or all of (*Pr–P*) will be retained by producers. This will be all the more so if the regulations increase barriers to entry – due to specialised knowledge required to negotiate them, the higher costs of land, banking and other operations, and so on.

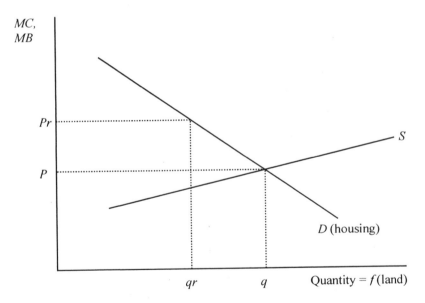

Figure 7.6   Regulations and premium prices

The practical implication is that government should be wary of introducing regulations in uncompetitive markets and seek ways of reducing perverse price effects.

There is a second set of reasons why producers may prefer regulations to taxation methods of externality abatement. Regulations require the regulating agency to create information in order both to design efficient regulations and to monitor them. Where the information is made public it will often serve as useful (free) market intelligence for producers.

In the early 1980s the reforming Thatcher government took steps to reduce the scope and strength of the statutory urban planning function of British local authorities (Thornley, 1991). By the end of that decade, however, land use regulations were stronger than at its start and the developer and house building industry were among the interests lobbying for stronger plans. Stronger public land use plans mean greater certainty, reduced risk, lower private information-gathering costs and lower market transaction costs (Alexander, 1992).

Regulations may confer advantages upon producers but they are, by nature, less flexible than taxation approaches. *Tradable* quotas, on the other hand, allow producers to make their own decision within a regulatory regime to the advantage of the industry but without compromising the goals of the regulations. Figure 7.7 shows two developers' demand schedules for additional floors (F) in a building on a standard plot. Developer A produces apartments and B produces offices. B can profitably build more floors than A and can also bid a higher price for each. Imagine that a municipal authority imposes a broad-brush density regulation aimed principally at controlling traffic and related congestion and pollution externalities. It sets a limit of five floors for any type of use, represented in the diagram by the right-most dotted line.

This is inefficient from the point of view of the two firms since it leaves gains from trade unrealised. It may be efficient in the aggregate analysis of reducing traffic towards some acceptable total but its lack of discrimination leads to avoidable losses to society. With the regulation strictly applied to all buildings, both developers have to reduce output (build at lower heights than they would like to) but B's loss is greater than A's. Below five floors, B values additional floors more than A values a reduction in floors and this holds up to point F. If the two were permitted to trade property rights over building height they would both gain without compromising total traffic volumes. F is the trading equilibrium. Between five and F, firm B is willing to pay anything up to ($C+D$) for additional floors, and firm A is willing to accept anything over D to give up its right over those floors. Bargaining would yield a minimum price of D for the exchanged property rights plus a portion of C, depending on the negotiating strengths of the two firms.

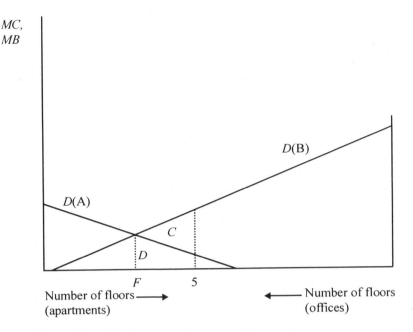

MC,
MB

D(B)

D(A)

C

D

F   5

Number of floors ⟶
(apartments)

⟵ Number of floors
(offices)

Figure 7.7   Tradable quotas

We may conclude that producers would prefer tradable to fixed quota approaches to regulating externalities so long as the costs of trading do not exceed the gains – an empirical question.

Consumers

Using the same argument, consumers also stand to benefit from tradable quotas, where this allows gains from trade between them – transferable rights to congested recreational facilities not equally valued by all, for example. In regard to consumers' preference for fiscal or regulatory control of externalities, they are likely to prefer approaches that appear to raise their welfare by the greater amount. Locally hypothecated taxation has the double advantage of reducing externality costs plus transferring wealth from the polluter to the polluted community. Tax controls that have little detectable local benefit, even if they are effective at a system-wide scale, are likely to be viewed as inferior to regulatory measures. Fuel taxes and land use controls might be effective in reducing total travel-related externalities but are not as efficient as road closures, speed limits and traffic calming. Detailed regulations that reassign property rights over contested neighbourhood resources have immediate impact. They may be costly to administer but that cost is often borne by the wider community. Residents gain the full benefits while sharing only a fraction of the costs.

Governments

Governments are made up of many groups, whose interests are differently served by different types of institution. Politicians might generally be said to seek to maximise votes. In an efficient liberal democracy this means aligning themselves with the preferences of the median voter – the class of voter capable of tipping political power by transferring allegiance to the nearest centrist party. In theory, however, politicians have a lot of scope for remaining unresponsive to externality issues, hiding behind more important issues or simply taking risks and playing games with electorates. Although the politics of specific issues are unique, some general propositions may be posed.

Central governments may be expected to be more sensitive than local governments to cost-efficiency and cost-effectiveness comparisons between alternative solutions. Local governments typically receive a proportion of their revenues as transfer payments from higher tax jurisdictions (state, regional, national or transnational governments) and are likely to be more sensitive to local impact and net transfers into the locality than to costs. They receive the full benefit of any policy to reduce local externalities but share the costs with higher governments.

From this analysis, it might be concluded that when considering taxation and regulatory institutions that broadly deliver a similar outcome, central governments will prefer taxes. To see why, consider Figure 7.8, which compares the efficiency of tax and regulatory approaches to tackling the externalities associated with two factories. The firm's demand schedules are Dn and Dm and, for convenience, have a common supply schedule S and generate a common level of externalities E.

If the factories have the economic right to produce as much as they wish, output is at qn and qm respectively. A tax on output equal to E would raise the firms' marginal cost curves to $S+E$ and output would adjust to qn' and qm' respectively. A regulation judiciously designed to move both factories near to qn' and qm' might be set at qr. This is inefficient for both factories, however, for different reasons. The regulation permits factory n to produce too much – by the triangle B. Factory m produces too little – by triangle A. This is the same situation faced by the two developers in Figure 7.7. The current point is that a government seeking value for money from tax revenue in the sense of maximising welfare in the economy will prefer the tax solution, since it avoids a welfare loss equal to $A+B$.

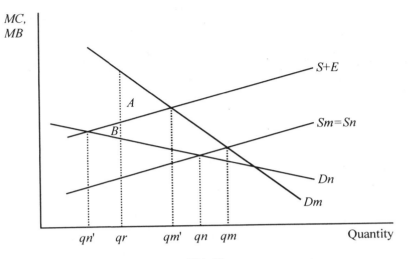

Source: Adapted from Cullis and Jones (1994: 49)

Figure 7.8   *Regulations incur welfare losses compared to Pigovian taxes*

Developing the local–central government theme further, consider one reason why local governments consistently demand strong local regulatory powers over land use. Figure 7.9 shows the marginal private benefit (*R*) derived from increasing the density of a major commercial development and the traffic and other externalities (*E*) that it generates. If the developer has economic property rights because there are no effective planning controls, then density will be *q*3, which is socially inefficient to the degree given by the height of curve *E*.

A regulatory regime that assigns development rights to the community would give a local government powers to impose a density regulation of *q*2, should it be in the improbable position of having accurate knowledge about *R* and *E*. In practice, density controls are likely to be derived from imprecise evaluations of urban infrastructure capacity and more arbitrarily from standards borrowed from elsewhere. They may not vary randomly around some notional social optimal, however, since local authorities can gain from setting standards artificially low. Commercial use densities regulated at a consciously artificially low level, say *q*1, will give a local government greater power when negotiating exactions from developers. As in many other countries, British planning laws permit the exaction of compensation for externalities that are directly related to a particular development project. Compensation can be negotiated via payments and works in kind, for example via traffic engineering works. An artificially low density regulation allows the regulating authority not only to exact compensation equal to C but also to negotiate relaxation of densities in the knowledge that this will not lead to excessive externalities. With property rights on its side, a tough local authority in a bullish development market might be able to exact profits from the negotiated density increase in excess of the extra externalities caused (that is C plus a portion of A). There is anecdotal evidence that some Southern Chinese cities coded artificially low densities into their development plans during the post-liberalisation boom years in order to negotiate lucrative gains from foreign direct investment projects.

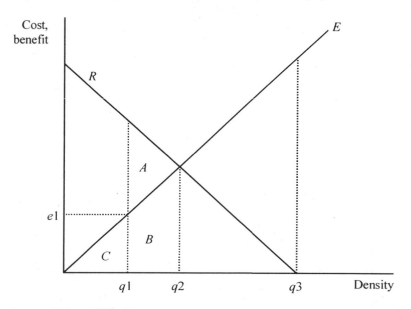

Source: Webster (1998: 66)

Figure 7.9   Regulations confer local authorities with monopoly rights

Regulations assign monopoly powers to local government therefore, which can be used to pursue objectives other than those relating to the reduction of externalities. We develop this theme in the next chapter, where we consider the costs of government action in a more systematic way.

Institutional order is contested by different groups seeking to address different externality problems with different approaches. Each has its own reasons for favouring particular kinds of solution. Over time it might be supposed that with sufficient openness in government, sufficient competition, trial and error and sufficient information, society learns which approaches are better fitted to particular problems. This knowledge will not of itself prevent different interests seeking to capture rent for themselves in externality solutions but it will tend to limit the scope for rent-seeking behaviour.

7.8 KEY ARGUMENTS OF CHAPTER 7

• Externalities are by-products of private consumption or production decisions that are consumed by third parties. They are third party effects that remain unpriced due to the high transaction cost of exclusion. At the heart of the phenomenon of externality are ill-defined property rights, incomplete information and the problem of a poorly-ordered public domain, vulnerable to wasteful competitive behaviour.

• Property rights ambiguities over externalities are problematic because:

(a) There are likely to be unexploited gains to be made from trading in them – gains that might be realised if certain transaction costs can be lowered.
(b) Resources will be employed by individuals in competing for control of externalities. Institutions arise in the process.
(c) These institutions impose their own costs.
(d) Some externalities are judged as morally wrong.

• There are many ways by which externalities may be managed:

(a) do nothing;
(b) voluntary solutions – negotiation, mediation, litigation and unitisation;
(c) information and persuasion;
(d) direct government investment;
(e) subsidise transaction costs;
(f) fiscal intervention;
(g) regulations.

• A corollary to the Coase theorem states: *If information is not perfectly distributed and transaction costs are not zero, then the outcome for any externality problem depends on the distribution of property rights.* If rights and liabilities over externalities could be clearly established and accurate information obtained about their incidence and value, then markets might develop and they would cease to be externalities.

- Recapping from Chapter 1: *The total value of a contract or of any collective action is maximised when agents with an ability to influence the value of the contract or the outcome of collective action bear the full effects of their actions. This will be achieved when agents are residual claimants over the resources they influence – such that they have an incentive to deploy their resources efficiently in the attainment of the contract of collective action goal (the subsidiarity rule).* Applied to contracts and agreements designed to resolve externality problems, the rule suggests that rights and liability should be assigned in a way that gives all parties an incentive to seek the desired result (lower externalities). The efficient allocation of property rights in a solution to an externality – or more generally a public domain – problem, invariably involves a division of ownership and liability between polluter and polluted. The externality should be internalised by all major parties to the problem, in proportion to their ability to influence the outcome.
- All interventions involve re-distribution of wealth and certain measures will inevitably favour certain groups. This would shape their rent-seeking behaviour. Producers, consumers and local governments prefer regulations such as those over outputs, whereas central governments prefer taxation.

8. Conclusion

In this final chapter we reflect upon, exemplify and summarise points made in preceding chapters. We reflect on the importance of transaction costs in influencing on the one hand, the spontaneity and on the other hand, the choice of governance system and style. We conclude that when the costs of transacting with government are low, policy experimentation should lead relatively rapidly to the dominance and spread of more efficient institutional, proprietary, spatial organisational and public domain order.

In this context we then consider three illustrations or stories of efficient governance. The first illustration involves governance of a single piece of equipment used by two co-owners to supply a private good – taxi-rides. The second illustration asks the same question – how should ownership be efficiently divided, but this time over a large and complex firm producing a public good – an urban transit system. The third illustration asks the question in respect of a complex externality problem – how should rights and liabilities over shared resources be allocated within urban neighbourhoods? The case studies cover the principal points made more theoretically in earlier chapters and are purposefully detailed in order to give illustrations of the relevance of those points to practical policy making. In particular, we emphasise in each 'story' the idea that property rights are efficiently ordered when they give resource owners an incentive to use their resources efficiently in pursuit of shared goals.

Following these case studies, we consider by way of a diagram and an illustration, how the five kinds of urban order discussed in the book interact. The interaction effects make cities complex systems, the behaviour of which is difficult, if not impossible to predict. Finally, we provide a summary of our property rights model of urban planning, markets and the management of spontaneous cities before closing the book with an epilogue on the art of property rights inquiry into urban planning and management.

8.1 TRANSACTION COSTS AND GOVERNMENT SPONTANEITY

There is an important relationship between the transaction costs of government and a society's ability to order itself efficiently. Competitive markets yield beneficial spontaneous order because of accurate information (prices). That order is defective, however, to the extent that certain resources are left in the public domain. It is the lack of information about the valuation of unpriced resources (public goods and externalities) that gives rise to disorder and to wasteful competition costs even when markets are otherwise functioning efficiently. Government often steps in to impose solutions by regulation, taxation or other methods of assigning rights and liabilities. But the information deficit problem is never fully resolved unless a competitive market develops for resources that previously lay in the public domain. Even then a new set of public domain problems will arise, as we have seen. Imperfect information means any planned intervention has a high chance of getting it wrong. Failed planned interventions, like failed market innovations are ultimately judged as such by the intended beneficiaries. The more efficiently government collects information in order to monitor impact and the more open it is with that information, the more spontaneous will the process of institutional refinement be.

Government administrative and decision making systems which impose high transaction costs on the *voice* option reduce government responsiveness to its own failures. The costs of transacting with government rise when voting systems blunt the power of the vote; when lines of responsibility and accountability are unclear; when politicians and bureaucrats have too much constitutional or informal power; and when government is heavily centralised. On the other hand, transaction costs also rise with the degree of democracy. In the extreme, if all decisions were made by referenda and other forms of direct democracy, government would grind to a halt under information and administrative overload. The various styles of representative democracy and liberalising autocracy are compromises that seek an equilibrium between information and transaction costs on the one hand and responsiveness and spontaneity on the other.

The high transaction costs of information collection, the costs of administering hierarchical organisations and the hidden agency costs of rent-seeking behaviour within government all act as barriers to spontaneity in the political market. If these are low it might be expected that over time, institutions and the order they produce evolve in a sequence of Popperian 'experiments' and converge towards more efficient solutions – ones in which property rights over a resource are assigned to those most able to influence the resource's contribution to private and social wealth.

Conversely, when the costs of transacting with and within government are high, institutional responsiveness is lower and spontaneous evolution of social order is slower. Feedback takes longer, is misunderstood and misapplied. Long and noisy feedback loops can distort intention–action–outcome processes as action is applied after it is needed or in inappropriate contexts. Resistance to institutional reforms constrains beneficial organisational, proprietary and spatial order. It can keep cities on low evolutionary paths and distorts system-learning and spontaneous resource reallocation. Dysfunctional feedback and misinformed local learning can easily bring steady-state urban systems (equilibriated urban economies) into crisis. Urban neighbourhoods can spin into decay because public domain institutions do not assign rights and liabilities efficiently. Markets and whole economies can collapse because institutions fail to make banks and investors accountable for undisciplined lending during times of property boom. Cities can lose opportunities to adopt a more efficient and sustainable spatial growth strategy because the institutions governing planning and infrastructure investment rely on inadequate information and fail to give decision makers sufficient incentive to search for the most efficient policies.

High government transaction costs also mean that the institutions of government that create those high costs will be resistant to change. Unresponsive governments and constitutions can be long-lived, therefore, and often have to be broken by various forms of popular revolt.

In the next section we draw together points we have made in previous chapters concerning the costs of government.

8.2 TRANSACTION COSTS AND THE CHOICE OF GOVERNMENT

Institutions, as human means of avoiding conflict and making peaceful social life possible, are never perfect. The reason is not only that the creations of imperfect human beings are innately limited but also that selection of one system inevitably incurs the opportunity cost of forgoing another possible system. At the level of personal introspection, one might be attracted to Thomas More's Utopia, Huxley's Brave New World, Plato's Republic, a Franciscan community or some form of econtopia. But in areas of practical decision making, individual experiences and human history are replete with examples of problems arising from bad choices of government.

If there were no artificial restrictions on immigration so that individuals could choose to enter and exit whatever governmental jurisdiction and economic system they liked, a process of natural institutional selection might prevail. The institutions most suitable for collective human existence would succeed – those that maximise individual liberty at the least collective cost – while other less effective arrangements would eventually be eliminated.

The institution of the market, viewed in this light, can only be imperfect, for clearly, most individuals are far from perfectly mobile. Unlike a community in which every one knows each other and monitors each other, the modern market is impersonal and oppressive of the less powerful. Resource allocation decisions are largely driven by the more resourceful (in terms of financial or human capital).

A market system, however, confers the greatest freedom to the greatest majority in the sense that the *status* of a person does not decisively dictate how much say he or she has in resource allocation decisions – as is the case with co-operation based on personal relationships. Market-led cities will always be plagued by social problems of alienation, anomie and powerlessness, yet they accommodate the generally peaceful and co-operative co-existence of a huge number of individuals with different characters and ways of life. Such a variety could not be tolerated in the close-knit communities of more traditional settlement. Neither could it be tolerated in a society that allocates resources by central planning, consensus and administrative decision. Centrally planned organisations require consensus and cannot easily tolerate diversity of views. Repression always follows a move towards centralisation – even in liberal democracies. Markets may not be perfect but they democratise resource allocation in the most thorough sense.

Visionaries promoting socialist institutions have often taken inspiration from the success of small communities run in a hierarchical manner, as in the case of religious orders and experimental communities. The Jesuit Fathers, with a strong hierarchical order and rich human capital that launched the Counter-Reformation, were able to establish an egalitarian Christian community in Paraguay. This utopian experiment far from Europe eventually succeeded and lasted until members of the Society of Jesus were expelled by the nationalist monarchs in Europe for political reasons.

Socialism of this kind is clearly possible but would appear to be rendered so by voluntarism. Even in voluntary communities, sustained centrally-planned communal life apparently requires institutional coercion when the community grows. Saint Francis of Assisi started a grass roots religious movement in thirteenth century Italy. It began as a spontaneous spiritual community and grew rapidly as Italian peasants voluntarily aligned themselves with Assisi's radical liberating message. It took only two years for the mystic to (reluctantly) write his first law – the 1210 Rule (Sabatier, 1924) and 13 years for a full constitution to emerge – the Rule of 1221. The former was a three-page minimalist institutional framework that was little more than a statement of faith; an inspirational rallying call: 'Come follow me, leave everything and follow God' (Sabatier, 1924: 263). Such was the movement's growth, however, and so strong the internal and external pressure to formalise it that by the time the ten-page 1221 Rule had been approved by the Pope in 1223, it had little of the spontaneity of Assisi's original message or of his 1210 Rule. It became instead, a reciprocal contract in which the call to submission of individual rights to community was viewed as a divine command to those who choose to accept it. As with other religious orders, acceptance carried something of binding commitment and the communal contract became coercive by assent. Where the informal institutions of culture and custom provide their own sanctions for breaking vows, the so-called voluntary socialism within religious communities can be truly coercive where there is no exit option. Where there is no problem of using internal coercion to maintain solidarity, a voluntary community without an apparatus of violence as a means to protect internal rights and liberties, may run the risk of being subverted by external forces. The eventual demise of the Jesuit Paraguay community is a good example. Modern religious bodies are able to flourish best in states in which the legal rights to worship and not worship are protected by the civil state.

There is an interesting parallel between the kind of spontaneous voluntary community observed in the first decade of the Franciscan movement and the spontaneous voluntary exchanges of the market place. Perhaps even the socialist ideals of submitting individual rights in favour of the rights of others can only be sustained by voluntary exchange and co-operation. Arguably Francis' movement began to die as soon as the ruling institutions of the day insisted on replacing the proscriptive 'rules' of spontaneous compassion (don't act selfishly) with the intrusive prescriptive rules of the Order.

There is a more general principle here, which arguably is a danger for all institutions that attempt to impose beneficial resource allocations. Prescriptive rules – those that prescribe outcomes – can easily crush the spontaneous individual creative activity that is needed to deliver and sustain those outcomes. Rent control, imposed racial segregation or imposed racial mixing and attempts to ban trade, for instance, work against fundamental ordering processes in society and tend to inhibit economic and social growth and development. They cannot easily survive the operation of the forces of demand and supply. Involuntary prescriptive impositions of government tend to lead to rebellion. The Continental System of Napoleon Bonaparte (a system of imposed protectionism devised to starve Britain), ultimately collapsed when Tsarist Russia learnt the cost of protectionism. The treaty ports in China (a system that conferred rights to free trade) suffered a long period of stagnation after forcibly being 'liberated' but have now re-opened voluntarily after learning costly lessons of centrally planned economics.

The system of forced labour, or serfdom in the USSR collapsed not by tipping the psychological balance by propaganda, or by a nuclear war, student uprising, or espionage. It collapsed because the employees of expensive war and police machines could no longer be paid and the working population could no longer be fed enough to turn the machines of state organised industry. That started a rapid process of dismantling the huge state apparatus that had withstood the White Army and the Wehrmacht.

Stephen Cheung in his work *Will China Go Capitalist* (1982) used Coasian arguments to explain the collapse of the twentieth century's centrally planned regimes. Recall from our discussion in Chapter 5 the Coase Theorem: 'where costs of operating institutions (or, simply, transaction costs) are zero, then the ways in which rights and liabilities are assigned will not affect the patterns of resource allocation (and hence outputs or productivity)'. By similar argument, the theorem also provides a theoretical explanation of Coase's theory of the firm. Stated simply: where transaction costs are zero, the choice between market and the firm is indifferent with respect to output. The market provides a way of co-ordinating the division of labour based on the freedom of contract. The firm is a way of co-ordinating the division of labour based on the commands of a hierarchy. A centrally planned economy as put into practice by the USSR is one single firm encompassing the whole society, a point made by Hayek in *Road to Serfdom* (1944). Cheung argues that the theorem can be extended to discuss matters as general as the whole economy, with the original formulation reinterpreted as follows: 'Where the costs of operating institutions (or, simply, transaction costs) are zero, then the *choice of economic systems* would not affect the patterns of resource allocation (and hence outputs or productivity)'. With perfect information and the corollary, zero transaction costs, central economic planning is as good as a free market economy or any other system, such as a mixed economy. Extending this to alternative varieties of mixed economy we can say that if information costs are zero, then the choice between a relatively low tax government administration (such as Hong Kong), a middling tax government (US or UK) and a strongly interventionist high tax government (France, Sweden or the newly formed East Timor) is indifferent with respect to economic output. At an urban level, the choice between a high and low intervention municipal government will not influence urban growth, wealth and welfare.

The reality is that transaction costs are not zero and are dependent on the choice of institutions at all levels. Thus, a bad choice of institutional arrangements is likely to have different economic consequences, in terms of resource allocation and productivity. At a system level, the market economy is demonstrably superior to a centrally planned economy. Cheung predicted that the centrally planned economic system of China would disintegrate due to high transaction costs. The market is more efficient than the plan in allocating goods that have the technical capacity to be rendered excludable. The former is based on the system of private property rights and the rule of law. It allows the maximum possible degree of individual liberty subject to certain prohibitions that are necessary for collective existence. The latter relies on state commands and obedience to instructions for specific actions for an infinitely large amount of requirements co-ordinated by the plan.

That is not to argue that all forms of transaction should be co-ordinated by the *invisible hand* and that all planning is inefficient. Our discussion in Chapters 5 to 7 demonstrates that planned collective action is necessary to tackle the public domain problems that are an unavoidable consequence of economic growth and urbanisation. The need for planned action will never go away.

Society will demand planning, (including land use planning, other forms of sectoral planning and spatial planning) in situations where the transaction costs of using the market are greater than using commands – the gist of Coase's theory of the firm. This is the *combination rule* in Chapter 1.

Society will prefer anarchy where the costs of creating an institution for a public domain resource are unjustifiably high. Some resources are efficiently left out of the market or of planned command entirely, as happens for most oceanic resources and some public spaces in cities and the countryside. This is the *public domain rule* in Chapter 1.

Many resources for which a degree of anarchy is planned (free-access and public domain by policy) are in reality congested and would be better organised by either efficient planned governance or markets. Most urban public spaces and other free-access urban infrastructure and services come into this category. This is the *subdivision rule* in Chapter 1.

The polar choice between a market economy and a centrally planned order is remote from most contemporary political or academic agendas. However, the popular contempt for the idea of a free market in a context of globalisation is a relevant political issue in countries with many different political systems. The choice between central planning and markets also manifests itself in contemporary debates about public service privatisation; denationalisation and deregulation of strategic industries; and about the desirable size and shape of the welfare state.

8.3   OPTIMAL SUBDIVISION AND ASSIGNMENT OF RIGHTS AND LIABILITIES

Central to these debates is the question of how rights and liabilities over civic goods and services are allocated. We have argued in this book that cities evolve as property rights combine and subdivide. We have also argued that competition and experience tends to improve the efficiency of these combinations and subdivisions. This applies in market and planned systems; in firms and in governments; with private goods and collective goods. Public domain problems will always persist, however, and the task of governance is to address these problems by clarifying rights and liabilities. This is true whether the governance is by elected politicians, appointed state officials, or decision-makers in private firms and other organisations. The limits to order are transaction costs, however. Some resources will be left in the public domain because of the high cost of assigning clear and enforceable rights. Some resources will be misallocated because of the high cost of planned order. To underline these ideas we offer three illustrations. They relate to a private good, a public good and a complex set of externality problems.

Private Goods: The Case of the Taxicab

We elaborate an illustration given by Barzel when discussing the division of ownership of equipment (Barzel, 1997: 57). We use to it to make the point that any new combination or subdivision of property yields new public domain problems that can only be addressed by collective action. When an organisation is created to produce a good or service, rules will be needed to supplant market transactions. Those rules will be able to clearly allocate rights over some resources but other resources, by virtue of the measuring and monitoring costs, will be left in the public domain. In this sense firms are like governments. The optimality of resource allocation within a firm, within the markets in which firms participate and within governments may be judged by what we termed in Chapter 1, the *subsidiarity rule*:

> The total value of a contract or of any collective action is maximised when agents with an ability to influence the value of the contract or the outcome of collective action bear the full effects of their actions. This will be achieved when agents have a residual claim on the benefits created by the resources that they influence. This way, they have an incentive to deploy their resources efficiently in the attainment of the contract of collective action goal.

Two taxi drivers share ownership of a taxicab. Apart from the personal knowledge and skills of the two drivers, the firm's main capital asset is the cab and the partnership question is 'how will ownership be divided?'. More specifically, how will property rights over the cab's various attributes be assigned: which will become exclusively divided between the two co-owners, which will be assigned to passengers, which to third parties and which will remain in the public domain?

The answers lie in the ease with which consumption of the cab's attributes can be monitored or measured and the various transacting parties' relative knowledge specialisation. Consider first, which attributes the two taxi drivers choose to take individual ownership of. If they pooled ownership of *fuel*, leaving fuel in the public domain for the two of them, each is likely to free ride at the expense of the other. Each pays only half of the fuel cost but will be tempted to use more than half the fuel by working more intensively during his time slot and by using the cab for personal journeys. Assuming the fuel gauge is accurately calibrated, they are likely to own their own fuel, therefore. This makes each a full residual claimant in respect of fuel owned encouraging efficient use; lowering wasteful competitive attempts to capture the common good; and reducing conflict.

Wear and tear on *tyres* cannot easily be measured directly but correlates well to mileage. Property rights over tyres might therefore be allocated by share of miles driven but since driving style and road surface can also influence wear and tear, the drivers are more likely to agree to leave tyres as a common good. Public domain problems will occur since each driver has a liability for half the tyre costs but can fully capture the time saved by careless driving. This might partially be solved if rights over visible tyre damage were allocated by adopting a convention by which each checks for visible damage before taking their time slot. Car-hire firms use this method.

Using the same argument, the *engine* is likely to become common property (rather than allocated on the basis of miles driven for example); more likely perhaps since it is less possible to perform visible checks for damage caused by careless driving or using substandard fuel. In regard to the latter, if the structure of fuel prices were such that each driver is tempted to buy cheaper fuel (saving the full price difference but paying for only half of the engine damage), the individual ownership of fuel is not a sufficient property rights solution to the public domain problem. In a bigger taxicab firm the problem may result in central control being taken over refuelling, or more likely, the purchase of lower specification taxis with engines better suited to cheap fuel.

Driving the taxi incurs an inevitable risk of accidental damage to the car, driver and third parties. The *accident risk* attribute is most efficiently allocated individually by each taking out separate insurance. In doing so, however, the taxicab nexus of contracts ('firm') extends beyond the two drivers. Accident risk is too costly an attribute for either to own and so they sell it to a third party – an insurer – who has expert knowledge in accommodating this kind of risk.

The *taxicab* itself is a capital good that has to be financed. Assuming that the drivers have insufficient means to purchase outright, they enter into an agreement with another 'partner' – a loan agency – who becomes a co-owner of the cab. The loan contract ensures that in the event of payment defaults, the cab is repossessed. The financier retains ownership of part of the cab's capital value until all payments are met.

Consider wear and tear of upholstery – or the converse, the attribute 'cleanliness'. This is difficult to monitor and is likely to become common property. Economic rights over *cleanliness*, however, are shared with all of the cab's riders. The drivers may attempt to limit the scope of public domain problems arising by agreeing on rules such as placing a *no smoking* sign and agreeing not to pick up passengers with food or who are drunk. Such rules attempt to assign rights over 'cleanliness' more clearly – by attenuating the rights of passengers and the rights of drivers to take fares. All parties may attempt to capture benefit from the public domain resource, however. A driver who hasn't had many fares during the day may be tempted to pick up a rowdy party late at night. A passenger may light up a cigarette after a ride has been agreed. If a valet is employed weekly to keep the cab interior in good condition the drivers will face the question of what rights and liabilities to pass on to the cleaner. If he is paid by result (the contract specifies a standard of cleanliness) then the 'cleanliness' attribute has been fully passed on to the valet. This is not the most efficient division of ownership however, since the cab drivers are in a position to influence the degree of dirtiness. Without retaining some degree of ownership of the attribute, they are likely to capture benefit for themselves by taking risky passengers in the knowledge that the valet bears all of the costs of cleaning up the mess. Ownership of wear and tear is likely therefore to be shared between drivers, valet and passengers, by a cleaning contract that specifies respective responsibilities including the drivers' responsibility to place prohibitive notices and enforce the rules.

Finally, consider the ownership of the attribute *frequency and pattern of use*. Imagine that lucrative business is to be had at a busy train station but that open access to taxis means (a) congestion at the taxi rank, (b) long waits for passengers and (c) mixed quality service resulting from inexperienced taxi drivers picking up rides to unfamiliar parts of the city. In such circumstances a franchise arrangement is likely to emerge in which drivers pay the station a weekly fee to use its rank. Property rights to station pick-ups will be allocated to a limited number of drivers, perhaps selected on the basis of length of experience or even a test. Since it is too costly for the station operator to collect information about the quality of individual drivers, it is likely to contract with a taxicab firm who subcontracts with individual drivers. The franchisee and the station operator share ownership of the station taxi customer base and they will each attempt to capture wealth from this common resource. The station will seek to maximise the franchise fee while the taxicab firm will seek to maximise the weekly fee charged to cab drivers. If either fee is too high, passengers will face a taxi shortage. If it is too low, the congestion and quality problems may return. The taxi firm is likely to have superior knowledge about demand and supply of taxi rides and is therefore likely to come out the winner as the contract evolves over time by trial, error, industrial action and negotiation. Assuming our jointly owned cab signs up with the station franchise, its *income stream* attribute is now partially owned by both the taxicab firm and the station operator. The division of ownership is efficient to the extent that contracts allocate customer revenue (via the two levels of fees) in proportion to the three parties' (drivers, taxicab firm and station operators) respective ability to influence the value of the station forecourt taxi business.

Urban Transit System: A Public Good Example

As we showed in Chapters 5 and 6, two *efficiency* arguments are usually employed to justify the public supply of major urban infrastructure. First, infrastructure such as roads and transit systems are said to be public goods by virtue of the non-excludable benefits they confer on urban populations and the non-rival manner in which they are consumed (below congestion). Goods with these characteristics are likely to be under-supplied or not supplied at all because of the problems of preference revelation and free riding. Market failure arguments assume that only government can supply to the aggregate demand curve because only it can coerce payments via taxation. Second, suppliers of urban infrastructure are said to enjoy natural monopolies by virtue of their captive markets, economies of scale and barriers to market entry. Governments should intervene (via direct supply or via indirect means), it is argued, to ensure that suppliers do not engage in monopoly pricing and perhaps also to ensure adequate investment.

In addition, urban infrastructure debates tend to generate strong feelings about equity issues – such as affordability and the distribution of ownership and control. This is the case with the recently announced London Underground public–private partnership (PPP) – the largest public–private contractual agreement ever attempted. The major opposition has rallied under a banner appealing to the idea of local control. Many distributional issues can also be thought of as efficiency issues if the 'fairness' considerations underlying them are taken to be attributes of the infrastructure or service for which there is a widespread demand. Affordability and comprehensive spatial coverage may, for example, be a widely demanded characteristic of an

MRT system. Such intangible attributes are public goods, as we have argued in Chapter 6, and are likely to be under-provided in an MRT supplied by an entrepreneur – just as affordable housing will be under-supplied by entrepreneurs in competitive housing markets.

Compelling though these rationales are in principle, public goods and natural monopoly arguments have been challenged by modern developments in technology – and by experience. The arguments provided a crucial intellectual foundation, which allowed modern urban government to emerge in the twentieth century; but circumstances have changed. Both are less powerful arguments as a result of advances in computer and information technology and in the light of the widespread experience – which suggest that government is as prone to fail in the efficient supply of civic goods and services as is the market.

Non-excludability is the principal public goods argument for state-supplied infrastructure. If a good cannot be made excludable it cannot easily be priced and there is no method by which consumers are required to reveal their true preferences. Non-rival consumption is not, on its own, an argument for government supply, but rather, an argument for supplying goods in clubs. So long as a good can be made excludable it can be supplied by an entrepreneur. If it is non-congested (in infinite supply for a group of included people), then it will not be in the entrepreneur's interest to assign rights within the co-consuming group and it will be efficient to supply it as a public domain good for a group who shares its consumption – as with a non-congested swimming pool for example. New technology has extended the class of goods that can be supplied in clubs. From water and electricity metering to road pricing using in-car tagging systems, technology means that many goods and services previously classed as non-excludable may now be viable commercial projects.

The same technology has transformed natural monopolies into arenas of competition. So long as a system of property rights is clearly defined, there is nothing now stopping a competitive market emerging to supply water, electricity, gas and telecommunication services. There appear to be advantages to commercial suppliers as well as customers in separating the rights to supply services from the rights to own and maintain the lines. It is now technically feasible to make roads, housing estates, shopping malls, working and recreational spaces excludable. It is a matter of time before cultural values and institutions adapt to make them more widely so in practice. As they do, new markets arise in civic goods and services. What remains is for the state to organise the supply of two classes of goods: 'fairness' goods and goods for which the costs of organising a payment system (including technology and institutions) outweigh the benefits of so doing. (The former is really a sub-class of the latter since if information were sufficiently complete to fully assign individual rights to a civic good, say transport, then it would also be possible to make decisions about pricing structures that meet agreed standards of fairness).

In the context of this analysis, transit systems like the London Underground stand in something of an ambiguous position, and this often clouds and confuses public and professional debate. The transport services they provide are clearly excludable. Rides can therefore be priced at levels that reflect marginal benefits to travellers, and entrepreneurs can make operating profits. It appears difficult, however, to operate complex metro systems on the basis of ticket revenue only. The London, Paris and New York metros all require substantial subsidies, for example. The Underground recovers only 70 per cent of running costs from ticket and advertising revenue and this is without adequate provision for re-investment.

Technology's potential for reducing natural monopoly effects are less in rail transit systems than with other urban infrastructure systems, largely due to the nature of the technology. Train lines cannot easily be used by competing train companies in quite the same way as telephone lines or gas pipes can be opened up to competitive use or bus routes opened to competing bus firms (buses can overtake each other). Strong public goods and monopoly arguments remain therefore for at least a partial government ownership of rail transit systems.

If conventional arguments for public–private supply are outdated, what is the optimal organisational arrangement for supplying urban goods and services? This question is at the heart of the public–private partnership (PPP) contract design problem: how should the supply of civic goods be best organised? Cheung, as we saw in Chapter 3, suggested that the concept of a firm is less helpful than the idea of a nexus of contracts as a focus for economic analysis. This is very pertinent to the study of modern urban governance. By rephrasing the organisational question in terms of contracts rather than firms and partnerships, focus shifts to the nature of the transactions embodied in the legal agreements that create economic organisations and ultimately to a consideration of property rights (contracts allocate property rights to exchange partners).

An economic analysis of property rights suggests, as we have seen, that:

a. optimal division of property rights is achieved when individuals best able to influence the income associated with particular attributes also have ownership of those attributes;

b. the optimal allocation may leave certain attributes in the public domain (rights unallocated) if the transaction costs of obtaining information about use of those attributes is too costly.

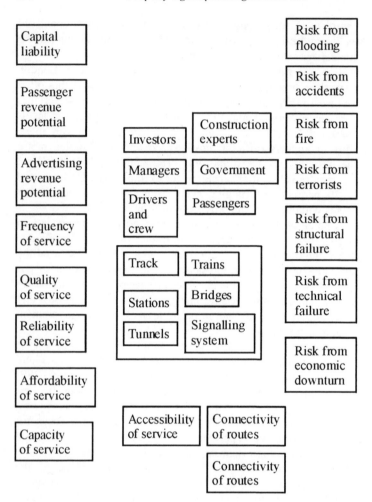

Figure 8.1 Key attributes of a mass rapid rail transit system

Applying these propositions to the specific case of a complex system of urban infrastructure we need to observe that where there are many operators or users of the infrastructure, there are many opportunities for public domain problems to arise. A public domain problem exists where, in the absence of clear property rights over an attribute, individuals attempt to capture wealth from that attribute by strategies and in so doing, dissipate resources. This leads to proposition (c) that elaborates propositions (a) and (b) above and is another version of the subsidiarity rule:

c. In an infrastructure supply problem, the structure of rights to emerge or to be designed may be expected to allocate ownership of individual attributes of the infrastructure system such that the parties who have a comparative advantage in affecting the income flow resulting from attributes that are susceptible to the public domain problem will obtain rights over them.

Now consider how the attributes of the London Underground, mentioned earlier in Chapter 6, might be efficiently subdivided.

First, consider the pattern of attributes of an MRT system (Figure 8.1). The model is arbitrary in its level of detail but captures key features. The central boxes are the main infrastructure components; the upper central boxes are the key groups of stakeholder; and the outer boxes are attributes of the infrastructure that influence service and revenue.

Capital Liability

At the commencement of the public–private partnership in 2002, the London Underground has an accumulated maintenance and investment backlog of $US1.8 billion. One reason for this is the inability of successive central government administrations to secure adequate funds via political methods of decision making. There is no certainty that this will change, even though transport is now higher on the political agenda of the UK government. Governments are contractually bound to their electorates on a number of issues, urban transport being just one. Votes are the principal incentive that drives government action, and politicians are residual claimants of voter goodwill: they seek to maximise voter approval at least cost in terms of budgets and political risk. This suggests that central governments are not the best placed agents to take principal responsibility for capital financing an MRT. The incentive structure is simply not in place for them to perform this task efficiently.

Whether local governments are in a better position to assume ownership of capital liability was the question at the heart of the Mayor of London's counter proposal to the central government's public–private partnership scheme. That proposal argued that under-investment started when liability was shifted from the Greater London Council (the former metropolitan regional government of London) to central government in the mid 1980s. It proposed that a municipal government agency (Transport for London – TFL) assume ownership of the capital liability of the Underground and financed this by issuing long-term bond-financed debt, secured on future ticket sales.

There are two issues at stake in comparing the local government plan with the central government plan: the cost of debt and the competence and costs in managing it. The local government agency TFL could borrow more cheaply (by say about 3 per cent) via bonds than the PPP can via the capital markets. On the other hand, TFL had no experience in bond-financing. There were not even laws in place at the time to allow it to raise finance in this way (the British government prohibits government departments from issuing debt). In contrast, the consortia bidding for the PPP included experts practised at financing large infrastructure projects using capital markets and might therefore be expected to perform this task with less organisational and other transaction costs.

The argument between central government and local government was therefore partly about the most efficient allocation of the capital liability attribute. A very public debate had the positive effect of exposing the details of each party's claim – down to publishing 'confidential' financial reports on the Web.

An interesting dimension to the debate was the lack of precise knowledge about the state of assets and therefore about the precise size and scheduling of maintenance and investment expenditure. Rival PPP consortia made their bids without this knowledge. The local government's TFL quickly made efforts to create an up-to-date asset inventory and claimed superior knowledge. For such a complex infrastructure system as the Underground it may well be that quality of knowledge about the assets for which capital is required is more important than a track record of managing large-scale debt financing.

Whichever is, in principle, the more efficient owner of the capital liability, both organisations – PPP consortia and local government – made it clear that central government needs to retain a degree of ownership. Both financial plans required subsidy. This was an important outcome from the process and all the more significant in that the PPP and the municipal plans required about the same amount of subsidy. The size and existence of the subsidy gap itself is a function of accumulated under-investment arising from property rights ambiguity over recent decades. In this sense it is a measure of the government failure resulting from ownership being passed back and forth between two tiers of government. The central government's willingness to subsidise also reflects the external benefits of the Underground to the wider economy. The efficient level of public ownership (degree of subsidy from general taxation) should reflect the wider value of the Underground as a public good. This is impossible to measure, of course, although the annual subsidies over the past 20 years may broadly reflect politicians' views about how much the general taxpayer is willing to pay for these positive externalities.

Equipment

When the main-line railways were re-privatised in Britain during the 1990s, ownership of tracks, trains and stations was fragmented. The subdivision of property rights was far from optimal, however, and hard lessons have been learned. Ownership of train track, for example, went to a company that for the first few years of operation had not a single engineer on the Board. A series of disasters linked to maintenance problems revealed the track company's incompetence in influencing the train system's essential attributes of safety and reliability. The London Underground PPP learnt from this experience and partitioned liability for equipment maintenance and improvement into three infrastructure companies (infracos), each of which owns the liability for all equipment for an entire set of Underground lines and has demonstrable competence. The infracos are contractors to a public company, London Underground Limited, which owns stations and operations and is under the control of London's new regional government. Infracos are entirely new organisations created by partnerships between transport, construction and engineering companies. By placing ownership of assets in the hands of a unitary organisation and giving the organisation a simple incentive structure, the PPP potentially (a) removes many of the public domain problems that occurred in the new main-line railway market and (b) overcomes the incentive problem that led to under-investment while the Underground was under public ownership. The PPP uses a performance measure that takes into consideration three key performance criteria: *availability* (measure of delay attributable to infrastructure), *capability* (journey times) and *ambience* (cleanliness and general conditions of trains). During the first seven years of the 30-year contract, London Underground Limited will pay the infracos $US4.5 for every passenger hour of benefit created (improvements in journey times multiplied by passengers affected). The payment – referred to as infrastructure service fee (ISF) – is made monthly with penalties for performance falling below agreed baseline levels. This is the sole source of revenue for the infracos.

Infracos are residual claimants of the ISF fee revenue they receive from London Underground Limited. They have considerable freedom in the way in which they meet performance targets and they gain from discovering and adopting more efficient ways and abandoning works and procedures that do not measurably raise performance.

Since the performance measures and payment schemes are simple and clear with no inherent measurement or information problems, the ownership of equipment seems efficiently allocated in the PPP contract. For this reason perhaps, there was no great debate about this aspect of the PPP proposal.

The one debate that did arise concerned the scheduling of infrastructural improvements. During the course of the PPP negotiation process, major improvements shifted to more distant time horizons, partly in response to adjusted predictions of revenue in the light of falling operational surpluses in the years since the bids were first prepared. The first new trains, for example, are not scheduled to appear until 2008 – year six of the contract. The problem partly arose from poor information about assets but led to predictions that infracos will schedule works to meet budgets that they set themselves and thus avoid any meaningful financial risk (see below). It has to be said that infracos have considerable scope for discovering ways of capturing benefit (rent seeking) using their discretion over capital works programmes. This will only partly be offset by London Underground Limited's periodic re-specification of investment priorities. The only way of overcoming this would be for LUL to specify conditions on the scheduling of infrastructure improvements. To stand firm on these at a negotiating table, however, LUL would have to outlay considerable information costs in creating realistic schedules. From this point of view it may be efficient to leave investment scheduling in the public domain, accepting that in so doing, the infracos will use their information advantage to capture some of the benefit.

Revenue

The PPP allocates ownership of revenue to London Underground Limited (and therefore ultimately to the Mayor of London) and this has been relatively uncontroversial. The government-owned company has the property rights to ticket and advertising revenue, which it uses for its own operations and to pay infrastructure service fees to the infracos. LUL is thus made residual claimant of the non-equipment side of the transport operation. It has the incentive to find more efficient ways of running stations, scheduling trains, and indeed, managing the infracos contracts.

Staff

Since it is staff that actually deliver the service, the allocation of ownership of staff assets and liabilities is crucial to the efficiency of the partnership. The PPP transferred 6000 staff from the former Underground organisation to the infracos (with protected terms of employment), leaving 8000 staff including management, drivers and crew in London Underground Limited. The infracos could be expected to design employment contracts and working practices that maximised performance improvement at minimum cost. They alone have the knowledge required to do this accurately. They may have been constrained in this by the protected terms of transferred staff, but one would expect any problems in this respect to have worked themselves out in the earlier years of the PPP.

The relationship between the drivers, crew, station staff and managers in London Underground Limited on the one hand and the infracos-owned equipment on the other has more potential for public domain problems, however. There is no incentive structure in place for the drivers or managers to use equipment in the most efficient way and one might expect problems to arise as public domain attributes (including revenue) are competed for. Indeed, the Mayor of London's alternative proposal, which was backed by the trade unions, predicted conflicts and resulting inefficiencies as a result of unclear relationships between LUL and infracos staff.

Risk

The ownership of risk is the most controversial issue for a contract with the size and complexity demanded by a mass rapid transit system. Several observations may be made about the way the London Underground PPP attempted to allocate risk. First, the central government promoted its initial case for the PPP in terms of the private sector being better able to assume many of the risks of the Underground's business. As negotiations proceeded, however, more and more of the risk was passed back to the local government-owned LUL and to central government. Risk is multi-dimensional and we consider selected dimensions in the following.

From the outset, London Underground Limited and central government assumed a large part of the ownership of the *safety* attribute (*risk from accident*). The Health and Safety Executive (HSE), a government agency, ultimately owns the right to pronounce working practice 'safe'. When it approves a 'Safety Case' submitted by one of the parties to the PPP it temporarily transfers partial ownership of the safety attribute back to the organisation. So when the HSE approved LUL's Safety Case, for example, LUL became responsible for safety as per the details of the Safety Case – which is a kind of contract between HSE and LUL. It is not a full assignment of liability, however, and the HSE retains some of the risk since an accident victim could take it to court for negligence in following due process or making a bad decision. Nevertheless, LUL, as holder of the Safety Case has the incentive to design and police safe working practices in its own operations and also to ensure efficient co-ordination with the infracos, each of which has to submit its own Safety Case to the HSE. There are, however, undoubtedly public domain problems at the boundaries of the respective responsibilities.

LUL and the government will also retain much of the *risk of revenue variation, changes to health and safety laws* and some *environmental risks*. It is this list that grew during negotiations – a process that could have been expected, especially with a central government that was ardently committed to the PPP for political reasons. The private sector consortia argued that the PPP contract would be prohibitively expensive if major external risks were fully costed in. For example, it would be difficult to find someone to insure the risk from a failure of the Thames flood barrier, or for the consortia to cover the risk itself. Similarly, risks from economic recession and terrorist action were not priced and either remain in the public domain (if they do not appear in the contract) or are owned by government in its role as residual subsidiser.

More creative arrangements might have been possible in some areas of risk where external agencies have clear purchase on that risk. For example, the operators of the Thames flood barrier and the water authorities responsible for rivers and pipes have a major influence on flood risk. If the assignment of liability for protecting London Underground's assets are insufficiently specified, then some risk could be transferred to these agencies. The same may be said of policing and fire services.

While it may be reasonable for the government to assume risks as diffuse and expensive as this (as it did in 2001 in respect of terrorism in the airline industry), some of the capital risk transferred to the government during the course of negotiating the PPP could undoubtedly have been assumed by the private partners. The over-allocation of risk to central government is likely to lead to a weaker incentive for the private infracos to perform efficiently (since they stand to make full gains from their investments but share unanticipated costs with the government).

Urban Neighbourhoods: An Externality Example

Consider the ownership pattern of a neighbourhood's attributes. To the extent that housing and capital markets are efficient, property rights over the private goods components of neighbourhoods will be subdivided according to tastes and levels of prosperity. Private rights may have become established over the use of parts of plots and parts of buildings and those rights may be distributed over time as well as space. Private rights will also have been established over individual buildings' risk from fire, theft and structural failure and over the capital value of buildings.

As we have shown in Chapters 5–7, property rights over shared neighbourhood attributes are generally less well defined than rights over building attributes because shared attributes are more costly to render excludable. Neighbourhood prestige, for example, is a function of the socio-economic attributes of neighbours in residential neighbourhoods and the profile of other firms in commercial or industrial neighbourhoods. The property right to prestige is jointly owned in as much as all can benefit from it directly or by exchange. Similarly, neighbours share economic property rights over attributes such as street cleanliness, security, visual amenity and access to shops, services and employment: they benefit directly from such amenities and indirectly through exchange (sale of their property). There may be a degree of legal protection of these rights – the right to citizen and corporate participation in land use planning, third-party rights over planning decisions and minimum service standards stipulated in citizens' charters for example – but legal rights over collectively consumed goods can be difficult to define and enforce.

Most collectively consumed goods are capable of being congested and the various *risks of congestion* may also be viewed as neighbourhood attributes. Any household or firm has the economic right to cause a nuisance to others and this right may or may not be restricted by custom, contractual agreement or state law. Conversely, the economic rights over a household or firm's risk of neighbour-related nuisance (a form of congestion) is owned by the household or firm's neighbours. The degree to which an aggrieved party can attenuate that right will depend on the existence and effectiveness of appropriate laws and social convention. In the absence of either, inter-neighbour conflict may result as both parties to a dispute attempt by various kinds of force to assert their own property rights and capture attributes of peace and goodwill that lie in the public domain. Access to on-street parking or loading space, use of air, open space and water-courses are attributes which many property owners assume a right to but have little control over in practice. All others who have a demand for these resources, share ownership of the economic rights to them and resources will be wasted contesting these economic rights. Non-resident users of a neighbourhood's facilities have the economic right, and if not constrained by regulation the legal right, to litter, to vandalise, to contribute to a sense of insecurity or security (depending on their characteristics and frequency) and to free ride on locally-supplied benefits. When neighbours possess no effective legal rights over the risk of neighbourhood congestion, neighbourhood quality and viability are at the mercy of outsiders and non-conforming insiders.

Consider five classes of neighbourhood attribute, each consumed at a different spatial scale and each produced and consumed by a particular group of agents. Together these attribute–agent categories characterise the joint production–consumption organisation that constitutes the neighbourhood. A set of transactions made via implicit and explicit contracts is required for the continued supply of the attributes. We comment on the efficiency of property rights assignments within neighbourhood 'organisations' by considering the pattern of residual claims in these contracts.

Application of the subsidiarity rule to the typically loose, yet important nexus of agreements, understandings and conventions that create and sustain distinct urban neighbourhoods, suggests the following version of the subsidiarity rule:

> The total value of neighbourhood welfare, or the sum of the value of private property rights, is maximised when agents with an ability to influence that value bear the full effects of their actions such that they are residual claimants over the share of the value that they can influence. This gives them the incentive to deploy their resources to maximum benefit. This implies that they should have a claim not only on the residual value of their privately owned neighbourhood assets but also on the total neighbourhood value.

(a) Micro-neighbourhood attributes

These are attributes that are produced and consumed jointly between small numbers of adjacent properties. We have said that a firm or household has the economic right to cause a nuisance to its neighbours. Specifically it has the economic right to benefit from activities that reduce the welfare of its immediate neighbour by noise, air, water and visual pollution, unfriendly or threatening behaviour (social pollution) and 'image' pollution. Conversely, a firm or household's immediate neighbours own the economic rights to impose upon it a range of near-neighbour externalities and associated costs. *An efficient allocation of property rights would seem to require that immediate neighbours have a share in the value of each other's properties.* If this were so, each would have an incentive not to over-consume at the expense of others and each would deploy its resources efficiently in seeking micro-neighbourhood welfare as well as private welfare. The proposition seems less bizarre when the reciprocity of relationships between close neighbours is considered. When neighbours are willing to collaborate, collective agreement can be expected over mutually acceptable behaviour. Voluntary codes of conduct that govern the use of shared space, access, noise levels, refuse disposal, building maintenance and so on, commonly develop between adjacent neighbours. Since restrictions are mutual and reciprocal a building user shares a claim on the 'good neighbour' attributes collectively consumed. It has no direct economic ownership of its neighbour's welfare or property value, but it experiences its own welfare and value premiums as its neighbours abide by the code. The external costs of its actions are internalised by reciprocal action and it becomes a residual claimant of the shared 'peace'. If it reneges then so might its neighbour and it will lose out. By reducing its own anti-social activities it stands to make its own welfare gains.

Efficient assignment of rights does not rely on identical tastes and the mutually agreed restriction does not have to be equal for both or all parties.

However, the greater the difference in tastes, the less stable the property rights are and the greater scope for voluntary assignment of rights to break down. It might also be asserted that the transaction costs of negotiation increase not only with numbers but also with the heterogeneity of preferences since there are additional communication, informational and psychic costs incurred when making agreements with dissimilar neighbours.

Given small numbers, similar, but not necessarily identical tastes, and sufficiently low transaction costs, adjacent neighbours may therefore be expected to make voluntary agreements that *efficiently* assign property rights over micro-level externalities. Conversely, in the presence of high transaction costs, resulting for example, from a lack of shared values, voluntary solutions to near-neighbour externalities may persist. Many individually trivial externalities can add up to significant neighbourhood problems that can trigger unpredictable city-wide changes in land values, land use patterns and neighbourhood economic fortune.

The institutions required to support efficient assignment of rights over micro-level externalities include spontaneous conventions and culture; contractual agreements via covenants and legal restrictions on deeds; contractual agreements via private neighbourhood rules; municipal land use regulations; and mediation. Land use regulations are blunter instruments than contractual arrangements since they are less able to completely assign property rights over local externalities (Fischel, 1978, 1987).

(b) Meso-neighbourhood (street) attributes

The actions of an immediate neighbour do not, other than in extreme cases, seriously jeopardise a property's value. The collective, aggregated actions of other neighbours do, however. It is typically at street level that neighbourhood identity is formed, that distinct housing market and commercial areas develop, and that the distinctive collective consumption and production behaviour that determines a neighbourhood's social, commercial and environmental quality develops. Tiebout-style homogenisation occurs at a street as well as jurisdictional level with land premiums operating as a spatial price for street-level local public goods. Unlike the micro-neighbourhood between small groups of land users in which a firm or household can co-determine, with others, the levels of shared attributes, neighbourhood dwellers are welfare-takers at the street level. They are one among many and their actions will not, on their own, change the character of the neighbourhood. The higher numbers at this scale render the efficiency analysis different to the case already discussed.

Take for example, the visual amenity and prestige attributes of a residential neighbourhood. Nature and the actions of others determine a household's visual amenity. If there is only foreground in the view from a house then the view is entirely determined by the previous actions of neighbouring landowners and occupiers. Welfare and property value derived from the street scene is therefore entirely dependent on the investment decisions of others. Similarly, a household is entirely dependent on the actions of others in sustaining the prestige value of the street. If others in the neighbourhood sell to entrepreneurs who convert properties to multi-occupation or non-residential use then a household may suffer welfare loss. If the level of local externalities increases as a result of a tenure and use change then property value relative to previously similar neighbourhoods might fall. *The dependence of a household's welfare on the actions of others in the neighbourhood suggests that an efficient allocation of property rights would require all property owners in the street to have a claim on the value of every other property. Under such conditions individual owners have an incentive to use their own resources efficiently in a way that increases the positive externalities arising from their actions and reduces the negative externalities. They become co-residual claimants of the nexus of positive externalities that create 'neighbourhood'.*

Condominiums and other forms of proprietary neighbourhoods achieve this to a degree. Individual owners combine property rights over common facilities, which in the case of apartments may include external and internal structures. The condominium's constitution may also effectively give co-owners a pro rata right in deciding the type of residents – at least indirectly through restrictions on age and behaviour and through the type of common goods supplied. In a traditional open neighbourhood street however, there is no legal assignment of rights over other properties. There is, however, a voluntary set of obligations and expectations that under certain conditions can achieve the same incentive to maximise shared value. The argument is similar to the micro-neighbourhood argument but differs in that (a) free riding is a greater risk, (b) entrepreneurs (estate agents) assume a share of the neighbourhood value in exchange for promoting consensus on mutual responsibilities and (c) the reciprocity is less obvious and less direct.

Each household has a pro rata influence over the quality of the neighbourhood. The influence is probabilistic, not deterministic, in the sense that an individual's actions in under-investing, over-consuming, or selling to a potentially intruding use carry a probability of negatively affecting the whole neighbourhood. In turn, each household is vulnerable to the prob-abilistic outcome of other households' actions. A household may take alternative views of this set of relationships. It may have a positive preference for neighbourly behaviour and willingly adjust its consumption and investment to benefit the neighbourhood as a whole. It may make the adjustments, motivated by fear that if it does not, others might follow suit and the whole neighbourhood suffers. It may free ride on the assumption that others will make the adjustments necessary to sustain a good neighbourhood and it may simply not care what happens to the neighbourhood. Households understanding the importance of maintaining a shared and reciprocated set of values and neighbourhood attributes will act as co-residual claimants in the same way as will two neighbours agreeing on noise levels, shared access or a shared water source. The only difference in this respect is the directness of the reciprocal effect. A reneging household will not be immediately punished: the punishment can only be predicted with a certain degree of probability. Strong neighbourhood codes of conduct may be found in high- and low-income areas alike and may be explained by a shared sensitivity to the consequences of letting the neighbourhood down. Sensitivity is likely to be stronger the greater the household's residual claim on neighbourhood welfare. Residents of neighbourhoods characterised by owner-occupation, long-term tenancies and resident management institutions are more likely to attenuate their individual rights voluntarily and enjoy a pro rata share in the outcome of their actions.

Existing households have no such incentive to act in the interests of other neighbourhood residents. However, estate agents acting on the latter's behalf, can help guard against neighbourhood damage caused by those leaving the club. Estate agents' fees are usually proportional to sale value and agents typically specialise with respect to locality. This makes them residual claimants when a household exchanges its right to live in a neighbourhood. They have the incentive to act in a way that maintains and improves neighbourhood value. It has long been recognised that estate agents have a conservative influence on housing markets and act to stabilise neighbourhoods. The allocation of a share of a neighbourhood's property rights to a third-party entrepreneur is an efficient one in the sense that it helps maximise the total value of the neighbourhood.

(c) Macro-neighbourhood attributes – access to shops and services

District and local service centres typically serve a number of contrasting neighbourhoods. Conversely, high- and low-valued residential streets and commercial and industrial clusters derive some of their value from proximity to shops, services and employment. Accessibility to local service infrastructure is an important neighbourhood attribute and local public goods supplied at local commercial centres are an important determinant of neighbourhood welfare – a point articulated in traditional urban economic models. *This suggests that an efficient allocation of property rights within the city should make entrepreneurs and other service providers claimants of the welfare enjoyed by surrounding neighbourhoods. This would give them the incentive to seek to increase positive externalities created by their activities and reduce negative externalities.*

Exceptional cases exist where this relationship is a direct one. In single employer towns and districts where the employer owns much of the land including houses and secondary services, the claim is a direct one via rental income and asset value. In all cities, however, there is an equivalent indirect sense in which service suppliers are claimants via the mutual benefits that accrue when services, including labour, are exchanged. The welfare derived by households from accessibility to services is mirrored in the welfare derived by service suppliers from accessibility to customers.

In an efficient market, goods and services purchased are exchanged at a price that reflects both the marginal cost of supply and the marginal benefit of consumption. So there is, in theory, a precise mutuality in welfare exchange (leaving aside for a moment the issues of distance and market boundaries) between supplier centre and consumer neighbourhoods. When service suppliers in a local centre invest, they not only increase the welfare of surrounding residents but, by definition, and assuming the investment is well made, they reap an equivalent increase in welfare. In this sense they have claim on the accessibility value they create. They have the incentive to deploy their resources efficiently in a way that increases the accessibility value of surrounding neighbourhoods. They have no claim on the capitalised land value resulting from greater accessibility but share in the benefits that give rise to that capitalisation.

Expressing this mutuality as property rights propositions: households and firms within the catchment of a commercial centre possess economic rights to the services supplied in the sense that they can enjoy them directly or benefit indirectly via the locational premium obtained when selling their location to another household. On the other hand, entrepreneurs and government service suppliers have an economic right to the custom of the local population. Local firms and local population are bound in a kind of informal contract based on the latter's assumption that local services will persist and the former's assumption that local patronage will persist.

As with reciprocal benefits between neighbours, the rights both ways are economic and not generally legal. This gives rise to similar kinds of uncertainty, and under certain conditions, instability. Residents, for example, may take their custom elsewhere – to out-of-town retailers – if they no longer value the economic right to local shop accessibility. The value of the attribute changes and the economic right is no longer exercised. This is not a problem for the residents who choose to behave in this way but it might be for less mobile groups. The local traders' claim on the accessibility attribute that they provide is lost and they disinvest, go out of business or move. When service suppliers change or remove their services to the detriment of local neighbourhoods or groups, they break the implicit contract that provides surrounding neighbourhoods with service accessibility. That an implicit contract exists is evidenced by the kind of complaint heard when shops or local employers cease to provide services to which local residents have become accustomed and by the kind of complaints made by shop owners when residents desert them. Entrepreneurs have a self interest in maintaining the contract where there is a demand for their service but may be forced to renege through exogenous influences – recession or restructuring of the retail or service industry.

Local services provided by government rather than entrepreneurs are additionally vulnerable to policy change. When high schools were selectively closed in the UK in the late 1980s, for example, and school catchments realigned, an important neighbourhood attribute suddenly changed. In principle, governments are claimants on the neighbourhood attributes they provide in the sense that they reap voter support and higher property taxes by improving those attributes. Local services, however, are vulnerable to wider policy objectives and in a planned system of resource allocation, local demand is subservient to central demand. The claim on a particular neighbourhood's political value can sometimes be insufficient incentive when compared to claims on other neighbourhoods or on the overall welfare in the jurisdiction.

(d) Central services – ubiquitous neighbourhood attributes
A distinction is made in urban economics between local public goods and those supplied ubiquitously to all within a jurisdiction. Ubiquitous services contribute to the welfare of all citizens and may also be thought of as attributes common to all neighbourhoods in the jurisdiction. *This suggests that an efficient set of property rights would give the municipal government a claim on the neighbourhood welfare generated by this set of attributes.*

Unlike the meso and macro neighbourhood levels examined above, such property rights are typically better defined legally and economically. Also in contrast to the local situations, the claim is direct, through property taxes, as well as indirect through voluntary reciprocal exchange – in this case of votes in exchange for economic and (incomplete) legal rights over public goods. A responsive and well-run municipal government makes policies that enhance the welfare of its citizens. We have referred to this as a spontaneous political market in previous chapters. In return, it can expect to receive continued support. In addition, assuming the welfare is capitalised into land values as the city competes successfully with surrounding cities, the municipal government benefits through increased property tax revenues. It may also benefit from sales, development and other tax resulting from a more popular and prosperous city. Taxation laws give it a legal right to a claim on the ubiquitous neighbourhood attributes it creates and at a city-wide level this is an efficient assignment of rights. It has a residual claim on tax revenue (and by analogy on voter goodwill), giving it the incentive to deliver prosperity-enhancing interventions efficiently. If it fails to make good policy or fails to do so efficiently it will suffer; if it is visionary, entrepreneurial and uses tax revenue and voter goodwill prudently, it will prosper.

Though this is efficient for the city as a whole, there will always be inefficiencies at the neighbourhood level. An urban development plan, zoning ordinance, transport plan or local education investment plan assigns economic and incomplete legal property rights to discrete areas. Even if it is an optimal assignment, say in terms of maximising the welfare of the largest number of citizens, there will always be neighbourhoods that suffer some kind of loss. In general, whenever city-wide policy is re-distributive there will be loser-neighbourhoods for whom it seems that property rights over local public goods are inefficiently assigned.

The various property rights assignments discussed in Chapters 5–7 provide creative ways of addressing the inevitably selective local inefficiency of city-wide policies. The right to public participation in planning decisions is a method designed to ensure better outcomes in the sense of fewer losers. It cannot prevent loss, however, since planning is nearly always re-distributive and as we have seen it has high transaction costs. Giving aggrieved residents a right to monetary or fiscal compensation is another approach. Fiscal compensation may involve tax rebate or the right to impose local compensation or betterment tax on development. Pollution tax or developer exactions with the right to hypothecate (spend on neighbourhood public goods) might redress some local inefficiencies without further redistribution of tax revenues. The redistribution would instead be between polluter and polluted. Another approach would give neighbourhoods rights over detailed local resource allocations. This might include the right to traffic-calm local roads congested by a strategic road proposal; the right to make local development control decisions; the right to levy local charges for local improvements – as with New York's Business Improvement Districts for example; and the right to vire between individual quotas in the application of local regulations, for example by trading density quotas. These are all potentially Pareto-improving property rights assignments. They have in common the assignment of additional rights over public domain neighbourhood attributes. A responsive municipal government wishing to maximise the value of property rights it assigns via various styles of intervention has an incentive to explore such options and it does so because it has a residual claim on neighbourhood welfare – via tax and votes.

(e) Outsiders – dispersed free riders

Each of the neighbourhood attribute providers discussed above can be associated with a particular spatial scale. There is one other important set of providers that it is easier to group together as outsiders. They could of course be assigned to some spatial unit, such as visitors from adjacent or far-off neighbourhoods or from other cities but from the point of view of a neighbourhood they are free riders. Outsiders are actually very important in determining neighbourhood quality. Visitors to a popular park in a prestige neighbourhood can endorse the sense of prestige residents enjoy since prestige requires comparison and comparison favourable to residents' sense of well-being is made both ways – by visitors and residents. Frequent passers by of the right type can increase residents' sense of security. Too many passers by or visitors with obviously different behaviour or appearance can have the opposite effect, as fear of the unknown replaces surveillance benefits. Passing pedestrians have less sense of ownership and are likely to enjoy neighbourhood benefits with less inclination to abide by the codes of conduct that help sustain them. Passers by can be a source of negative or positive externalities and have, as a group, considerable influence on neighbourhood welfare. *Does this mean that an efficient property rights allocation would make them claimants of that welfare? In theory the answer is yes and there are various ways in which this is attempted.*

Singapore's famous spot fines for littering, spitting, jaywalking and other pedestrian misdemeanours are attempts to internalise the social costs of street-users' actions. Effectively enforced fines make passers by accountable for their own actions – if they desist from littering they receive the benefit of not being fined. Since their desisting results in an increase in neighbourhood welfare, the pedestrian effectively has a residual claim on that welfare. Where state policing is ineffective, vigilantes try to reduce externalities from outsiders and non-conforming insiders. They have a personal interest in the security of a neighbourhood and will thus deploy their efforts efficiently, being residual claimants of the welfare thus gained. Protection racketeers provide a commercial version of the vigilante service, overcoming the collective action problem by force and fear. It may be immoral but victims may collude because there is a perverse efficiency to the solution.

These are extreme cases. Neighbourhood watch schemes are an acceptable form of vigilantism and the rights to exercise resident police power may even be endorsed in law. Private policing of excludable or non-excludable space is even more efficient because it involves commercial contracts enforceable in law which pay a security company to produce a desired outcome. Like the estate agent, the company becomes a co-claimant of neighbourhood welfare. Its residual claim on the fee provided encourages it to police efficiently so long as there are performance measures in its contract that discourage shirking. Public policing is viewed as more equitable by many and can be as efficient if the controlling political authority has sufficient resources and is responsive enough to residents' demands for security. Where public policing is inadequate, as now seems ubiquitously to be the case, the property rights may be efficiently assigned in the sense of an agreeable exchange of police and security for votes and property taxes but the public authority fails to deliver on its contract for lack of resources. This illustrates the idea that capital is required to guarantee the contracts that create a successful neighbourhood.

Where the agent in the best position to influence a particular input to neighbourhood quality is under-capitalised to do so, then the property right is either more efficiently assigned to another or the agent's property rights are more efficiently combined with others who control capital. In Britain's ailing ex-public sector low-income and mixed tenure housing estates, residents have the detailed knowledge necessary for efficient estate management. However, they generally possess neither adequate management knowledge nor capital. The municipal governments that used to own them had management knowledge but inadequate commercial knowledge and insufficient access to capital for maintenance and investment. It was inevitable in time therefore that new forms of organisation would emerge that combined the property rights of residents (tenants and owner occupiers), specialised estate management companies and specialised financing companies.

It was inevitable in a responsive market and a responsive political market that the planned order governing public sector housing estates would be supplanted by a more efficient spontaneous order. Government had a crucial role in this latest evolutionary development of low-cost housing provision, however: it provided the institutional framework that permitted a new kind of organisational and proprietary order to emerge and flourish.

8.4   COMPLEX SYSTEMS, INTERDEPENDENT URBAN ORDERS AND THE PROBLEM OF PLANNING

The efficiency of one form of order affects all other forms of order. Inefficiently assigned property rights arise from inefficient institutions and efficient institutions lead to efficient organisations and spatial order. Spatial order reflects land market practices, or in the absence of a land market, government priorities. The more efficient land market institutions are, the more efficient the spatial distribution of activities. Imperfections in capital markets impact the efficiency of labour and land markets.

When China reformed land ownership in the early 1990s it had to use capital from Hong Kong and Taiwan. The improved land market institution couldn't realise gains because of an underdeveloped capital market. China's capital and land market institutions and organisations rapidly improved in parallel. By the end of the 1990s individuals were borrowing on the basis of land to finance education – contributing to improvements in the labour market. In addition, the mass redistribution of housing to occupants and the creation of housing market institutions in 1998 meant that the seeds of capitalism were sown deep and wide. The first-hand knowledge gained from managing a substantial asset and participating in the housing market may be expected to improve the supply of capitalist knowledge in the economy and increase the supply of entrepreneurs.

Improved institutions lead to improvements in the pattern of organisations that govern a city's private resources and its collective action. Government structure adjusts to more efficient rules governing public voting and internal decision-making. Firms form, merge and divide as the state creates facilitating institutional frameworks and more efficient legal frameworks create more efficient market structures. Clear systems of rights and liabilities allow voluntary associations to form and transform into entrepreneurial firms and give rise to new kinds of organisations that combine the property rights of governments, entrepreneurs, residents, the travelling public, consumers, neighbourhood members.

Patterns of private ownership become more efficient as organisational and institutional order evolve upwardly. Public domains become more efficiently ordered as superior mechanisms of intervention are discovered; as government functions are distributed more efficiently over different levels of governance; as public goods become club goods; and as externalities are internalised through organisations that efficiently combine rights and liabilities.

Table 8.1   Interactive urban orders

Type of order	Organisational	Proprietary	Public domain	Spatial	Institutional
Organisational	O–O	O–P	O–D	O–S	O–I
Proprietary	P–O	P–P	P–D	P–S	P–I
Public domain	D–O	D–P	D–D	D–S	D–I
Spatial					
Institutional					I–I

Table 8.1 cross-tabulates the five kinds of urban order we have discussed in this book. The interactions represented by the cells capture distinctive processes at work as cities evolve. Each cell is a distinct nexus of cause–effects and each interacts with the processes in other cells in a non-deterministic fashion. Linear sequences of cause–effects can be traced (for example increased congestion leads to changes in institutions and property rights reassignment) but by and large the various discrete processes interact

in non-linear ways and the whole system evolves unpredictably, characterised by local learning in space and time; spontaneous local feedback;
and chaotic behaviour. We demonstrate this with an example that starts with
an exogenous organisational change – falling household size – and we
comment briefly, by way of illustration, on the cells labelled in the table.

Household size in the United Kingdom has been falling in recent years
and this has caused significant pressure on the country's heavily constrained
land supply. During the 25-year period starting in 1995, 4 million extra
households have been predicted by central government. Consider the
following interactions. Changes in transaction costs cause change in one kind
of order, which leads to further changes in transaction costs and to changes in
other forms of order.

O–O: Rising incomes, falling birth rates, delayed child-bearing and
institutional changes, for example laws and conventions governing marriage,
have all contributed to falling average household size. The basic
organisational unit in society changes as individuals weigh up the costs and
benefits of alternative living arrangements. This is a process analogous to the
Coasian idea of firms and industries configuring themselves in response to
the relative costs of transacting within the market and transacting by
organisation and planning. In response to the organisational change of
household structure, new entrepreneurial opportunities arise; new products
are created for single person households; new firms start up and other firms
reorganise themselves to newly emerging markets. The transaction costs of
searching for customers and suppliers determines the organisational structure
of suppliers of new products oriented to the young professional market, the
working mother market and the empty-nester market.

O–P: With greater numbers demanding exclusive living space, land and
building values rise and there is a demand to subdivide these resources into
smaller proprietary units. Land fragments, buildings subdivide, homes get
smaller, per capita land consumption falls and property rights are assigned to
some resources that previously lay in the public domain. School playing
fields, for example, are subdivided and sold for private housing; property
rights to lofts and garages are partitioned and sold off; large houses are
subdivided into apartments or demolished and sites redeveloped with multi-
occupant buildings co-owned by residents, developers, management companies and other interests.

O–D: Rising household numbers potentially means urban sprawl; green
land-take; higher numbers of cars, trips and demand for road space. At a
general level, the change in household organisation leads to increasing
congestion of shared resources, increasing competition costs and new
collective action problems. An immediate public domain problem created
concerns the spatial allocation of the 4 million new households. They are a

'resource' (or more accurately a liability) that congested local authorities will expend valuable resources competing to avoid.

O–S: To reduce the costs of searching for co-consumers and suppliers of goods and services, the rising number of smaller households cluster to form new communities. They outbid secondary office users and create residential quarters in city centres and they form new suburban and ex-urban neighbourhoods. The spatial structure within cities and within metropolitan regions changes in subtle ways in response to household re-organisation.

O–I: Faced with an alarming number of new households competing for space and local governments in the congested areas increasingly hostile to the idea of giving up more land for housing, central government responds with minimum housing allocations for each jurisdiction. In principle, this institutional response has the potential benefit of lowering transaction costs in the development process – by cutting developer–local government negotiation costs, developer search costs and intra-jurisdiction decision making costs.

P–O: The greater fragmentation of property rights leads to organisational adjustments. For example, new suburban neighbourhoods create new local commercial opportunities and entrepreneurial individuals set up new businesses, combining property rights of land labour and capital. Local estate management companies form, grow and diversify as a city's central-area apartment market takes off.

P–P: Innovative products formed by the subdivision of property rights spread as entrepreneurs and resource owners copy and adapt innovations. Loft-living, and high density, high specification suburban complexes spread from one city to another. Evolution of proprietary order spreads by fashion and news of success.

P–D: Higher density city centre living and the filling up of land within urban boundaries raises the frequency, variety and severity of externality problems. Land shortage means that house builders can sell homes next to motorways, industrial and waste sites but in so doing they create new externality problems. The shape and value of local public domains change therefore as local resource ownership patterns change. Resources that once had little or no value (motorway noise for example) become valued but unpriced resources and give rise to new public domain problems.

P–S: The local subdivision of land has a direct spatial manifestation. Fewer direct interactions arise for example as increasing car ownership and increasing per capita expenditure on leisure and home improvement induce locational changes in commercial activities.

P–I: New institutions form around new patterns of proprietary order. Customs, conventions, neighbourhood association and condominium rules arise to protect property.

D–O: Re-configured and new public domain problems induce organisational changes within neighbourhoods and within local authorities. Local authorities for example may create new divisions to tackle traffic congestion in residential quiet zones; strengthen conservation sections; or work with developers on creative solutions for brown-field regeneration. Neighbourhood organisations form to lobby for schools or to tackle externality problems.

D–P: Changes in public domain problems lead to changes in proprietary order. Increasing traffic flows on access roads to new suburban housing estates lead to changes in ownership. Houses at road intersections change from owner occupation to rented tenure. Land at the centre of new residential clusters changes hands as it is bought by the commercial sector.

D–D: One public domain change can lead to another. Increasing congestion on one route diverts commuters elsewhere and spreads congestion throughout the system.

D–S: New suburban communities and expanded towns create new agglomeration economies and change the incidence of distance-related transaction costs. Once formed they continue to grow, if allowed, as individuals move in search of public goods.

D–I: The new public domain problems created by individuals living in city centres give rise to new government policies (for example the fear of up-market condo-ghettos and social fragmentation externalities may lead to social housing quotas on new developments). Contractually organised rules emerge in private neighbourhoods.

The illustration makes the point that the interactions between the different kinds of order are complex. The cause–effect relationships are non-linear. Local feedback and recursion is possible with any particular change. This means that it is impossible to predict with any degree of certainty how cities will accommodate Britain's anticipated extra households. Although central government has allocated minimum quotas, congested local governments have retaliated with defensive maximum 'capacity' arguments (an I–I interaction). There is no knowing how government institutions will evolve during the process of negotiations over the next 20 years. Nor how markets will respond spontaneously to demand and to government policy. There is no certainty even that the predicted increase in households will materialise. A crisis in the global economy or in international security could fundamentally change the basis of prediction. We can only predict on the basis of known trends and anticipated events. When it comes to predicting local behaviour in order to prescribe policies to guide urban growth and deal with public domain problems, the best that urban planners can do is to invent the future where the market wants a future invented (to underwrite the risk of collective action). Governments can do this best by growth strategies supported by major infrastructure investment. They should do so, however, with maximum exposure to the anticipated behaviour of markets and in a way that permits markets to do what they can do best – allocate private goods and services on the basis of price. Inventing the future in too great a level of detail gives hostage to fortune and threatens to bring a plan and a government, and planning and governance into disrepute.

8.5 A PROPERTY RIGHTS MODEL OF URBAN DEVELOPMENT, PLANNING AND MANAGEMENT

We conclude this chapter and the book with a summary of our property rights model of urban development, planning and management, followed by a survey of the landscape of property rights research in urban planning and management. The model is illustrated in the stories told in this chapter and elaborated in considerable detail in the preceding chapters.

Planned versus Spontaneous Order

The distribution of individuals, firms and cities across the world is largely an unplanned order. It is one that has been highly successful in generating wealth, however. Cities and systems of cities are the spatial manifestations of co-operative acts, indicating a universal compelling advantage of:

- spatial concentration; and
- economic specialisation.

How should these co-operative acts best be ordered, planned, managed, administered, organised?

Two kinds of order have co-existed and competed throughout human civilisation:

- planned order (imposed, centralised, government, within-firm); and
- spontaneous order (voluntary, decentralised, market, individual, arising from millions of individual exchanges).

Paradoxes:
- the more complex the system, the greater the need for simple rules to achieve order; but
- the greater the apparent need for co-ordination, the more difficult the task of imposing planned order.

The information problem for planned order:

- planned order requires centralised information; and
- the costs of acquiring information are excessive and the information guiding planned order is always partial or defective.

The information advantage of spontaneous order lies in the fact that:

- decentralised exchange decisions are made on the basis of local subjective information;
- individuals face the costs of information search; and
- in competitive markets price acts as an efficient signal of benefit.

Spontaneous order requires rules that protect:

- freedom to enjoy private property by use or exchange;
- freedom from undue interference with private property by theft, slavery, violence, unreasonable government exaction;
- freedom from opportunism by exchange partners in markets or by government; and
- freedom from unreasonable levels of external costs arising from other individuals' property rights exchanges (a form of violence).

Within an appropriate framework of rules, individual decision making is capable of ordering highly complex systems such as world cities.

The Benefits of Co-operation

The creative nature of competitive markets (catallaxis) is characterised by two features:

- competitive markets induce suppliers to outlay resources looking for better ways of meeting other people's needs (inducing them to search for and test new knowledge); and
- competition controls problems of errors as new knowledge is discovered and tested (poor products and processes tend to fail).

The co-operative nature of markets is characterised by two features:

- in pursuit of self-interested goals, individuals contract to exchange with others and in so doing provide other individuals with goods and services that they need; and

- even a simple item such as a pin, a pencil or a cup of coffee requires the co-operation of a multitude of individuals dispersed across the world and linked in a nexus of exchanges that have little to do with the end product.

The Costs of Co-operation

The costs of co-operating with others (costs of owning and using property rights) include:

- exclusion costs (costs of protection from third party opportunism);
- transaction costs (costs of using markets); and
- organisation (or agency) costs (costs of managing co-operation and planning within an organisation).

These are often collectively termed transaction costs or exchange costs. But in the specific definition of transaction cost used in this list, transaction costs include both:

- information search costs (search for exchange partners, their location, product description and quality); and
- negotiating costs, concluding, monitoring and policing contracts.

The Emergence of Spontaneous Order in Cities

Maximising individuals and firms tend to seek co-operative arrangements that minimise such costs. As they do, order emerges in society and space. The following kinds of order emerge to reduce the costs of co-operation:

- institutional order (patterns of rules and sanctions governing ownership, exchange and combination of property rights);
- proprietary order (patterns of property rights resulting from institutions);
- organisational order (patterns of combined property rights);
- spatial order (spatial patterns of property, resources, organisations and institutions); and
- public domain order (patterns of resources left with unclear property rights).

Institutional Order

Co-operation is forged by agreements and contracts. Agreements and contracts are created and upheld by *institutions* (systems of rules and sanctions). These are created:

• spontaneously (informal and voluntary rules emerging over time):
   – conventions (violation sanctioned by harmed self interest);
   internalised rules (violations sanctioned by bad conscience);
   – customs and manners (violations sanctioned by response of others);
• by formal private agreement (violations sanctioned by agreed procedures
   – e.g. rules of behaviour in a leisure club or profession);
• by governments (formal, imposed by government, violations sanctioned
   by legal penalty backed by the state's monopoly control of violence):
   – universal rules of conduct (freedom from…);
   – specific directives (freedom to… specific outcomes); and
   – procedural directives (rules governing government processes).

Proprietary Order

• Institutions have the purpose and effect of reducing the costs of co-operation by creating and protecting exclusive ownership rights (property rights).
• Exclusive property rights lower the costs of competition, preventing in the extreme the complete dissipation of a resource's value by anarchy.
• Resources and commodities have multiple attributes, the rights to which may be separated.
• Property rights may be economic and/or legal:
   – *Economic right*: the ability to derive direct or indirect income or welfare from a resource (or more generally, from an attribute since rights can be assigned to abstract attributes – such as intellectual value-added – as well as physical resources and commodities).
   – *Legal right*: legally protected economic right achieved by:
      – *private contractual rules*;
      – *common law*; and
      – *statutory law*.
• Rights are exchanged by formal *contracts* and by *agreements* with varying degrees of formality (see Institutional order above).
• The degree to which ownership is established over a resource or commodity's separate attributes depends on the cost of creating and policing contracts that establish ownership – *transaction costs*.

- Property rights and institutions therefore emerge to reduce the costs of transacting in markets. But their creation incurs additional transaction costs.
- Property rights assignment will occur if the additional resource value thus created is greater than the transaction costs of assignment.

Organisational Order

- Institutions are administered by *organisations* (government, firms, households, communities, clubs), which are created by individuals ceding certain economic and legal property rights to a collective entity in exchange for certain benefits – the benefits of institutions, the benefits of wages and the like.
- Organisational order is a function of the costs of transacting in the market and the costs of organising co-operation by collective action and hierarchical decision making. Organisations exist because they are able to govern transactions at a lower cost than the market.
- If this ceases to be the case in a particular organisation, organisational structure changes – companies are spun-off, merged or closed; governments are reorganised.

Spatial Order

- Human settlements form under the dual influence of aversion to travel and attraction to opportunities for co-operation. These are both transaction cost arguments.
- Agglomeration economies exist because spatial concentration of complementary individuals and firms lowers certain kinds of transaction cost – particularly search and contracting costs.
- Travel costs are another kind of transaction cost.
- Cities – their size and internal morphology – may therefore be said to be shaped by an aversion to transaction costs.

Public Domain Order

- Resources are left in the public domain by design or because the transaction cost of assigning rights is too costly.
- As a resource becomes congested demand will arise for property rights to be assigned more clearly.
- Cities are local theatres of conflict over a vast number of public domain issues. Individuals and firms live close together and externalities of

consumption and production are many and dense. Urban infrastructure is under-supplied by markets and easily congested.

- Collective action is required to govern the orderly consumption of congested public domain resources; to reduce transaction costs where contested resources have unclear economic and legal property rights.
- Without collective action anarchy prevails, leading to wasteful competition costs that in the extreme can dissipate the positive value of a resource.
- Collective action strategies require organisation and give rise to institutions. Households, firms, clubs and governments create rules to govern public domains.
- All organised (planned as opposed to spontaneous) order, particularly government, has a tendency to become increasingly costly. This is ultimately due to the rent-seeking behaviour permitted within systems that allocate resources by administration, discretion and rule rather than by price.
- Governments tend to expand interventions without due regard to the costs of bureaucracy; to the opportunity costs of budget spent on interventions; to the benefits of intervention; and to the social costs of unforeseen consequences of intervention.
- In addition, it is impossible for any but a despotic government to avoid redistributing resources towards vocal and usually powerful groups.
- As organisations (firms as well as governments) get larger, information problems get more severe and at some point the transaction costs–saving advantages of transacting within an organisation reduce to zero at the margin. At that point, some transactions should be taken back into the market.
- This explains the move towards private urban governance and public–private partnership in ordering public domains (supplying public goods and tackling externalities).
- Spontaneity in political markets (responsiveness to the public) can lead over time to progressively efficient mechanisms for allocating property rights over shared and contested resources.
- As in economic markets, however, spontaneity in political markets is impeded when there is a lack of competition and high transaction costs (costs of transacting with and within governments – the two are related).
- To the extent that these impediments are overcome, rights and liabilities over urban resources will tend to become progressively finely defined and efficiently allocated.
- Some public domain resources will become club domain resources, shared by smaller groups; smaller 'publics'.
- Others will become private goods protected by exclusive property rights.

- Others will be governed by regulations that confer incomplete property rights but nevertheless introduce a degree of order to shared consumption problems.
- The greater the information, feedback, learning and spontaneity of governing authorities, the more efficient will be the allocation of rights and liabilities.
- Whatever the organisational context, efficient ownership division rests on a variant of the same principle: the subsidiarity rule.
- This rule is a *positive* one in the sense that institutional, organisational, proprietary, spatial and public domain order may be expected to yield to it over time through evolutionary processes of trial, error, experimentation, democratic accountability and popular revolt.
- It is also a *normative* rule in the sense that it provides guidance in the design of collective action, be it governed by informal agreements, private contracts, government interventions using regulation, taxation and subsidy, and state laws.
- Notwithstanding a society's ability to tackle its urban management problems responsively and efficiently, public domain problems will never go away, since the assignment of property rights always creates new public domains. As property rights subdivide, externalities densify.
- Governments and societies may become wiser and cities may become better at ordering themselves, but there will be ever-increasing opportunities to apply such wisdom. If a government is responsive to the voice of the individuals it serves, however, there is a sense in which the political market evolves spontaneously in an analogous way to economic markets. Over time, better methods of ordering public domain problems emerge and replace less cost effective methods. Because of the inherent informational handicap of planned action, the spontaneous ordering of a city's public domain resources is inevitably slower and less efficient. Nevertheless, as with proprietary order, public domain order might be expected over time to move towards greater efficiency. The efficiency rule is similar in both cases – rights and liabilities are best assigned to agents in positions of economic influence with respect to the desired outcome.
- As a consequence, urban governance has by and large passed through the municipal socialism experiment of the last century to be delivered by an ever-changing organisational configuration. Governments, firms, non-profit organisations, entrepreneurial clubs, informal groups, households and partnerships between these deliver urban governance.
- It was a fatal conceit to think that government could order cities. The wise municipal government is the one that understands its role as reducing the costs of market transactions and reducing the public domain

problems that inevitably arise. It will inevitably find itself in a dual relationship with the market as it does this – partner in the supply of public goods and partner in the control of externalities. Partnership is demanded in both types of public domain problem since the best outcomes are achieved when all parties to a problem take a share of the responsibility for ordering contested resources.

Interactive Urban Orders

Each of the five types of urban order discussed in this book interacts with the others. The interactions are non-linear, characterised by local learning and feedback, and cities are therefore complex systems that behave chaotically. Given the information disadvantage of centralised decision making, prediction as a basis of planning would be insecure with the simplest of system. With unpredictable complex systems prediction is just one way of inventing a future. Governments should be wary of inventing futures. There are strong rationales for doing so – particularly where investment risk is a public good (public bad) and when the transaction costs of co-ordination can be significantly reduced by providing collective agreement on strategic market issues including pace, direction and general shape of city growth. Inventing planned utopias in contradistinction to market-driven utopias is imprudent, however, and misses the point. Markets create wealth and distribute it widely. They need the state in order to do this, however. The state can best promote the creation of utopian cities by efficiently but justly assigning and attenuating private property rights.

8.6   EPILOGUE

With hindsight, Burton's criticism of the 'Pigovian formula' for town planning in the monograph *The Myth of Social Cost* (Cheung, 1978) raised a curtain for the new institutional economics to make a contribution to urban planning and management theory and research.

Initially, the impact was hardly spectacular and textbooks in the field, other than the notable exceptions of William Fischel's *The Economics of Zoning Laws: a Property Rights Approach* (1985) and K.G. Willis' *The Economics of Town & Country Planning* (1980), seldom made reference to the ideas of this paradigm.

However, from the early 1990s onwards, the Coasian transaction costs theme began to make its appearance more widely in the planning and public administration literature. An important early contribution was Ernest Alexander's 'A transaction cost theory of planning' in the *Journal of the*

American Planning Association (1992), and more recent monographs include Eric Heikkila's *The Economics of Planning* (2000) and Mark Pennington's *Planning and the Political Market* (2000). The interest in institutional economics can be partly explained by the elevation of the so-called Chicago School economists, especially Ronald H. Coase, to Nobel laureate status. However, the more forceful explanation must lie in the fact that conventional paradigms had run out of credit at a time when the accepted understanding of the role of urban government was being radically challenged by practice. The old political–economic structures within which planning was highly regarded had generally long gone. Nowhere is this more starkly illustrated than in Mainland China, home to one sixth of the world's population. Property rights and transaction costs economics have become something of the new currency of economic dialogue. Translations of all the main works are inspiring fresh public and academic debate on foreign policy, the domestic economy, the land market and local governance. The intellectual vacuum in China is greater than in most other countries, but the West and other developing countries have their own versions. In particular, the challenges posed by the ideas of sustainable development, smart growth and globalisation, have created an intellectual atmosphere and a set of ideological and practical policy tensions that are conducive to the evolution of new ideas.

In this book, we have sought to develop an approach to the analysis of urban planning and management that uses the language and ideas of the new institutional economics. The four rules set out in Chapter 1 and elaborated throughout the book come close to a general theory of urban development and planning (Mandelbaum, 1979). That is far too grand a claim, however. More modestly we offer a framework of clear and refutable propositions capable of being applied in both explanatory and normative enquiry. These should be regarded as a catalyst in the generation of new analytical and operational concepts that help shape the role and practice of urban planners, manager, administrators and governments at the start of the urban century.

Bibliography

Abercrombie, P. (1948), *Hong Kong: Preliminary Planning Report*, Hong Kong: Government Printer.

Alchian, A.A. and Allen, W.R. (1977), *Exchange and Production*, Belmont, CA: Wadsworth.

Alchian, A.A. and Demsetz, H. (1973), 'The property rights paradigm', *Journal of Economic History*, **3** (1), 16–27.

Alexander, E.R. (1992), 'A transaction cost theory of planning', *Journal of American Planning Association*, **58** (2), 190–200.

Alexander, E.R. (1995), *How Organisation Acts Together: Inter-organisational Co-ordination in Theory and Practice*, Amsterdam: Gordon and Breach.

Alexander, E.R. (2001), 'Why planning vs. markets is an oxymoron: asking the right question', *Planning and Markets*, **4** (1), http://www-pam.usc.edu/index.html

Alonso, W. (1964), *Location and Land Use*, Cambridge, MA: Harvard University Press.

Alonso, W. (1971), 'The economics of urban size', *Regional Science Association Papers*, **26**, 68–83.

Arrow, K.J. (1951), *Social Choice and Individual Values*, New York, NY: John Wiley.

Arrow, K.J. (1970), 'The organisation of economic activity: issues pertinent to the choice of market versus non-market allocation', in R.H. Haverman and J. Margolis (eds), *Public Expenditure and Policy Analysis*, Chicago, IL: Rand McNally, pp. 59–73.

Barzel, Y. (1974), 'A theory of rationing by waiting', *Journal of Law and Economics*, **17** (1), 73–96.

Barzel, Y. (1982), 'Measurement cost and the organisation of markets', *Journal of Law and Economics*, **25**, 27–48.

Barzel, Y. (1997), *Economic Analysis of Property Rights*, Cambridge, MA: Cambridge University Press.

Batty, M. (2001), 'Polynucleated urban landscapes', *Urban Studies*, **38** (4), 635–55.

Baumol, W.J. (1972), 'On taxation and the control of externalities', *American Economic Review*, **62**, 307–22.

Beito, D.T. (1989), 'Owning the "Commanding Heights": historical perspectives on private streets', *Essays in Public Works History*, **16**, 1–47.

Berki, R.N. (1976), *The History of Political Thought: a Short Introduction*, London: Rowman and Littlefield.

Berneri, M.L. (1950), *Journey Through Utopia*, London: Freedom Press.

Blakely, E. and Snyder, M. (1997), *Fortress America*, Washington, DC: The Brookings Institute Press and Cambridge, MA: Lincoln Institute of Land Policy.

Bottomley, A. (1963), 'The effect of the common ownership of land upon resource allocation in Tripolitania', *Land Economics*, **40**, 91–5.

Bowyer, J. (1992), 'The economics of planning gain', *Urban Studies*, **29**, 1329–39.

Buchanan, J. (1965), 'An economic theory of clubs', *Economica*, NS **32** (125), 1–14.

Buchanan, J. (1968), *The Demand and Supply of Public Goods*, Chicago, IL: Rand MacNally.

Buchanan, J. (1993), *Property as a Guarantor of Liberty*, Aldershot, UK and Brookfield, US: Edward Elgar.

Buchanan, J.M. and Stubblebine, W.C. (1962), 'Externality', *Economica*, NS **29** (116), 371–84.

Calderon Cockburn, J. (2002), 'The mystery of credit', *Land Lines*, **14** (2), 5–8.

Chau, K.W., Lai, L.W.C. and Wong, K.C. (1993), 'Will labour only subcontracting lead to exploitation and inefficiency?', in Conference proceedings, *Changing Roles of Contractors in the Asia Pacific Rim*, Chartered Institute of Building (CIOB), Hong Kong Branch, HK, pp. 171–82.

Cheung, S.N.S. (1969), *A Theory of Share Tenancy*, Chicago, IL: University of Chicago Press.

Cheung, S.N.S. (1973), 'The fable of the bees: an economic investigation', *Journal of Law and Economics*, **16**, 11–33.

Cheung, S.N.S. (1975), 'Roofs or stars: the stated intent and actual effects of a rents ordinance', *Economic Inquiry*, **13** (1), 1–21.

Cheung, S.N.S. (1978), *The Myth of Social Cost*, Hobart Paper 82, London: The Institute of Economic Affairs.

Cheung, S.N.S. (1982), *Will China Go Capitalist?*, London: Institute of Economic Affairs.

Cheung, S.N.S. (1983), 'The contractual nature of the firm', *Journal of Law and Economics*, **24** (2), 1–21.

Clarke, E.H. (1971), 'Multi-part pricing of public goods', *Public Choice*, **11**, 17–33.

Coase, R.H. (1937), 'The nature of the firm', *Economica*, NS, 4 (16), 386–405.

Coase, R.H. (1959), 'The Federal Communications Commission', *Journal of Law and Economics*, 2, 1–40.

Coase, R.H. (1960), 'The problem of social cost', *Journal of Law and Economics*, 3, 1–44.

Coase, R.H. (1974), 'The lighthouse in economics', *Journal of Law and Economics*, 17, 357–76.

Cornes, R. and Sandler, T. (1996), *The Theory of Externalities, Public Goods and Club Goods*, 2nd edn, Cambridge: Cambridge University Press.

Corporation of London (2001), *London's Contribution to the UK Economy*, London: Corporation of London.

Cullis, J.G. and Jones, P. (1992), *Public Finance and Public Choice*, London: McGraw Hill.

de Búrca, G. (1999), *Reappraising Subsidiarity's Significance after Amsterdam*, Jean Monnet Working Papers 7/99, Harvard Law School/New York School of Law Jean Monnet Centre.

De Long, J.B. (1998), *Estimating World GDP, One Million B.C. – Present*, http://www.j-bradford-delong.net/TCEH/1998_Draft/World_GDP/Estimat ing_World_GDP.html (accessed October 2001).

Demsetz, H. (1967), 'Towards a theory of property rights', *American Economic Review*, 57, 347–59.

Eggertsson, T. (1990), *Economic Behaviour and Institutions*, Cambridge: Cambridge University Press.

Fischel, W.A. (1978), 'A property rights approach to municipal zoning', *Land Economics*, 54, 64–81.

Fischel, W.A. (1987), *The Economics of Zoning Laws: a Property Rights Approach to American Land Use Controls*, Baltimore, MD: Johns Hopkins University Press.

Foldvary, F. (1994), *Public Goods and Private Communities*, Aldershot, UK and Brookfield, US: Edward Elgar.

Frantz, K. (1999), *Indian Reservation in the United States*, Chicago, IL: University of Chicago Press.

Frantz, K. (2000), 'Gated communities in the USA', *Espace, Populations, Sociétés*, 2000 (1), 101–13.

Friedman, M. and Friedman, R. (1990), *Free to Choose: A Personal Statement*, London: Harcourt Brace.

Fujita, M. (1989), *Urban Economic Theory*, Cambridge: Cambridge University Press.

Fujita, M., Krugman, P. and Venables, A. (1999), *The Spatial Economy*, Cambridge, MA and London: MIT Press.

George, S. (2000), *Liverpool Park Estates*, Liverpool: Liverpool University Press.

Grant, M. (2000), *Environmental Court Project: Final Report*, London: Stationery Office.

Guy, C. (1998), 'Controlling new retail spaces: the impress of planning policies in Western Europe', *Urban Studies*, **35**, 953–79.

Gwartney, James D. and Stroup, Richard L. (1982), *Economics: Private and Public Choice*, New York, NY: Academic Press.

Hall, P. (1999), *Cities of Tomorrow: an Intellectual History of Urban Planning and Design in the Twentieth Century*, updated edn, Oxford: Blackwell.

Hall, P., Thomas, R., Gracey, H. and Drewett, R. (1973), *The Containment of Urban England*, London: Allen and Unwin.

Hart, O. and Moore, J. (1990), 'Property rights and the nature of the firm', *Journal of Political Economy*, **48**, 1119–58.

Hayek, F.A. (1944), *The Road to Serfdom*, Chicago, IL and London: University of Chicago Press.

Hayek, F.A. (1967), *Studies in Philosophy, Politics and Economics*, London: Routledge & Keegan Paul.

Hayek, F.A. (1978), *New Studies in Philosophy, Politics, Economics and the History of Ideas*, London: Routledge & Kegan Paul.

Hayek, F.A. (1988), *The Fatal Conceit: the Errors of Socialism*, Chicago, IL: University of Chicago Press.

Hayek, F.A., Friedman, M. and Stigler, M.J. (1972), *Verdict on Rent Control: Essays on the Economic Consequences of Political Action to Restrict Rents in Five Countries*, London: Institute of Economic Affairs.

Heikkila, E.J. (1996), 'Are municipalities Tieboutian clubs?', *Regional Science and Urban Economics*, **26**, 203–26.

Heikkila, E.J. (2000), *The Economics of Planning*, New Brunswick, NJ: Rutgers University, Centre for Urban Policy Research.

Herington, J. (1984), *The Outer City*, London: Paul Chapman.

Herington, J. (1990), *Green Belts*, London: Jessica Kingsley/Regional Studies Association.

Hirschman, Albert O. (1970), *Exit, Voice, and Loyalty*, Cambridge, MA: Harvard University Press.

Howard, E. (1902), *Garden Cities of Tomorrow*, 2nd edn, London: S. Sonnenschein.

Hu, J. (1988), *A Concise History of Chinese Economic Thought*, Bejing: Foreign Languages Press.

Huang, R. (1990), *China: a Macro History*, Armonk, NY: M.E. Sharpe.

Hume, D. (1739), *A Treatise of Human Nature*, edited by L.A. Selby-Brigge and revised by P. Nidditch (1976), Oxford: Oxford University Press.

Jack, A. (2002), 'Russia's industrial towns long for the good old days', *Financial Times*, 17 May, p. 16.

Jacobs, J. (1964), *Life and Death of Great American Cities*, Harmondsworth: Penguin.

Jänicke, M. (1990), *State Failure: the Impotence of Politics in Industrial Society*, Cambridge: Polity Press.

Jones, M. and Lowrey, K. (1995), 'Street barriers in American cities', *Urban Geography*, **16** (2), 112–22.

Kasper, W. and Streit, M.E. (1998), *Institutional Economics: Social Order and Public Policy*, Cheltenham, UK and Northampton, MA, USA: Edward Elgar.

Krugman, P. (1995), *Development, Geography and Economic Theory*, Cambridge, MA and London: MIT Press.

Kwong, Jo Ann (1990), *Market Environmentalism: Lessons for Hong Kong*, Hong Kong: Chinese University Press.

Lai, L.W.C. (1993), 'Marine fish culture and pollution – an initial Hong Kong empirical study', *Asian Economic Journal*, 7 (3), 333–51.

Lai, L.W.C. (1994), 'The economics of land use zoning: a literature review and analysis of the work of Coase', *Town Planning Review*, **65** (1), 77–98.

Lai, L.W.C. (1996), *Zoning and Property Rights: a Hong Kong Case Study*, Hong Kong: Hong Kong University Press.

Lai, L.W.C. (1997), 'Property rights justifications for planning and a theory of zoning', *Progress in Planning*, **48** (3), 161–246.

Lai, L.W.C. (1998), 'The leasehold system as a means of planning by contract: the case of Hong Kong', *Town Planning Review*, **69** (3), 249–75.

Lai, L.W.C. (2000a), 'Hayek on town planning: a note on Hayek's views towards town planning in *The Constitution of Liberty*', *Environment and Planning A*, **31**, 1567–82.

Lai, L.W.C. (2000b), 'The Coasian market–firm dichotomy and sub-contracting in the construction industry', *Construction Management and Economics*, **18** (3), 355–63.

Lai, L.W.C. (2002), 'Fifty years no change: land use planning and development in Hong Kong under constitutional capitalism', in M. Chan (ed.), *China's Hong Kong into the 21st Century: Transformations in the Hong Kong Special Administrative Region*, Armonk, NY: M.E. Sharpe, pp. 404–47.

Lai, L.W.C. and Yu, M.K.W. (2001a), 'The rise and fall of discriminatory zoning in Hong Kong', *Environment and Planning B: Planning and Design*, **28**, 295–314.

Lai, L.W.C. and Yu, B.T. (2001b), 'The Hong Kong fish marketing organisation: a case study of the financial problem of a legal monopoly', *Pacific Economic Review*, 7 (1).

Lai, L.W.C. and Yu, B.T. (2002), *The Forces of Demand and Supply: Thinking Tools and Case Studies for Students and Professionals*, Hong Kong: Hong Kong University Press.

Lin, S.Y. (1940), 'Fish culture in ponds in the new territories of Hong Kong', *Journal of the Hong Kong Fisheries Research Station*, **1** (1), 161–92.

Mandelbaum, S.J. (1979), 'A complete general theory of planning is impossible', *Policy Sciences*, **11** (1), 59–71.

Mark, Johnathan H. and Goldberg, Michael A. (1981), 'Land use controls: the case of zoning in the Vancouver area', *AREUEA Journal*, **9**, 418–35.

Maser, Steven M., Riker, William H. and Rosett, Richard N. (1977), 'The effects of zoning and externalities on the prices of land: an empirical analysis of Monroe County, New York', *Journal of Law and Economics*, **20**, 111–32.

McGinn, A.P. (1998), 'Aquaculture growing rapidly', in L.R. Brown, M. Renner, C. Flaivin, *Vital Signs 1998*, New York, NY: Norton, pp. 36–7.

Meade, J.E. (1973), *The Theory of Economic Externalities*, Leiden and Geneva: Sijthoff.

Metton, A. (1995), 'Retail planning policy in France', in R.L. Davies (ed.), *Retail Planning Policies in Western Europe*, London: Routledge, pp. 62–77.

Mises, L. von (1943), *Human Action*, English translation by Bettina B. Greaves (1996), Irvington: Foundation for Economic Education, http://www.mises.org/humanaction.asp (accessed 1 May 2002).

Mises, L. von (1949), *Human Action: a Treatise on Economics*, Edinburgh: W. Hodge, reprinted (1978), Chicago: Contemporary Books.

Mishan, E. (1988), *Cost Benefit Analysis*, London: Allen & Unwin.

Miyao, T. (1981), *Dynamic Analysis of the Urban Economy*, New York, NY: Academic Press.

Molho, I. (1997), *The Economics of Information: Lying and Cheating in Markets and Organisations*, London: Blackwell.

Morris, J. (1997), *Hong Kong: Epilogue to an Empire*, London: Penguin.

Mueller, D. (1989), *Public Choice II*, Cambridge: Cambridge University Press.

Nelson, R.R. (1995), 'Recent evolutionary theorization about economic change', *Journal of Economic Literature*, **33** (1), 48–90.

Nelson, R.R. and Winter, S.G. (1982), *An Evolutionary Theory of Economic Change*, Cambridge MA: Belknap Press.

Noongo, E.N. (2001), 'Spatial pattern of soil erosion hazard in North Central Namibia', unpublished M.Sc. Dissertation, Department of Geography, University of Durham.

North, D.C. (1990), *Institutions, Institutional Change and Economic Performance*, Cambridge and New York, NY: Cambridge University Press.

North, D.C. (1992), *Transaction Costs, Institutions and Economic Performance*, San Francisco, CA: International Centre for Economic Growth.

North, D.C. and Thomas, R.P. (1973), *The Rise of the Western World: a New Economic History*, Cambridge, MA: Cambridge University Press.

Olson, M. (1965), *The Logic of Collective Action*, Cambridge, MA: Harvard University Press.

Olson, M. (1982), *The Rise and Decline of Nations: Economic Growth, Stagflation and Social Rigidities*, London: Yale University Press.

Olson, M. Jr. and Zeckhauser, R. (1970), 'The efficient production of external economies', *American Economic Review*, **60**, 512–17.

Panayoutou, T. (2001), 'Population and environment', in Tom Tietenberg and Henk Folmer (eds), *The International Yearbook of Environmental and Resource Economics 2000/2001*, Cheltenham, UK and Northampton, MA, USA: Edward Elgar.

Pennington, M. (1996), *Conservation and the Countryside: by Quango or Market?*, London: Institute of Economic Affairs.

Pennington, M. (2000), *Planning and the Political Market*, London and New Brunswick, NJ: Athlone Press.

Pennington, M. (2002), *Liberating the Land*, London: Institute for Economic Affairs.

Pigou, A. (1920), *The Economics of Welfare*, London: Macmillan.

Pigou, A. (1932), *The Economics of Welfare*, 4th edn, London: Macmillan.

Popper, K. (1974, originally 1945), *The Open Society and its Enemies*, London: Routledge and Kegan Paul.

Popper, K. (1999), *All Life Is Problem Solving*, London: Routledge.

Racheter, D.P. and Wagner, R.E. (1999), *Limiting Leviathan*, Cheltenham, UK and Northampton, MA, USA: Edward Elgar.

Rawls, J. (1971), *A Theory of Justice*, Cambridge, MA: Harvard University Press.

Read, L.E. (1958), 'I, Pencil', in W. Kasper and M.E. Streit (eds), *Institutional Economics: Social Order and Public Policy*, Cheltenham, UK and Brookfield, US: Edward Elgar, pp. 490–93.

Richardson, H.W. (1978), *Regional and Urban Economics*, London: Penguin.

Sabatier, P. (1924), *Life of St. Francis of Assisi*, London: Hodder and Stoughton.

Samuelson, P.A. (1954), 'The pure theory of public expenditure', *Review of Economics and Statistics*, **36**, 387–9.

Samuelson, P.A. (1955), 'Diagrammatic exposition of a pure theory of public expenditure', *Review of Economics and Statistics*, **37**, 350–55.

Shibata, H. and Winrich, J.S. (1983), 'Control of pollution when the offended defend themselves', *Economica*, NS **50** (200), 425–38.

Simmie, J. (1996), *Planning at the Crossroads*, London: UCL Press.

Smith, A. (1776), *An Enquiry Into the Nature and Causes of the Wealth of Nations*, reprinted in R.H. Campbell and A.S. Skinner (eds) (1976), Oxford: Oxford University Press.

Stigler, G.J. (1971), 'The economics of information', in D.M. Lamberton (ed.), *Economics of Information and Knowledge*, Harmondsworth: Penguin, pp. 61–82.

Stubbs, J. and Clarke, G. (eds) (1996), *Megacity Management in the Asian and Pacific Region*, Vol. 1, Manila: Asian Development Bank.

Thornley, A. (1991), *Urban Planning under Thatcherism*, London: Routledge.

Thorson, J.A. (1996), 'An examination of the monopoly zoning hypothesis', *Land Economy*, **72**, 43–55

Thrall, G.I. (1987), *Land Use and Urban Form*, London and New York, NY: Methuen.

Thünen, J.H. von (1826), *Von Thünen's Isolated State*, English translation by C.M Wartenberg (1966), Oxford: Pergamon Press.

Tideman, T.N. and Tullock, G. (1976), 'A new and superior process for making social choices', *Journal of Political Economy*, **84**, 1145–59.

Tiebout, C.M. (1956), 'A pure theory of local expenditures', *Journal of Political Economy*, **64**, 416–24.

Timms, D.W.G. (1971), *The Urban Mosaic*, Cambridge: Cambridge University Press.

Tollison, R.D. (1982), 'Rent seeking: a survey', *Kyklos*, **35** (4), 575–602.

Townsend, I. (2002), 'Age segregation and gated retirement communities in the Third Age', *Environment and Planning B: Planning and Design*, **29**, 371–97.

Tullock, G. (1993), *Rent Seeking*, Aldershot, UK and Brookfield, US: Edward Elgar.

Umbeck, J. (1977), 'The California God rush: a study of the formation and initial distribution of property rights', *Economic Enquiry*, **19** (1), 38–59.

United Nations (1995), *World Urbanisation Prospects*, New York, NY: United Nations.

United Nations (1998), *World Distribution of Cities Map*, www.un.org/Depts/unsd/demog/globcity.htm (accessed 12 July 2002).

Walker, R.M. and Jeanes, E. (2001), 'Innovation in a regulated service: the case of English housing associations', *Public Management Review*, **3**, 525–50.

Warner, Sam Bass (1962), *Streetcar Suburbs: the Progress of Growth in Boston 1870–1900*, Cambridge, MA: Harvard University Press.

Webster, C.J. (1998a), 'Public choice, Pigovian and Coasian planning theory', *Urban Studies*, **35**, 53–75.

Webster, C.J. (1998b), 'Sustainability and public choice: a theoretical essay on urban performance indicators', *Environment and Planning B: Planning and Design*, **25**, 709–29.

Webster, C.J. (2001a), 'Gated cities of to-morrow', *Town Planning Review*, **72** (2), 149–70.

Webster, C.J. (2001b), 'Contractual agreements and neighbourhood evolution', *Planning and Markets*, **4** (1), http://www-pam.usc.edu/index.html.

Webster, C.J. and Wu, F. (2001), 'Coase, spatial pricing and self-organising cities', *Urban Studies*, **38**, 2037–54.

Willis, K.G. (1980), *The Economics of Town and Country Planning*, Oxford: Granada Publishing.

Witt, U. (1991), 'Reflections on the present state of evolutionary economic theory', in G.M. Hodgson and E. Screpanti (eds), *Rethinking Economics: Markets, Technology and Economic Evolution*, Aldershot, UK and Brookfield, US: Edward Elgar, pp. 83–102.

Wong, R.Y.C. (1998), *On Privatizing Public Housing*, Hong Kong: City University of Hong Kong Press.

Wu, F. and Webster, C.J. (1998), 'Simulation of natural land-use zoning under free-market and incremental development control regimes', *Computers, Environment and Urban Systems*, **22**, 241–56.

Yap, K.S. and Sakchai, K. (2000), 'Bangkok's housing boom and the financial crisis in Thailand: once only the sky was the limit', *Housing Studies*, **15** (1), 11–27.

Yu, B.T., Shaw, D., Fu, T.T. and Lai, L.W.C. (2000), 'Property rights and contractual approach to sustainable development', *Environmental Economics and Policy Studies*, **3**, 291–309.

Index